Threat Level Red

Cybersecurity Research Programs of the U.S. Government

T0187905

Threat Level Red
Cybersecurity Research Programs
of the U.S. Government

Michael Erbschloe

CRC Press
Taylor & Francis Group
Boca Raton London New York

CRC Press is an imprint of the
Taylor & Francis Group, an **informa** business

AN AUERBACH BOOK

CRC Press
Taylor & Francis Group
6000 Broken Sound Parkway NW, Suite 300
Boca Raton, FL 33487-2742

First issued in paperback 2020

© 2017 by Taylor & Francis Group, LLC
CRC Press is an imprint of Taylor & Francis Group, an Informa business

ISBN 13: 978-0-367-65784-0 (pbk)
ISBN 13: 978-1-138-05280-2 (hbk)

Library of Congress Cataloging-in-Publication Data

Names: Erbschloe, Michael, 1951- author.
Title: Threat level red : cybersecurity research programs of the US government / Michael Erbschloe.
Description: Boca Raton : Taylor & Francis, CRC Press, 2017. | Includes bibliographical references.
Identifiers: LCCN 2017010262| ISBN 9781138052802 (hardback : acid-free paper) | ISBN 9781315167558 (electronic)
Subjects: LCSH: Computer networks--Security measures--Research--United States. | Cyberspace--Security measures--Research--United States. | Federal aid to research--United States. | United States--Administrative and political divisions.
Classification: LCC TK5105.59 .E7323 2017 | DDC 005.8072/073--dc23
LC record available at https://lccn.loc.gov/2017010262

Visit the Taylor & Francis Web site at
http://www.taylorandfrancis.com

and the CRC Press Web site at
http://www.crcpress.com

Contents

Foreword

In the late 1990s, the U.S. Commission on National Security in the twenty-first century concluded that if the United States does not invest significantly more in public research and development, it will be eclipsed by others. Failure to do so may return to haunt the nation and in the judgment of the Commission; the U.S. government had not taken a broad, systematic approach to investing in science and technology R&D, and thus will not be able to sustain projects of sufficient scale and boldness. To keep pace with changes in technology, the commission recommended that the President of the United States should propose, and the Congress should support, dramatically increasing the U.S. government's investment in science and technology research and development by 2010.[1] The looming challenge was to be able to master cyberspace and at that time it was not realized to what extent the added dimension of cyberspace would change the world as drastically as it has over the last two decades.

The increasing dependency on information technology systems and networked operations pervades nearly every aspect of our society. While bringing significant benefits, this dependency can also create vulnerabilities to cyber-based threats. Underscoring the importance of safeguarding critical information and information systems and weaknesses in such efforts, federal information and network security as well as private security efforts supporting our nation's critical infrastructure are designated a high-risk area.

From buying products to running businesses to finding directions to communicating with the people the online world has fundamentally reshaped our daily lives. But just as the continually evolving digital age presents boundless opportunities for the economy, businesses, and people, it also presents a new generation of threats that we must adapt to meet. Criminals, terrorists, and countries who wish to do harm have all realized that attacking online is often easier than attacking in person. As more and more sensitive data is stored online, the consequences of those attacks grow more significant each year. Nation states can become more secure but to stay that way they need to develop the capability to defend against cybersecurity attacks. The same is true for government agencies and private corporations.

Reference

1. U.S. Commission on National Security 21st Century. *Road Map for National Security: Imperative for Change the Phase III Report of the U.S. Commission on National Security 21st Century.* February 15, 2001. Retrieved December 17, 2016, http://govinfo.library. unt.edu/nssg/PhaseIIIFR.pdf

Acknowledgments

The author acknowledges Richard O'Hanley, Publisher at CRC Press, and his publishing team for their support and assistance which helped getting this book from concept to print. The author also acknowledges his sister for her never-ending support of his efforts.

About the Author

Michael Erbschloe worked for more than 30 years performing analysis of the economics of information technology, public policy relating to technology, and utilizing technology in reengineering organization processes. He has authored several books on social and management issues of information technology most of which covered some aspects of information or corporate security. Mr Erbschloe has also taught at several universities and developed technology-related curriculum. His career has focused on several interrelated areas: technology strategy, analysis, and forecasting; teaching and curriculum development; writing books and articles; speaking at conferences and industry events; publishing and editing; and public policy analysis and program evaluation. He currently works as a consultant on technology and security issues.

Introduction

Cyberspace and its underlying infrastructure are vulnerable to a wide range of risk stemming from both physical and cyber threats and hazards. Sophisticated cyber actors and nation states exploit vulnerabilities to steal information and money and are developing capabilities to disrupt, destroy, or threaten the delivery of essential services. Cyberspace is particularly difficult to secure due to a number of factors: the ability of malicious actors to operate from anywhere in the world, the linkages between cyberspace and physical systems, and the difficulty of reducing vulnerabilities and consequences in complex cyber networks. Of growing concern is the cyber threat to critical infrastructure, which is increasingly subject to sophisticated cyber intrusions that pose new risks. As information technology becomes increasingly integrated with physical infrastructure operations, there is increased risk for large-scale or high-consequence events that could cause harm or disrupt services upon which our economy and the daily lives of millions of Americans depend. In light of the risk and potential consequences of cyber events, strengthening the security and resilience of cyberspace has become an important homeland security mission.[1]

Cyberattacks can instantly squander billions of dollars worth of private investments in intellectual property and research and development, or disrupt crucial business operations. Governments face unique challenges in defending national in such a threat environment. The vast majority of the infrastructure that underpins the digital economy, from financial systems to telecommunications networks, is owned and operated by private industries. When Iran launched denial-of-service attacks on U.S. banks, when North Korea infiltrated Sony Pictures, when cyber-criminals injected ransomware into a California hospital's patient management system, they targeted privately owned infrastructure. Neither government nor industry can confront the cyber challenges alone. To realize the vast potential of the digital economy, the public and private sectors need to work together to improve and maintain cybersecurity.[2] This cooperation may have become even more important since Russia has been accused by many of hacking the U.S. presidential election of 2016.

The United States and other technology-dependent nations are challenged with continuing to defend current systems and networks and at the same time attempt to get out in front of adversaries and ensure that future technology can better protect critical infrastructures and respond to attacks. Government-funded and government-led research and development (R&D) plays an increasing role to meet these challenges and protect national and economic security. The research, development, test, evaluation, and other life cycle considerations required reaches from technologies that secure individuals and their information to technologies that will ensure that critical infrastructures are more resilient.[3]

This book examines a wide range of cybersecurity research activities being conducted by the U.S. Science Laboratories, branches of the military and civilian agencies. The research activities examined are representative of what the U.S. government is doing in cybersecurity research but it is not exhaustive. In other words, there are activities not covered and the examination of the research that is included is brief in many areas because of both time and space. The coverage in each chapter is summarized below.

Chapter 1: The U.S. Federal Government Initiatives on Cybersecurity Research. This chapter traces some of the significant actions on the part of the government that has led to the current state of affairs on cybersecurity and cybersecurity research. The cybersecurity efforts of the U.S. government are slowly maturing and starting to show more solid progress including the coordination and prioritization of cybersecurity research activities. There are several national laboratories and federal agencies that will apply their unique capabilities to research programs designed to address the goals and challenges outlined in the Strategic Plan. The major legislation and executive actions of President Obama that have impacted the progress of these efforts include

- The Comprehensive National Cybersecurity Initiative of 2009
- The Federal Information Security Modernization Act of 2014
- The Cybersecurity Act of 2015 and Automated Indicator Sharing (AIS)
- The Strategic Plan for the Federal Cybersecurity Research and Development Program of 2011

Chapter 2: The Department of Homeland Security Cybersecurity Research Programs. The Homeland Security Advanced Research Projects Agency (HSARPA) supports research in technologies, new capabilities, and threat and risk assessments for the Homeland Security Enterprise (HSE).[1] The Department of Homeland Security (DHS) Science and Technology Directorate Cyber Security Division (DHS S&T CSD) focuses on applied research and development, test, evaluation, and transition for technologies to support civilian federal, state, and local governments and private sector unclassified needs to protect the cyber infrastructure. Of particular interest to DHS are technologies that can be developed and transitioned to commercial products or used in federal, state, and local government systems.[4] To maintain the focus on research programs and projects, there are numerous partnerships, industry coordination efforts, and transition projects going on in DHS that are not covered in this chapter. Research areas covered in this chapter are

- Anonymous Networks and Currencies
- Assessment and Evaluation (see Cybersecurity Metrics)
- Cyber Analytics Behavior and Resilience (see Cybersecurity Metrics)
- Cyber Economic Incentives (see Cybersecurity Metrics)
- Cyber-Physical Systems Security (CPSSEC)
- Cyber Security Forensics
- Cybersecurity Competitions (see Talent Development)
- Cybersecurity Incident Response Teams (CSIRT) (see Talent Development)
- Data Privacy Technologies
- Distributed Denial of Service Defense (DDoSD)
- Distributed Environment for Critical Infrastructure Decision-Making Exercises (DECIDE) (see Talent Development)
- Enterprise-Level Security Metrics and Usability (see Cybersecurity Metrics)
- Experimental Research Testbed (DETER)
- Experiments and Pilots
- Insider Threat
- Internet Measurement and Attack Modeling
- Mobile Device Security
- Security of Cloud-Based Systems

Chapter 3: The National Institute for Standards and Technology. The National Institute of Standards and Technology (NIST) was founded in 1901 and is part of the U.S. Department of Commerce and is one of the oldest physical science laboratories in the United States. The Congress established the agency to remove a major challenge to U.S. industrial competitiveness at the time which was the country's second-rate measurement infrastructure that lagged behind the capabilities of the United Kingdom, Germany, and other economic rivals.[5]

Innumerable products and services rely in some way on technology, measurement, and standards provided by the National Institute of Standards and Technology. NIST measurements support the smallest of technologies to the largest and most complex of man-made creations from *nanoscale* devices so tiny that tens of thousands can fit on the tip of a single strand of human hair up to earthquake-resistant skyscrapers and global communication networks. NIST's cybersecurity program supports the promotion of innovation and industrial competitiveness of the United States by advancing measurement science, standards, and related technology through research and development in ways that enhance economic and national security.[6] Research areas covered in this chapter are

- The Cybersecurity Framework
- Advanced Network Technologies
- Computer Security
- Standards for High-Impact System Security

- Smart Grid
- Cyber-Physical Systems

Chapter 4: The Defense Advanced Research Projects Agency. The Defense Advanced Research Projects Agency (DARPA) is the principal agency within the Department of Defense for high-risk, high-payoff research, development, and demonstration of new technologies and systems that serve the warfighter and the defense of the United States. DARPA's R&D efforts in cybersecurity strongly support the *Moving Target Defense* and *Tailored Trustworthy Spaces* themes. In particular, DARPA's Information Assurance and Survivability Program draws upon biological and immune systems as inspiration for radically rethinking computer hardware, software, and system designs. Such systems will be able to detect, diagnose, and respond to attacks by using their own innate and adaptive immune systems. Furthermore, in response to attacks, such systems will also be capable of dynamically adapting and improving their defensive capabilities over time. As in biological systems, the cyber systems will dynamically diversify, increasing their resiliency and survivability, and that of their individual, constituent computers.[7] This chapter covers some of the unclassified cybersecurity research of DARPA including

- Active Authentication and Active Cyber Defense (ACD)
- Automated Program Analysis for Cybersecurity (APAC)
- Clean-Slate Design of Resilient, Adaptive, Secure Hosts (CRASH)
- Cyber Fault-tolerant Attack Recovery (CFAR) and Transparent Computing
- Edge-Directed Cyber Technologies for Reliable Mission Communication (EdgeCT)
- Enhanced Attribution and Extreme DDoS Defense (XD3)
- High-Assurance Cyber Military Systems (HACMS)
- Integrated Cyber Analysis System (ICAS)
- Mission-oriented Resilient Clouds (MRC)
- Rapid Attack Detection, Isolation, and Characterization Systems (RADICS)
- Space/Time Analysis for Cybersecurity (STAC)
- Vetting Commodity IT Software and Firmware (VET)

Chapter 5: Intelligence Advanced Research Projects Activity and In-Q-Tel. The Intelligence Advanced Research Projects Activity (IARPA) invests in high-risk, high-payoff research programs to tackle some of the most difficult challenges of the agencies and disciplines in the Intelligence Community (IC). IARPA collaborates across the IC to ensure that research addresses relevant future needs. This cross-community focus ensures the ability to address cross-agency challenges, leverage both operational and R&D expertise from across the IC, and to coordinate transition strategies with agency partners. IARPA does not have an operational mission and does not deploy technologies directly to the field. Instead, IARPA facilitates the transition of research results to IC customers for operational application. In-Q-Tel is investing in research and development projects that are of interest to IC. This chapter covers the unclassified cybersecurity research information provided by IARPA and In-Q-Tel.[8]

Chapter 6: U.S. Military Cybersecurity Research and Deployment. The U.S. military has several diverse challenges in cybersecurity research and development of cyber capabilities. First is the strategic research needs to develop leap ahead transforming technology to maintain cyber superiority which is largely handled by DARPA and other military research laboratories. Second is the combined strategic and applied research, development, and deployment of the technology required to protect the Department of Defense (DoD) at the enterprise level. Third is the applied research, development, and deployment of the technology required to enable and protect the missions of the diversity of the capabilities provided by the air force, army, navy, and marines. Fourth is the applied research, development, and deployment of the technology required to enable and protect the specific units and missions within the four branches of services. Finally, the tactical and action research required to enable and protect all military forces and missions that are in progress as they face emerging and possibly previously unknown cyber threats. Each military branch has developed cybersecurity goals and strategies which help to guide the type of research which is conducted internally or for which contracts are initiated with research partners. The Broad Agency Announcements, Other Transaction (OT) Agreements, and the Sources Sought Notices reviewed in this chapter are examples of how the DoD approaches the cybersecurity process.[9] This chapter examines how the U.S. military meets the challenges of cybersecurity research including the Military Cybersecurity Cross-Community Innovation Ecosystem.

Chapter 7: The National Security Agency. The National Security Agency (NSA) has several research efforts exploring the Tailored Trustworthy Spaces theme, including exploration of risk through behavioral analytics and large-scale data analysis, novel means to detect modifications to computing systems and network analytics, and efforts to customize system controls. NSA is also exploring Moving Target technologies. By conducting a full scope analysis of the Moving Target problem and solution space, NSA plans to develop movement prototypes and evaluate several critical enabling functions. In partnership with the DoD, the agency produced a survey of current Moving Target techniques, thereby enabling a cost–benefit analysis that will take into account different approaches and technologies, the potential impact Moving Target protections may have on mission operations, the costs and overheads associated with implementation, and the overall effectiveness of the movement response. In addition, NSA is supporting activities that foster an interdisciplinary collaborative community around the science of security, including a virtual organization and four university-based multidisciplinary research centers.[10] The nature of NSA is such that most things will happen in secrecy. However, NSA does do considerably cybersecurity research, which is applied in the development of advisories, guidance, and standards and selected areas are covered in this chapter. Topics also include: the Science of Security; Information Assurance (IA) Research; Information for IT Decision Makers, Staff, and Software/Hardware Developers; NSA's Technology Transfer Program; and the National Centers of Academic Excellence in Cyber Defense.

Chapter 8: The National Science Foundation. The National Science Foundation (NSF) invests in cybersecurity research through several programs, including the Directorate of Engineering (ENG) programs in Communications, Circuits, and Sensing Systems (CCSS) and Energy, Power, and Adaptive Systems (EPAS). A major program in cybersecurity is spearheaded by the NSF Directorate of Computer and Information Science and Engineering (CISE), in collaboration with the Directorates of Education and Human Resources (EHR), Engineering (ENG), Mathematical and Physical Sciences (MPS), and Social, Behavioral, and Economic Sciences (SBE). NSF's solicitation for the Secure and Trustworthy Cyberspace (SaTC) Program provides funding to university investigators for research activities on all four Strategic Plan thrusts, with an explicit option for transition to practice projects. NSF's program is distinguished from other agency efforts by its comprehensive nature, and by the strong role of research on cybersecurity foundations.[7] This chapter covers some of the relevant activities of the NSF including an overview of NSF, cybersecurity research activities, and cybersecurity research grants.[11]

Chapter 9: Federally Funded Research and Development Centers. Federally Funded Research and Development Centers (FFRDCs) are government-funded entities that have long-term relationships with one or more federal agencies to perform research and development and related tasks. FFRDCs are typically entirely federally funded, or nearly so, but they are operated by contractors or other nongovernmental organizations.[12] FFRDCs sponsored by the DOE are covered in Chapter 10. This chapter covers FFRDCs that are sponsored by other agencies.

Chapter 10: DOE-Funded Research and Development Centers. Founded during the immense investment in scientific research in the period preceding World War II, the National Laboratories have served as the leading institutions for scientific innovation in the United States for more than 60 years. The Energy Department's National Laboratories address large-scale, complex research and development challenges with a multidisciplinary approach that places an emphasis on translating basic science to innovation.[13] This chapter provides background on federally funded research and development centers (FFRDCs) and examines the cybersecurity research activities of the DOE-funded national laboratories including Argonne, Idaho, Lawrence Berkeley, Los Alamos, the National Renewable Energy Laboratory, Oak Ridge, Pacific Northwest, and Sandia.[14]

Chapter 11: Cybersecurity Research for the Critical Industry Sectors. Since the events of September 11, 2001, many governments have supported the implementation of stronger security measures in their country as well as in the countries of their treaty or trading partners. In the United States, the Department of Homeland Security (DHS) has provided a leadership role in promoting threat analysis and security efforts.[14] DHS and The Office of the President have identified 16 critical infrastructure sectors whose assets, systems, and networks are important to sustaining national interest including economic stability and sustainability.[8] This chapter reviews the critical sectors and the NIST cybersecurity framework being used to address cybersecurity issues as well as sector-specific agencies cybersecurity progress.

Chapter 12: Cybersecurity Research for Consumer Protection. A considerable amount of cybersecurity research is directed at protecting the national infrastructure and the military capability of the United States. However, there are several research initiatives that are definitely focused on protecting consumers. Agencies like the Food and Drug Administration (FDA), the National Highway Transportation Safety Administration (NHTSA), and the Federal Aviation Administration (FAA) have specific responsibilities to protect the general public. This chapter examines research efforts that are directed at protecting consumers some of the cybersecurity including automotive cybersecurity and automated vehicle research, enabled aircraft, medical devices and hospital networks, protecting personal technologies, and unmanned aircraft systems.

Chapter 13: Cybersecurity Usability Obstacles and Research. Usability has only recently become an important concern in the cybersecurity field, due to growing recognition of the fact that users themselves are a key component in organizational security programs. If users find a cybersecurity measure too difficult, they will try to circumvent it which, of course, harms organizational security. There are numerous obstacles to achieve cybersecurity usability but there are also proven methods to perform appropriate usability testing for cybersecurity applications. It is in every organization's interest to design cybersecurity measures in such a way that they take into account the perceptions, characteristics, needs, abilities, and behaviors of users themselves.[15] This chapter covers the security usability research of the U.S. government including: the NIST Usability of Cybersecurity Team, the basics of usability research, mobile device security usability, the growth in the use of handheld computers for Internet access and literacy in the United States.

Chapter 14: Conclusions. The cybersecurity efforts of the U.S. government are slowly maturing and starting to show more solid progress including the coordination and prioritization of cybersecurity research activities. The major legislation passed by the U.S. Congress and the executive actions of President Obama that have prompted greater progress in these efforts. It is likely that the Congressional actions will stay in place but it is also likely that the executive actions will be modified by incoming presidents and cabinets. The research goals and objectives will likely stay in place but how the organization of oversight and priority setting will be modified by the new cabinets. The changes will mostly be propaganda focused with new administrations criticizing past administrations and self-glorifying and laying claim to their new but not likely improved management approaches. This chapter provides an overview of the some major findings and conclusions of this research project.

References

1. U.S. Department of Homeland Security. *Cybersecurity Overview.* September 27, 2016. Retrieved November 13, 2016, https://www.dhs.gov/cybersecurity-overview
2. U.S. Department of Commerce. *U.S. Deputy Secretary of Commerce Bruce Andrews Delivers Keynote at the Internet Security Alliance's 15th Anniversary Cybersecurity Conference.* September 15, 2016. Retrieved November 13, 2016, https://www.commerce.gov/news/deputy-secretary-speeches/2016/09/us-deputy-secretary-commerce-bruce-andrews-delivers-keynote
3. U.S. Department of Homeland Security. *Roadmap for Cybersecurity Research.* November 2009. Retrieved November 13, 2016, https://www.dhs.gov/sites/default/files/publications/CSD-DHS-Cybersecurity-Roadmap.pdf
4. U.S. Department of Homeland Security. *Science and Technology CSD Projects.* Retrieved November 13, 2016, https://www.dhs.gov/science-and-technology/csd-projects
5. The National Institute of Standards and Technology. *About NIST.* Retrieved November 16, 2016, https://www.nist.gov/about-nist
6. The National Institute of Standards and Technology. *Cybersecurity.* Retrieved November 16, 2016, https://www.nist.gov/topics/cybersecurity
7. Defense Advanced Research Projects Agency (DARPA). *DARPA Offices.* Retrieved November 21, 2016, http://www.darpa.mil/about-us/offices
8. Intelligence Advanced Research Projects Activity (IARPA). *About IARPA.* Retrieved November 10, 2016, https://www.iarpa.gov/index.php/about-iarpa
9. The Networking and Information Technology Research and Development Program. *Report on Implementing Federal Cybersecurity Research and Development Strategy.* Retrieved November 11, 2016, https://www.nitrd.gov/PUBS/ImplFed-CybersecurityRDStrategy-June2014.pdf
10. U.S. National Security Agency. *Science of Security.* June 21, 2016. Retrieved November 28, 2016, https://www.nsa.gov/what-we-do/research/science-of-security/index.shtml
11. NSF. *At a Glance.* Retrieved November 28, 2016, https://www.nsf.gov/about/glance.jsp
12. United States Government Accountability Office. *Federally Funded Research Centers.* August 2014. Retrieved December 1, 2016, http://www.gao.gov/products/GAO-14-593
13. DOE. *Office of Electricity Delivery & Energy Reliability. Mission.* Retrieved December 1, 2016, http://www.energy.gov/oe/mission
14. Critical Infrastructure Sectors. *United States Department of Homeland Security.* October 2015. Retrieved December 8, 2016, https://www.dhs.gov/critical-infrastructure-sectors
15. NIST Security. *Usability of Security.* Retrieved December 10, 2016, http://csrc.nist.gov/security-usability/HTML/about.html

Chapter 1

The U.S. Federal Government Initiatives on Cybersecurity Research

It was not until after the September 11, 2001, terrorist attacks on the United States did the country start getting serious about cybersecurity. The Homeland Security Acts and the related legislation just barely started to address cybersecurity. The national leadership had very little understanding of anything cyber and the missteps in legislative efforts and attempts at building a robust organizational response to the cyber threat was at best inadequate. A decade later the understanding of cyber issues in Washington, DC finally entered its adolescence. The efforts of the U.S. government are slowly maturing and starting to show more solid progress including the coordination and prioritization of cybersecurity research activities. This chapter traces some of the significant actions on the part of the government that has led to the current state of affairs on cybersecurity and cybersecurity research.

1.1 Evolving toward Coordinated Cybersecurity Research

Since September 11, 2001, the United States and other countries have worked to improve security on all fronts including cybersecurity. This has been a slow and cumbersome process especially in the early years of the effort. Cybersecurity efforts have lagged behind in the public and private sectors even as the frequency of cyberattacks and hacking rose dramatically.

Cyber incidents reported by the U.S. federal agencies increased from 5,503 in the fiscal year (FY) 2006 to more than 48,000 in FY 2012.[1] The Internet Crime Complaint Center (IC3) which provides the public with a reliable and convenient reporting mechanism to submit information to the Federal Bureau of Investigation (FBI) concerning suspected Internet-facilitated criminal activity receives approximately 300,000 complaints of Internet crime incidents per year. In 2015, IC3 reported there were $55 million in losses from Internet crime incidents.[2] High-profile hacking and attack incidents have become common place with hacks or data thefts reported by Yahoo, Sony, the U.S. Office of Personnel Management, Target stores, and numerous others.

In 2009 and subsequent years, the U.S. government started to retool its approach to dealing with cyber threats and cybersecurity research and since then there has been improved legislation and a more coordinated effort to address cybersecurity issues.

1.2 The Comprehensive National Cybersecurity Initiative

In May 2009, President Obama accepted the recommendations of the Cyberspace Policy Review Initiative including the selection of an Executive Branch Cybersecurity Coordinator who was to have regular access to the President. The Executive Branch was then directed to work closely with all key players in the U.S. cybersecurity including state and local governments and the private sector to ensure an organized and unified response to future cyber incidents. This strengthening of *public/private partnerships* was designed to find technology solutions that ensure U.S. security and prosperity and to invest in the cutting-edge research and development (R&D) necessary for the innovation and discovery to meet the challenges of cyber threats.

The activities were designed to implement the recommendations of the Cyberspace Policy Review Initiative and further build on the Comprehensive National Cybersecurity Initiative (CNCI) launched by President George W. Bush in the National Security Presidential Directive and Homeland Security Presidential Directive 23 (NSPD-54/HSPD-23) in January 2008. The CNCI consisted of a number of mutually reinforcing cybersecurity initiatives with the following major goals:

■ To establish a front line of defense against immediate threats by creating or enhancing shared situational awareness of network vulnerabilities, threats, and events within the federal government and ultimately with state, local, and tribal governments and private sector partners as well as the ability to act quickly to reduce current vulnerabilities and prevent intrusions.

- To defend against the full spectrum of threats by enhancing the *counterintelligence (CI) capabilities* of the United States and by increasing the security of the supply chain for key information technologies.
- To strengthen the future cybersecurity environment by expanding cyber education; coordinating and redirecting R&D efforts across the federal government; and working to define and develop strategies to deter hostile or malicious activity in cyberspace.

The CNCI included funding for the federal law enforcement, intelligence, and defense communities to enhance the key functions of criminal investigation; intelligence collection, processing, and analysis; and information assurance (IA) critical to enabling national cybersecurity efforts. The CNCI initiatives included

- *Initiative #1.* Manage the Federal Enterprise Network as a single network enterprise with Trusted Internet Connections (TIC). The TIC initiative, headed by the Office of Management and Budget (OMB) and the Department of Homeland Security (DHS), covered the consolidation of the federal government's external access points (including those to the Internet).
- *Initiative #2.* Deploy an intrusion detection system of sensors across the federal enterprise. Intrusion detection systems using passive sensors form a vital part of U.S. government network defenses by identifying when unauthorized users attempt to gain access to those networks.
- *Initiative #3.* Pursue deployment of intrusion prevention systems across the federal enterprise. This initiative represents the next evolution of protection for civilian departments and agencies of the Federal Executive Branch. This approach, called EINSTEIN 3, was to draw on commercial technology and specialized government technology to conduct real-time full-packet inspection and threat-based decision making on network traffic entering or leaving Executive Branch networks.
- *Initiative #4.* Coordinate and redirect R&D efforts. No single individual or organization was aware of all of the cyber-related R&D activities being funded by the government. This initiative was to develop strategies and structures for coordinating all cyber R&D sponsored or conducted by the U.S. government, both classified and unclassified, and to redirect that R&D where needed.
- *Initiative #5.* Connect the current cyber operations centers to enhance situational awareness. There was a pressing need to ensure that government information security offices and strategic operations centers share data regarding malicious activities against federal systems, consistent with privacy protections for *personally identifiable information (PII)* and other protected information, as legally appropriate, in order to have a better understanding of the entire threat to government systems and to take maximum advantage of each

organization's unique capabilities to produce the best overall national cyber defense possible.

■ *Initiative #6.* Develop and implement a government-wide cyber CI plan. A government-wide cyber CI plan was necessary to coordinate activities across all federal agencies to detect, deter, and mitigate the foreign-sponsored cyber intelligence threat to government and private sector information systems.

■ *Initiative #7.* Increase the security of classified networks. Classified networks house the federal government's most sensitive information and enable crucial warfighting, being diplomatic, counterterrorism, law enforcement, intelligence, and homeland security operations. Successful penetration or disruption of these networks could cause exceptionally grave damage to the national security.

■ *Initiative #8.* Expand cyber education. While billions of dollars were being spent on new technologies to secure the U.S. government in cyberspace, it is the people with the right knowledge, skills, and abilities to implement these technologies who will determine success.

■ *Initiative #9.* Define and develop enduring "leap-ahead" technology, strategies, and programs. One goal of the CNCI was to develop technologies that provide increases in cybersecurity by orders of magnitude above the current systems and which can be deployed within five to ten years. This initiative sought to develop strategies and programs to enhance the component of the government R&D portfolio that pursues high-risk/high-payoff solutions to critical cybersecurity problems.

■ *Initiative #10.* Define and develop enduring deterrence strategies and programs. Senior policymakers were to think through the long-range strategic options available to the United States in a world that depends on assuring the use of cyberspace.

■ *Initiative #11.* Develop a multipronged approach for global supply chain risk management. Globalization of the commercial information and communications technology marketplace provides increased opportunities for those intent on harming the United States by penetrating the supply chain to gain unauthorized access to data, alter data, or interrupt communications. Risks stemming from both the domestic and globalized supply chain must be managed in a strategic and comprehensive way over the entire lifecycle of products, systems, and services.

■ *Initiative #12.* Define the federal role for extending cybersecurity into critical infrastructure domains. The U.S. government depends on a variety of privately owned and operated critical infrastructures to carry out the public's business. In turn, these critical infrastructures rely on the efficient operation of information systems and networks that are vulnerable to malicious cyber threats.[3]

1.3 The Federal Information Security Modernization Act of 2014

The Federal Information Security Modernization Act of 2014 (FISMA 2014) amended the Federal Information Security Management Act of 2002 (FISMA) to reestablish the oversight authority of the Director of the OMB with respect to agency information security policies and practices, and set forth authority for the Secretary of Homeland Security (DHS) to administer the implementation of such policies and practices for information systems.[2] The goals set out by FISMA 2014 fall into five major areas:

- Clarification of federal agency responsibilities
- Improved reporting of and response to security incidents by federal agencies
- Annual reporting to congress regarding the effectiveness of information sharing and compliance with security policies
- The application of uniform standards to cybersecurity efforts
- Improved coordination of security efforts and research to achieve cost savings[4]

1.4 The Cybersecurity Act of 2015 and Automated Indicator Sharing

The DHS's free Automated Indicator Sharing (AIS) capability enables the exchange of cyber-threat indicators between the federal government and the private sector at machine speed. Threat indicators are pieces of information like malicious Internet Protocol (IP addresses or the sender address of a phishing email although they can also be much more complicated). AIS is a part of DHS's efforts to create an ecosystem where as soon as a company or federal agency observes an attempted compromise, the indicator will be shared in real time with all partners, protecting them from that particular threat.

That means adversaries can only use an attack once, which increases their costs and ultimately reduces the prevalence of cyberattacks. While AIS was never expected to completely eliminate sophisticated cyber threats, it allows companies and federal agencies to concentrate more on them by clearing away less sophisticated attacks. Ultimately, the goal was to commoditize cyber-threat indicators through AIS so that tactical indicators are shared broadly among the public and private sectors, enabling everyone to be better protected against cyberattacks.

AIS is available for free through a DHS 24/7 cyber situational awareness, incident response, and management center which was designated as the central hub for the sharing of cyber-threat indicators between the private sector and the federal government by the Cybersecurity Act of 2015. This legislation also granted liability protection and other protections to companies that share indicators through AIS.

As mandated by the Cybersecurity Act of 2015, DHS certified the operability of AIS in March 2016 and released guidance to help private sector entities share cyber-threat indicators with the federal government. This guidance document can be found on www.us-cert.gov/ais.

AIS participants connect to a DHS-managed system in the Department's National Cybersecurity and Communications Integration Center (NCCIC) that allows bidirectional sharing of cyber-threat indicators. Each partner requires a technical capability (which can be built or bought from a number of commercial vendors) to allow them to exchange indicators with the NCCIC. Participants receive DHS-developed indicators, but can also share indicators they have observed in their own network defense efforts, which DHS will then share back out to all AIS participants.

Participants who share indicators through AIS are not identified as the source of those indicators to other participants unless they affirmatively consent to the disclosure of their identity. In other words, they are anonymous unless they want us to share their name. Indicators are not validated by DHS as the emphasis is on velocity and volume: partners vet the indicators they receive through AIS, so the goal of DHS is to share as many indicators as possible and as quickly as possible. However, when the government has useful information about an indicator, it will assign a reputation score.[5]

1.5 The Cybersecurity National Action Plan

To take further positive steps to improving security, detection, and response, President Obama directed his administration to implement a Cybersecurity National Action Plan (CNAP) that takes near-term actions and puts in place a long-term strategy to enhance cybersecurity awareness and protections, protect privacy, maintain public safety as well as economic and national security, and to take better control of their digital security.

The CNAP was the capstone of more than seven years of determined effort building upon lessons learned from cybersecurity trends, threats, and intrusions. The plan calls for is designed to foster the conditions required for long-term improvements to cybersecurity across all sectors as well as increasing education, training, and awareness on cybersecurity methods and issues. The CNAP actions included the following:

■ Establish the Commission on Enhancing National Cybersecurity: This commission was to be composed of top strategic, business, and technical thinkers from outside of government including members to be designated by the bipartisan congressional leadership. The commission is to make recommendations on actions that can be taken over the next decade to strengthen cybersecurity in both the public and private sectors while protecting privacy; maintaining economic and national security; fostering discovery and development of new technical solutions; and bolstering partnerships between federal, state, and local government and the private sector in the development, promotion and use of cybersecurity technologies, policies, and best practices.

■ Modernize government IT and transform how the government manages cybersecurity through the Information Technology Modernization Fund, which enables the retirement, replacement, and modernization of legacy IT that is difficult to secure and expensive to maintain, as well as establishing the position of the Federal Chief Information Security Officer.

■ Empower Americans to secure their online accounts by judiciously combining a strong password with additional factors, such as a fingerprint or a *single use code delivered in a text message*, to make their accounts even more secure. This focus on *multifactor authentication* will be central to a new National Cybersecurity Awareness Campaign launched by the National Cyber Security Alliance including partnering with leading technology firms like Google®, Facebook®, DropBox®, and Microsoft to make it easier for millions of users to secure their online accounts, and financial services companies such as MasterCard, Visa, PayPal, and Venmo that are making transactions more secure. In addition, the federal government is to take steps to safeguard personal data in online transactions between the citizens and the government, including through a new action plan to drive the federal government's adoption and use of effective identity proofing and strong multifactor authentication methods and a systematic review of where the federal government can reduce reliance on Social Security Numbers as an identifier of citizens.

■ Invest more than $19 billion for cybersecurity as part of the FY 2017 Budget. This represents a more than 35% increase from FY 2016 in overall federal resources for cybersecurity.

Meanwhile, DHS is enhancing federal cybersecurity by expanding the EINSTEIN and Continuous Diagnostics and Mitigation programs. DHS is also dramatically increasing the number of federal civilian cyber defense teams to a total of 48, by recruiting cybersecurity talent from across the federal government and private sector. These standing teams will protect networks, systems, and data across the entire Federal Civilian Government by conducting penetration testing and proactively hunting for intruders, as well as providing incident response and security engineering expertise.

The federal government, through efforts such as the National Initiative for Cybersecurity Education (NICE), plans to enhance cybersecurity education and training nationwide and hire more cybersecurity experts to secure federal agencies. This includes expanding the Scholarship for Service (SFS) program by establishing a CyberCorps Reserve program, to offer scholarships for Americans who wish to obtain cybersecurity education and serve their country in the civilian federal government. There is also an effort to strengthen the National Centers for Academic

Excellence in Cybersecurity Program to increase the number of participating academic institutions and students, better support those institutions currently participating, increase the number of students studying cybersecurity at those institutions, and enhance student knowledge through program and curriculum evolution.

The 2016 Federal Cybersecurity Research and Development Strategic Plan (RDSP) was called for in the 2014 Cybersecurity Enhancement Act, and it lays out strategic R&D goals for the nation to advance cybersecurity technologies driven by the scientific evidence of efficacy and efficiency. The plan was to reduce duplication of research efforts and enhance coordination between the agencies and laboratories on the direction of their research programs.[6]

1.6 The Strategic Plan for the Federal Cybersecurity Research and Development Program

In December 2011, the National Science and Technology Council (NSTC) released the Trustworthy Cyberspace: Strategic Plan for the Federal Cybersecurity Research and Development Program which is a framework for a set of coordinated federal strategic priorities and objectives for cybersecurity research. The Strategic Plan was the result of a continuing dialogue between federal agencies conducting cybersecurity research, agencies with cybersecurity as a critical facet of their mission, along with leading industry and academic experts.

The 2011 Strategic Plan was the culmination of many efforts within the federal government, spearheaded by the Office of Science and Technology Policy (OSTP) and the Federal Networking and Information Technology Research and Development (NITRD) Program. Three interagency forums coordinated the content of the report: the Cyber Security and Information Assurance Interagency Working Group (CSIA IWG), the Special Cyber Operations Research and Engineering (SCORE) IWG, and the Cyber Security and Information Assurance Research and Development Senior Steering Group (CSIA R&D SSG). Collectively, these groups represent efforts by the primary agencies conducting unclassified cybersecurity research within the federal government, including: the Defense Advanced Research Projects Agency (DARPA), Department of Energy (DOE), DHS, Intelligence Advanced Research Projects Activity (IARPA), National Institute of Standards and Technology (NIST), National Security Agency (NSA), National Science Foundation (NSF), Office of the Secretary of Defense (OSD), and Department of Defense (DoD) Service Research Organizations in the Air Force, Army, and Navy.

The four thrusts of the Strategic Plan and their corresponding areas of scientific research should not be taken as the whole of federal activities in the area of cybersecurity. In fulfilling their mission goals, NITRD agencies have and will continue to engage in a diverse set of supplemental cybersecurity R&D activities on topics not directly addressed in the Strategic Plan or covered in the document. Many of these activities may be critical for the secure functioning of cyber systems of specific interest to agencies, but may not fall into the purview of the harmonized set of current priorities for the federal cybersecurity R&D enterprise. Specifically, it is important to note that the unclassified research activities outlined are only one portion of the work of the federal cybersecurity R&D enterprise, of which classified activities are an important additional component.

In February 2013, the President issued Executive Order 13636 (EO 13636), Improving Critical Infrastructure Cybersecurity, and Presidential Policy Directive 21 (PPD-21), Critical Infrastructure Security and Resilience. EO 13636 states that the cyber threat to critical infrastructure continues to grow and represents one of the most serious national security challenges we must confront. The national and economic security of the United States depends on the reliable functioning of the critical infrastructure in the face of such threats. It is the policy of the United States to enhance the security and resilience of the critical infrastructure and to maintain a cyber environment that encourages efficiency, innovation, and economic prosperity while promoting safety, security, business confidentiality, privacy, and civil liberties.

Within these two documents, the President specified a new roadmap of activities and goals that the federal government must undertake to ensure the cybersecurity of the critical infrastructure, outlining a plan of policy coordination, information sharing, privacy and civil liberties protection, and the development of frameworks to identify and address cybersecurity risks. PPD 21 explicitly outlines the roles and responsibilities for different agencies within this directive, including for cybersecurity R&D, specifically

- Promoting R&D to enable the secure and resilient design and construction of critical infrastructure and the accompanying cyber technology
- Enhancing modeling capabilities for determining the potential impacts of incident or threat scenarios on critical infrastructure, as well as cascading effects on other sectors
- Facilitating initiatives to incentivize cybersecurity investments and the adoption of critical infrastructure design features that strengthen all-hazards security and resilience
- Prioritizing efforts to support the strategic guidance issued by the Secretary of Homeland Security

The Strategic Plan provides a framework of four strategic thrusts to organize activities and drive progress in cybersecurity R&D:

- Inducing change by utilizing game-changing themes to direct efforts toward understanding the underlying root causes of known current threats with the goal of disrupting the status quo with radically different approaches to improve the security of the critical cyber systems and infrastructure that serve society.

- Developing scientific foundations through developing an organized, cohesive scientific foundation to the body of knowledge that informs the field of cybersecurity through adoption of a systematic, rigorous, and disciplined scientific approach. Promoting the discovery of laws, hypothesis testing, repeatable experimental designs, standardized data-gathering methods, metrics, common terminology, and critical analysis that engenders reproducible results and rationally based conclusions.
- Maximizing research impact by catalyzing integration across the game-changing R&D themes, cooperation between governmental and private sector communities, collaboration across international borders, and strengthening linkages to other national priorities, such as health IT and the smart grid.
- Accelerating transition to practice by focusing efforts to ensure adoption and implementation of the powerful new technologies and strategies that emerge from the research themes, and the activities to build a scientific foundation so as to create measurable improvements in the cybersecurity landscape.

The Strategic Plan identifies high-priority cyber capabilities that hold promise for enabling fundamental improvements in the security and trustworthiness of cyberspace. To achieve these capabilities, the plan defined an R&D framework that organizes objectives and activities across a range of R&D efforts, including those that require coordination across multiple agencies and those that an individual agency might support in the context of its particular mission, capabilities, and expertise.

No single agency addresses all the priority areas in the Strategic Plan nor should it. Instead, it is the many different agency efforts comprising the federal cybersecurity R&D enterprise that, with guidance from the Strategic Plan and coordination through NITRD, enables progress toward the plan's goals. The unique aspects of agency research strategies for addressing the goals and challenges outlined in the Strategic Plan are as follows.

Air Force Research Laboratory (AFRL): AFRL's efforts in cybersecurity aim to create a firm, trustable foundation in cyberspace, and then to build assured mission capabilities upon it. New technologies are needed to be aware of the missions and threats, compute optimal assurance solutions, and implement protection as needed via mission agility or infrastructure reinforcement. The capabilities developed through this research will be more agile and resilient than current solutions, providing the ability to avoid, fight through, survive, and recover from advanced cyber threats. They will also be more effective at engaging and optimizing the role of humans in cyberspace operations (CSO).

Army Research Laboratory (ARL): ARL's mission is to provide the science, technology, and analysis that underpin full-spectrum military operations. Within its mission, ARL contributes to a number of the Strategic Plan objectives with a particular focus on Moving Target technologies within its Cyber Maneuver Initiative.

The Cyber Maneuver Initiative aims to improve defense against advanced persistent threats (APTs) by creating dynamic attack surfaces for protected systems, and includes research in dynamic operating system maneuverability, application diversity, network agility, cyber deception, predictive cyber-threat modeling, and cognitive reasoning and feedback to maximize maneuver effectiveness in tactical environments.

DARPA: DARPA is the principal agency within the DoD for high-risk, high-payoff research, development, and demonstration of new technologies and systems that serve the warfighter and National defense. DARPA's R&D efforts in cybersecurity strongly support the Moving Target and Tailored Trustworthy Spaces themes. In particular, DARPA's Information Assurance and Survivability Program seeks to draw on biological and immune systems as an inspiration for radically rethinking computer hardware, software, and system designs. Such systems will be able to detect, diagnose, and respond to attacks by using their own innate and adaptive immune systems. Furthermore, in response to attacks, such systems will also be capable of dynamically adapting and improving their defensive capabilities over time. As in biological systems, the Cyber Maneuver Initiative s will dynamically diversify, increasing their resiliency and survivability, and that of their individual, constituent computers.

DOE: A key mission of the DOE Office of Electricity Delivery and Energy Reliability (OE) is to enhance the reliability and resiliency of the national energy infrastructure. Within DOE OE's Cybersecurity for Energy Delivery Systems (CEDS) Program, cybersecurity R&D is tailored to the unique performance requirements, designs, and operational environments of the energy delivery systems (EDS). The CEDS Program operates with the goal that, by 2020, resilient EDS are designed, installed, operated, and maintained to survive cyber incidents while sustaining the critical functions. To help achieve this vision, OE fosters and actively engages in collaborations among energy stakeholders including utilities, vendors, national labs, and academia. Through these collaborations, OE seeks to solve hand-in-hand with industry the right problems, and to transition next-generation research from the national labs and academia into commercial products operating in the energy sector. The Strategic Plan research themes, particularly Designed-In Security and Tailored Trustworthy Spaces are strongly supported by the strategies and milestones outlined in the CEDS Program.

Other elements of DOE also perform related cybersecurity research. The Advanced Scientific Computing Research (ASCR) Program, which is part of the Office of Science, sponsors research to support DOE's world leadership in scientific computation. Security of networks and middleware is a critical element in the ASCR Next Generation Networking Research Program. The National Nuclear Security Administration (NNSA) within DOE also sponsors cybersecurity research to support its unique mission requirements.

DHS: The DHS Science and Technology Directorate Cyber Security Division (DHS S&T CSD) focuses on applied R&D, test, evaluation, and transition for technologies to support civilian federal, state, and local governments and private sector unclassified needs to protect the national cyber infrastructure. Of particular interest to DHS are technologies that can be developed and transitioned to commercial products or used in federal, state, and local government systems. DHS S&T CSD has promoted innovation and accelerated transition to practice by using Broad Agency Announcements (BAA) to solicit research proposals, supporting the Small Business Innovation Research (SBIR) program, participating in and initiating public–private partnerships, and collaborating with federal agencies and international partners through joint project funding and management. In FY 2011, DHS S&T CSD issued BAA 11-02 which solicited proposals for R&D in 14 technical areas (TAs), spanning all research themes of the Strategic Plan.

IARPA: IARPA's cybersecurity research is spearheaded by its Office of Safe and Secure Operations (SSO), which aims to counter emerging adversary potential to ensure the U.S. Intelligence Community's (IC) operational effectiveness in a globally interdependent and networked environment. SSO's research portfolio is organized into three areas: computational power, trustworthy components, and safe and secure systems. Objectives within the computational power area include developing revolutionary advances in science and engineering to solve problems intractable with today's computers, focusing on the fundamental elements of quantum computing systems, and exploring the feasibility of a superconducting computer. In the trustworthy components area, research programs focus on understanding and manipulating very small-scale electronics, obtaining mission-worthy chips from the state-of-the-art, but untrusted fabrication facilities, and gaining functionality from unpedigreed software without placing mission systems at risk. Finally, research in the safe and secure systems area has a broad objective of safeguarding the integrity of missions in a hostile environment. Some of the current projects focus on enabling collaboration without wholesale sharing of data through privacy-preserving search techniques. Research in both the trustworthy components and safe and secure systems areas contributes directly to the Tailored Trustworthy Spaces research theme.

NIST: NIST's Information Technology Laboratory (ITL) is a recognized thought leader in cryptography, identity management, key management, mobile security, risk management, security automation, security of networked systems, foundations of measurement science for information systems, secure virtualization, cloud security, trusted roots of hardware, usability and security, and vulnerability management. ITL is composed of six divisions. In particular, the NIST Software and Systems Division (SSD) works with industry, academia, and other government agencies to increase trust and confidence in the deployed software, standards, and testing tools for today's software infrastructures and tomorrow's next-generation software systems, and conformance testing. In addition, the NIST Computer Security Division (CSD) within the ITL leads the government's efforts in risk management, identity management, key management, security automation, mobile security, trusted roots for hardware, vulnerability management, and cryptography. CSD's activities in key management, multifactor authentication, and identity management strongly contribute to the Tailored Trustworthy Spaces theme. Among its recent priorities, CSD's efforts in information security continuous monitoring (ISCM) support the *Moving Target Defense* or theme by developing tools and specifications that maintain ongoing awareness of information security, vulnerabilities, and threats to support organizational risk management decisions. The NIST National Cybersecurity Center of Excellence (NCCoE) and National Strategy for Trusted Identities in Cyberspace (NSTIC) Program Management Office are focused on driving adoption of cybersecurity and identity management standards and best practices to support measurable improvements in the cybersecurity landscape.

NSA: NSA has several research efforts exploring the Tailored Trustworthy Spaces theme, including exploration of risk through behavioral analytics and large-scale data analysis, novel means to detect modifications to computing systems and network analytics, and efforts to customize system controls. NSA is also exploring Moving Target technologies. In partnership with the DoD, the agency produced a survey of current Moving Target techniques, thereby enabling a cost–benefit analysis that will take into account different approaches and technologies; the potential impact Moving Target protections may have on mission operations, the costs and overheads associated with implementation; and the overall effectiveness of the movement response. In addition, NSA is supporting activities that foster an interdisciplinary collaborative community around the science of security, including a virtual organization and four university-based multidisciplinary research centers.

NSF: NSF invests in cybersecurity research through several programs, including the Directorate of Engineering (ENG) programs in Communications, Circuits, and Sensing-Systems (CCSS) and Energy, Power, and Adaptive Systems (EPAS). A major program in cybersecurity is spearheaded by the NSF Directorate of Computer and Information Science and Engineering (CISE), in collaboration with the Directorates of Education and Human Resources (EHR), Engineering (ENG), Mathematical and Physical Sciences (MPS), and Social, Behavioral, and Economic (SBE) Sciences. NSF's solicitation for the Secure and Trustworthy Cyberspace (SaTC) Program provides funding to university investigators for research activities on all four Strategic Plan thrusts, with an explicit option for transition to practice projects. The solicitation provides funding for projects related to cybersecurity education, as well as SBE perspectives on cybersecurity. Another major program is CyberCorps: SFS led by the EHR Directorate. This program supports cybersecurity education and workforce development.

Office of Naval Research (ONR): ONR cybersecurity strategies focus on long- and medium-term scientific and technology areas that have the potential for delivering significant improvements in the robustness, resiliency, security, and operational effectiveness of cyber environments. ONR's cybersecurity research contributes strongly to be the objectives identified in the Moving Target, Tailored

Trustworthy Spaces, and Designed-In Security areas. The Moving Target theme is particularly supported by the Robust and Autonomic Computing Systems Program, a long-term initiative for exploring architectures and approaches for future adaptive computing systems. Research in the Tailored Trustworthy Spaces area is supported by the Fabric Project a medium-term project providing strong, principled security guarantees based on explicitly stated security policies, and does so for distributed systems with complex, incomplete, and changing trust between participants. Additional programs such as Automation in Cryptology, Software Efficiency Reclamation, Computer Network Defense and Information Assurance, and Quantum Information Sciences contribute to the Strategic Plan by developing novel capabilities and technologies across the research themes. At the Georgia Institute of Technology, ONR-funded researchers investigated the theory and models for botnets, and developed state-of-the-art algorithms, methods, and tools for detecting and tracking botnets and their command and control. Their research has been invaluable for the DoD, as well as the tools developed and now in use by the FBI for taking down botnets and tracking down botmasters and individual operators. In addition, ONR promotes underexplored research topics that have promising impacts on cybersecurity. For example, at the University of California, ONR is supporting a technical investigation of the underground economy that allows botnets to exist.

OSD: DoD's cybersecurity science and technology programs emphasize game-changing research over incremental approaches, and enhance the organizational ties and experimental infrastructure needed to accelerate transition of new technologies into practice. The Assistant Secretary of Defense for Research and Engineering (ASD(R&E)) formed the DoD Cyber S&T Community of Interest (DoD Cyber COI). The DoD has specialized needs in cybersecurity due to the nature of its national security and warfighting mission. The DoD Cyber COI was charged with developing a DoD Cyber S&T problem statement, challenge areas that address warfighter requirements, a research framework, priority technology areas, and, in particular, a Cyber S&T Roadmap of the current and needed research in cybersecurity.

The Cyber S&T Roadmap lays out four areas of research: Foundations of Trust, Resilient Infrastructure, Agile Operations, and Assuring Effective Missions. All four areas relate strongly to the Designed-In Security theme, strengthening different attributes of security through the development, design, and validation methods, component and system design, algorithms, protocols, and architecture. The Foundations of Trust area contributes particularly to the Tailored Trustworthy Spaces theme. The Resilient Infrastructure and Agile Operations areas support the Moving Target theme.[7]

There are numerous aspects of the NITRD that help drive the work of the program and more information can be found on the website (www.nitrd.gov/Index.aspx). The later chapters of this book will focus on the actual research being supported and conducted by the laboratories and agencies (Figure 1.1).

Networking and Information Technology Research and Development (NITRD) Member Agencies
Agency for Healthcare Research and Quality (AHRQ)
Defense Advanced Research Projects Agency (DARPA)
Department of Homeland Security (DHS)
Environmental Protection Agency (EPA)
Military Service Research Organizations (Air Force, Army, Navy)
National Aeronautics and Space Administration (NASA)
National Archives and Records Administration (NARA)
National Coordination Office for Networking and Information Technology Research and Development (NITRD/NCO)
National Institute of Standards and Technology (NIST)
National Institutes of Health (NIH)
National Nuclear Security Administration (DOE/NNSA)
National Oceanic and Atmospheric Administration (NOAA)
National Reconnaissance Office (NRO)
National Science foundation (NSF)
National Security Agency (NSA)
Office of Electricity and Energy Reliability (DOE/OE)
Office of Management and Budget (OMB)
Office of Science (DOE/SC)
Office of Science and Technology Policy (OSTP)
Office of the National Coordinator for Health Information Technology (ONC)
Office of the Secretary of Defense (OSD)

Figure 1.1 NITRD Member Agencies. (From The Networking and Information Technology Research and Development Program. Report on Implementing Federal Cybersecurity Research and Development Strategy. Retrieved November 11, 2016 from https://www.nitrd.gov/PUBS/ImplFedCybersecurityRDStrategy-June2014.pdf)

1.7 2016 Federal Cybersecurity RDSP

The NSTC's Federal Cybersecurity RDSP responds to Section 201 of the Cybersecurity Enhancement Act of 2014, which directs the NSTC and the NITRD Program to develop a Strategic Plan to guide federal cybersecurity R&D. It builds on Trustworthy Cyberspace: Strategic Plan for the Federal Cybersecurity Research and Development Program, which was released by the NSTC in December 2011.

State-of-the-art approaches to cyber defense typically focus on the detection of known cyber events and related artifacts in the later phases of malicious activity; analysis is often ex-post in order to investigate and discover new indicators from the earlier phases. As malicious cyber activities have increased and methods have evolved over the years, the established approaches (e.g., signature-based detection, anomaly detection) have not adequately enabled cybersecurity practitioners to stay ahead of these threats.

The gap between aspirations for detection and the current state of detection is striking. It is clear that defenders are not detecting malicious cyber activities at the earliest possible time. It seems very likely that many completed and ongoing malicious activities are never detected; some are probably completed and the tracks are cleaned up, while others likely continue to this day. To address these challenges, new technologies must be developed that

- Enable robust situational awareness to defend networks and systems that identify all critical assets contained within network when devices have been added or removed, as well as the attributes and anomalies associated with the users. Real-time change detection, including schemes that are flexible enough for dynamic network conditions and that enable comparisons against last known good system states, is essential.

- Identify weaknesses in systems when changes in system configuration, introduction of new applications, or discovery of new techniques may reduce the level of protection or create new vulnerabilities. Tools are required to identify the shortcomings in protection measures in near real time, so that the situation can be remediated.

- To reliably detect malicious cyber activities, research is needed to determine whether the security tools are ineffective or underutilized. Additional R&D is required to ensure that the techniques can reliably detect the full range of adversaries' malicious cyber activities and reduce the detection time. In particular, tools are needed that can detect zero-day malware and innovative sequences of operations with acceptable levels of false positives and negatives as well as behavioral intrusion detection and heuristic tools, which look for anomalies to system baseline activities, offer an avenue of promising research.

Near-term R&D objectives are to discover and apply automated tools to map networks, including entities, attributes, roles, and logical relationships between processes and behaviors as well as usable presentation interfaces that allow operators to better anticipate incidents, discover them in progress, and achieve better post-incident response.

While midterm R&D objectives are to use data analytics to identify malicious cyber activities and differentiate them from authorized user behavior with low false positive and false negative rates and apply predictive analysis techniques across a range of potential cyber-threat vectors (e.g., via software or hardware) and determine the probable course of action for each threat method. Predictive analysis supports all four defensive elements: deter, protect, detect, and adapt. The long-term R&D objectives is to develop automated tools for cyber-threat forecasting in order to assess the limitations of protective measures and better inform sensor deployment.

As cybersecurity technologies are integrated into complex systems and systems of systems, responses often have unforeseen dependencies and coupled interactions. Developers and users need visibility and insight into these system behaviors, as well as analytic techniques and response pathways that maintain clarity and trust and avoid unintended consequences.

Modern IT systems were often designed according to decades-old principles developed when compute cycles and memory were expensive resources that had to be conserved at the expense of other concerns including cybersecurity. Currently, compute cycles and memory are comparatively cheap, so new design principles can more readily take into consideration the ongoing cybersecurity research, the persistence of legacy systems, and the continued adoption of disruptive technologies (e.g., Internet of things [IoT]). While comparatively cheap compute cycles and storage establish new opportunities for each of the defensive elements, the opportunities for adaptation and resilience are particularly striking.

Ongoing cybersecurity research is exploring new clean-slate design approaches, including new hardware architectures that eliminate broad classes of exploitable vulnerabilities by explicitly maintaining the distinction between executable code and data, and new software that introduces diversity among instances of applications. Some approaches are inspired by biological immune systems, creating cyber systems that continue to function in the face of malicious cyber activities and acquire immunity to new methods by learning from past compromises. Systems designed with these clean-slate approaches will continue to interact with legacy systems and technologies, so new design principles must consider the need to achieve resilience in heterogeneous systems that contain suspect components.

Another challenge comes from the increasing use of autonomous systems, which must also be able to support response, recovery, and adjustment with little or no interaction with (or even knowledge on the part of) cyber defenders. Further, adversaries might co-opt or exploit autonomous functions, and the machine learning that underlies them. The implications of autonomy must be considered as resilience design principles and technologies are created.

Multi-scale risk governance presents technical challenges to current cyber defense activities. Decisions that increase, decrease, or shift factors that contribute to risk are made at many levels and at multiple scales. Decisions made at one level can affect other levels in complex and not always obvious ways. Technical approaches are needed to identify and understand risk dependencies and explore the resulting decision space. Another challenge is that the time within which decisions must be made and implemented continues to shrink. Therefore, to improve the overall ability of systems to adapt, R&D activities should improve the capacity of systems, enterprises, and critical infrastructure to respond, recover, and adjust in three ways:

■ Dynamic assessment measure the key properties and attributes of system components and assess the potential damage in a trustworthy manner, thereby enabling response and recovery to a known good state. Dynamic assessment means doing this in the context of evolving threat methodologies and system requirements. Focus areas include the following:

■ Real-time digital forensic analysis methods that can provide cyber defenders with insight and understanding of the tactics, techniques, and procedures used by adversaries. These include methods and tools for the analysis of digital media, data, devices, and network data, and that apply to newer technologies such as mobile, embedded systems, IoT, and distributed cloud services, as well as traditional IT and industrial control systems (ICSs).

■ Real-time assessment of changes, behaviors, and anomalies to enable cyber professionals and other decision makers to make accurate damage assessments, predict, and manage potential effects on operations, and determine when system anomalies indicate malicious activity.

Discovery and analysis of system components and interdependencies (including those injected by adversaries in supply-chain-based malicious cyber activities) to provide insight into how changes in them can affect missions or business functions at multiple scales and timeframes. Adaptive response requires methods to adjust to actual, emerging, and anticipated disruptions, so that mission and organizational needs can continue to be met, while unintended consequences and adversary return-on-investment are minimized. These methods will support risk trade-offs in homogeneous enterprise systems in the near-term, and integrated heterogeneous cyber-physical systems (CPSs) in the midterm. In the long term, they will enable integrated resilient architectures that are optimized for the ability to absorb shocks and speed recovery to a known secure operable state. Focus areas include the following:

■ Autonomous reconfiguration and movement of resources to enable changing cyber assets to be marshaled and directed in order to create a defensive advantage.

■ Transparent direct remediation and indirect mitigation of damage. Direct remediation mechanisms isolate damaged or compromised components and systems and provide (via alternate mechanisms, if necessary) essential functionality transparently to end users. Direct remediation will thwart irreparable harm to assets (e.g., destruction or indeterminate corruption) and degradation of critical operations. Indirect mitigation includes recovering, repairing, reconstituting, or replacing potentially compromised components, information flows, or systems, and applying supply chain analysis and reverse engineering so that components can be identified and at scale.

■ Application of social science for security, including manipulation of adversary perceptions of cyber effects (e.g., via denial and deception techniques) in order to influence the adversary's knowledge of, and confidence in, the effectiveness of their cyber operations.

Near-term R&D objectives are to develop the technologies and techniques that enable critical assets to adjust and continue operating acceptably, despite adversary actions. Midterm R&D objectives are to establish methods to achieve the timely recovery of functionality of interdependent systems even while adversary activity continues. Long-term R&D objectives are to build adaptive effective collective defenses informed by predictive analysis that minimize adversary-imposed effects, as well as unintended effects caused by defender actions.

It is estimated that 80% to 90% of current cybersecurity failures are due to human and organizational shortcomings. Comprehensive cybersecurity requires understanding the human facets of cyber threats and secure cyber systems. Much research in SBE disciplines has investigated the human aspects of cybersecurity problems. The field of cybersecurity economics examines adversaries' incentives and the means by which they profit from malicious cyber activities in the real world. The economic analysis of incentives helps explain why individuals and organizations do (and do not) take action to detect and mitigate cybersecurity threats. Social psychologists have investigated the impact of individual characteristics (e.g., age, gender, dispositional factors of personality) and social norms on promoting good practices in cyberspace.

Research on persuasion has identified the methods to train, incentivize, or encourage users to improve their cybersecurity behavior. Socio-technical investigations have expanded understanding of the role of trust and assurance in secure socio-technical systems as well as deception and adverse intentions in malicious cyber activities. While these are excellent examples of fruitful multidisciplinary research activities, many opportunities in the economic, human, and social research still exist for improving cybersecurity. Research is needed to support the following four elements:

■ Research in economic ecosystem externalities to enable understanding of the impact of trust and organizational design on cybersecurity decisions, as well as the role of microeconomics and macroeconomics in the design, construction, and operation of software, hardware, and systems.

■ Modeling and social and behavioral experimentation to help identify the strengths and weaknesses of incentive mechanisms to acquire and deploy cybersecurity measures.

■ Development of validated sociological models of human weaknesses and strengths for use in analyzing security properties in systems and the respective roles of users, developers, operators, defenders, and adversaries. There is also a need to identify and teach human behaviors that enhance security and identify the effective methods to encourage more cybersecure behavior in the design and operation of IT systems.

■ Modeling international norms, rules of engagement, and escalation dynamics of malicious cyber activities to cyberwarfare to enable identification of institutional and structural factors that promote or undermine a secure cyberspace.[8]

1.8 The Growing Necessity for Diverse and Specialized Research

It is widely accepted that cyberspace has moved well beyond websites and social media applications. We are now in the age of the IoT. Through the integration of computers, sensors and networking in physical devices, the IoT fuses the physical and digital worlds to develop new capabilities and services, which in turn create new opportunities. Innovators and entrepreneurs around the world are in the development phase and initial stages of deployment of IoT systems and services, extending the Internet beyond laptops and personal technology devices to everyday devices of all types from cars and clothing to homes and factories while adding the sensors and computing capabilities that make them smart.

While IoT devices incorporate many technologies people have used for decades including microprocessors, cameras, and other sensors this is only the beginning. Small, ordinary-looking devices placed in homes and businesses can help keep us secure, but they also open important privacy questions; sensors in cars, trucks, airplanes, and ships help identify and prevent failures or accidents before they happen but also open new cybersecurity vulnerabilities; and complex IoT software and operating systems may contain bugs or are not updated regularly, raising questions about safe deployment in critical health, infrastructure, and even everyday uses.[9]

As exciting as many people believe this to be, it is only the beginning and will eventually be dwarfed into a novelty. With the commercialization of space exploration and travel in the United States and the establishment of the Office of Space Commercialization in 2007 in the U.S. Department of Commerce, National Oceanic and Atmospheric Administration the government has developed a Strategic Plan to

- Facilitate an environment that enables increased space commerce investment
- Increase U.S. government use of commercial space goods and services
- Reduce U.S. government competition with industry
- Reduce legal, policy, and institutional impediments to space commerce
- Promote growth in the export of space-related goods and services
- Advocate free and fair trade practices in space commerce
- Increase communication between the U.S. government, commercial space industry, the media, and the general public on space commerce issues[10]

The new frontier will require resilient and secure networks for space operations, vehicles, and stations. They may very well have their own Internet which will facilitate commerce and industry in space.

The government of Luxembourg announced in early 2016 that the country will be investing in the as-yet-unrealized industry of asteroid mining. Luxembourg will be funding research into the extraction of minerals from objects in space, working on legal and regulatory frameworks to govern such activities and, potentially, directly investing in companies active in the field. The nation's ministry of the economy says in a statement that the measures are meant to position Luxembourg as a European hub in the exploration and use of space resources. Luxembourg is already home to SES, a satellite operator, and has previously moved to boost its international high-tech profile. There are technical challenges involved in finding promising targets, sending unmanned spacecraft to mine them, managing communications within the technology infrastructure, and returning exploited resources safely to Earth. Japan's space agency is working in a similar direction.

Asteroids are governed by the Outer Space Treaty which says space and space objects do not belong to any individual nation. What that means for mining activities has never been tested in international courts because, well, nobody's managed to mine an asteroid yet. The U.S. Space Act of 2015 says American companies are permitted to harvest resources from outer space. The law asserts that extracting minerals from an extraterrestrial object is not a declaration of sovereignty. However, it is not clear what happens if another country passes a contradictory law, or if treaties are arranged that cover extraction of minerals from space.

To research and develop cybersecurity and secure networking technologies for Earth-based enterprises and space activities as well as for future space exploration, a variety of U.S. government agencies will need to continue to research at the science, technology, and application levels to protect the future Internet infrastructure and networked activities.

1.9 Summary

The cybersecurity efforts of the U.S. government are maturing and starting to show more solid progress including the coordination and prioritization of cybersecurity research activities. This chapter traces some of the significant actions on the part of the government that has led to the current state of affairs on cybersecurity and cybersecurity research. The major legislation and executive actions that have impacted the progress of these efforts include

- The CNCI of 2009
- The FISMA of 2014
- The Cybersecurity Act of 2015 and AIS
- The Strategic Plan for the Federal Cybersecurity Research and Development Program of 2011

There are several national laboratories and federal agencies that will apply their unique capabilities to research programs designed to address the goals and challenges outlined in the Strategic Plan including

- Air Force Research Laboratory (AFRL)
- Army Research Laboratory (ARL)

- Defense Advanced Research Projects Agency (DARPA)
- Department of Energy (DOE)
- Department of Homeland Security (DHS)
- Intelligence Advanced Research Projects Activity (IARPA) National Institute of Standards and Technology (NIST)
- National Security Agency (NSA)
- National Science Foundation (NSF)
- Office of the Secretary of Defense (OSD)

This book examines a wide range of cybersecurity research activities being conducted by the U.S. Science Laboratories, branches of the military, and civilian agencies listed above as well as by cybersecurity research efforts in other agencies.

1.10 Seminar Discussion Topics

Discussion topics for graduate or professional-level seminars are

- What experience has seminar participants had working with or utilizing U.S. government cybersecurity programs or cybersecurity research efforts?
- What experience has seminar participants had with private corporations or nongovernmental organizations that have worked with U.S. government cybersecurity programs or cybersecurity research efforts?
- What areas of U.S. government cybersecurity research do seminar participants think are the most important? Why?
- What areas of U.S. government cybersecurity research do seminar participants think are the most relevant to the private sector? Why?

Key Terms

counterintelligence capabilities: are the knowledge, skills, technology, and organization that provide a comprehensive security program and constant evaluation of the intentions and targets of foreign intelligence services. CI capabilities and programs also work to detect and neutralize the impact of espionage against national interests

moving target defense: is a rotational environment that runs an application on several different operating system platforms to thwart attacker reconnaissance efforts and improve application resilience to the threat of zero-day exploits

multifactor authentication: uses a combination of two (or more) different methods to authenticate a user identity. The first is what users know, usually a password, but this can also include a user response to a challenge question which is generally known as knowledge-based authentication, and, by itself, is insufficient for authentication to sensitive information. The second is what users have such as a physical object (token), for example, a smart card, or hardware token that generates one-time-only passwords. It might also be some encrypted software token installed on an individual's system. The third is who users are, as indicated by some biometric characteristic such as a fingerprint or an iris pattern

personally identifiable information (PII): is information that can be used to distinguish or trace an individual's identity, either alone or when combined with other personal or identifying information that is linked or linkable to a specific individual

public/private partnerships: joint efforts for a mutual cause and benefit between government agencies and private corporations, foundations, or nongovernmental organizations

single use code delivered in a text message: is an authentication technique that is used to assure controlled access to online applications or databases by sending the user a text code that can be used only once to access an application and expires within minutes if not used

References

1. U.S. GAO. *Cybersecurity National Strategy, Roles, and Responsibilities Need to Be Better Defined and More Effectively Implemented.* February 2013. Retrieved November 10, 2016, www.gao.gov/products/GAO-13-187
2. Internet Crime Complaint Center (IC3). *2015 Internet Crime Report.* Retrieved November 10, 2016, https://www.ic3.gov/images/2015IC3Report.png
3. The White House. *The Comprehensive National Cybersecurity Initiative.* Retrieved November 8, 2016, https://www.whitehouse.gov/issues/foreign-policy/cybersecurity/national-initiative
4. S.2521—*Federal Information Security Modernization Act of 2014 113th Congress (2013–2014).* December 18, 2014. Retrieved November 8, 2016, https://www.congress.gov/bill/113th-congress/senate-bill/2521
5. U.S. Department of Homeland Security. *Automated Indicator Sharing (AIS).* Retrieved November 8, 2016, https://www.us-cert.gov/sites/default/files/ais_files/AIS_fact_sheet.pdf
6. The White House. *The Cybersecurity National Action Plan.* February 9, 2016. Retrieved November 8, 2016, https://www.whitehouse.gov/the-press-office/2016/02/09/fact-sheet-cybersecurity-national-action-plan
7. The Networking and Information Technology Research and Development Program. *Report on Implementing Federal Cybersecurity Research and Development Strategy.* Retrieved November 11, 2016, https://www.nitrd.gov/PUBS/ImplFedCybersecurityRDStrategy-June2014.pdf
8. National Science and Technology Council. *Networking and Information Technology Research and Development Program. 2016 Federal Cybersecurity Research and*

Development Strategic Plan. February 2016. Retrieved November 27, 2016, https://www.whitehouse.gov/sites/whitehouse.gov/files/documents/2016_Federal_Cybersecurity_Research_and_Development_Stratgeic_Plan.pdf

9. The White House. *Internet of Things: Examining Opportunities and Challenges.* August 30, 2016. Retrieved November 10, 2016, https://www.whitehouse.gov/blog/2016/08/30/internet-things-examining-opportunities-and-challenges

10. U.S. Department of Commerce, National Oceanic and Atmospheric Administration. *U.S. Leadership in Space Commerce Office of Space Commercialization Strategic Plan.* March 2007. Retrieved November 10, 2016, http://www.space.commerce.gov/wp-content/uploads/NOAA-2007-Space-Commercialization-Strategic-Plan-6-pages.pdf

Chapter 2

The Department of Homeland Security Cybersecurity Research Programs

The Homeland Security Advanced Research Projects Agency (HSARPA) supports research in technologies, new capabilities, and threat and risk assessments for the Homeland Security Enterprise (HSE).[1] The DHS S&T CSD focuses on applied R&D, test, evaluation, and transition for technologies to support civilian federal, state, and local governments and private sector unclassified needs to protect the cyber infrastructure. Of particular interest to DHS are technologies that can be developed and transitioned to commercial products or used in federal, state, and local government systems. DHS S&T CSD has promoted innovation and accelerated transition to practice by using BAA to solicit research proposals, supporting the SBIR program, participating in and initiating public–private partnerships, and collaborating with federal agencies and international partners through joint project funding and management. In FY 2011, DHS S&T CSD issued BAA 11-02 which solicited proposals for R&D in 14 TAs, spanning all research themes of the Strategic Plan.[2] To maintain the focus on research, there are several development programs and projects, numerous partnerships, industry coordination efforts, and transition projects going on in DHS that are not covered in this chapter.

2.1 DHS CSD Research

The DHS CSD creates and deploys information resources, standards, frameworks, tools, and technologies enabling seamless and secure interactions among homeland security stakeholders through a practitioner-driven approach. With a wide-range of partnerships across federal agencies, state and municipal administrations and first responders, critical infrastructure sectors, Internet security researchers, universities, national laboratories, and international organizations, CSD works to strengthen cybersecurity capabilities.

CSD funds cybersecurity R&D projects that result in a deployable solution. By using a cybersecurity R&D lifecycle process which includes research, development, test, evaluation, and transition to practice these unclassified solutions can be implemented in both public and private sectors. The goal is to bring innovative, usable technologies, tools, and techniques to defend, mitigate, and secure current and future systems, networks, and critical infrastructures against cyberattacks.[3] Areas that CSD funds cybersecurity R&D projects include:

■ Anonymous Networks and Currencies
■ Assessment and Evaluation (see Cybersecurity Metrics)
■ Cyber Analytics Behavior and Resilience (see Cybersecurity Metrics)
■ Cyber Economic Incentives (see Cybersecurity Metrics)
■ Cyber-Physical Systems Security (CPSSEC)
■ Cyber Security Forensics
■ Cybersecurity Competitions (see Talent Development)
■ Cybersecurity Incident Response Teams (CSIRT) (see Talent Development)
■ Data Privacy Technologies
■ Distributed Denial of Service Defense (DDoSD)
■ Distributed Environment for Critical Infrastructure Decision-making Exercises (DECIDE) (see Talent Development)
■ Enterprise-Level Security Metrics and Usability (see Cybersecurity Metrics)
■ Experimental Research Testbed (DETER)
■ Experiments and Pilots
■ Insider Threat
■ Internet Measurement and Attack Modeling
■ Mobile Device Security (MDS)
■ Security of Cloud-Based Systems

2.2 Anonymous Networks and Currencies

The emergence of Bitcoin and other virtual currencies has presented a number of unique opportunities and challenges. Building innovative platforms for conducting commerce can help improve the depth and breadth of a national financial system. However, there have also been instances where the cloak of anonymity provided by virtual currencies has helped support dangerous criminal activity, such as drug smuggling, money laundering, gun running, and child pornography.

If virtual currencies remain a virtual wild west for narcotics traffickers and other criminals, that would not only threaten the national security, but also the very existence of the virtual currency industry as a legitimate business enterprise. Thus, it is in the common interest of the public and the virtual currency industry to bring virtual currencies out of the darkness and into the light of day through enhanced transparency. It is vital to put in place appropriate safeguards for consumers and law-abiding citizens.

Firms engaging in money transmission are generally required by states to post collateral in order to better safeguard customer account funds. In addition, they are required to undergo periodic safety and soundness examinations, as well as comply with applicable anti-money laundering laws. These guidelines for money transmitters help protect consumers and root out illegal activity. In addition, putting in place appropriate regulatory safeguards for virtual currencies will be beneficial to the long-term strength of the virtual currency industry.

Safety and soundness requirements help build greater confidence among customers that the funds that they entrust to virtual currency companies will not get stuck in a digital black hole. Indeed, some consumers have expressed concerns about how quickly their virtual currency transactions are processed. Taking steps to ensure that these transactions, particularly redemptions, are processed promptly is vital to earning the faith and confidence of customers.

Virtual currency companies and the currencies themselves have received significant interest from investors and venture capital firms. Similar to any other industry, greater transparency and accountability is critical to promoting sustained, long-term investment. Taking steps to root out illegal activity is both a legal and business imperative for virtual currency firms serving as a money changer of choice for terrorists, drug smugglers, illegal weapons dealers, money launderers, and human traffickers who could expose the virtual currency industry to extraordinarily serious criminal penalties.[4]

Anonymous networks and *cryptocurrencies* have many legitimate applications to support the freedom of the press, protect human rights, and allow new methods of payments that protect individual privacy. However, criminals are exploiting the protections built into the encryption and the promise of near anonymity. Investigating anonymous networks and cryptocurrencies is resource intensive and difficult, requiring significant man-hours to investigate and prosecute criminals involved in illegal activities on anonymous marketplaces and websites.

DHS S&T is developing cost-effective solutions for law enforcement components to complement and expand their capabilities to investigate crimes. Strong partnerships with law enforcement results in requirements for solutions fitting specific investigative needs while protecting the privacy and the legitimate uses of anonymous networks and cryptocurrencies. Current anonymous networks and currencies efforts include the following:

- New Tor Service Protocol: Development of a new service protocol for The Onion Router (Tor) to provide stronger encryption and protections for law enforcement communications within the anonymous networks. This effort will improve security through protocol enhancements and provide end-to-end encryption.
- Safe Aggregation of Usage Statistics: Development of techniques to provide for a safe aggregation of usage statistics within anonymous networks while respecting and protecting the privacy and anonymity of anonymous network users.
- System Analysis, Requirements Gathering, and Tool Development: Implementation of system analysis of the broader anonymous network and cryptocurrency landscape to generate additional requirements and develop broader solutions to investigate criminal activities.
- Cryptocurrency Forensics: Development of tools to enable law enforcement to perform forensic analysis of cryptocurrency transactions and facilitate the tracing of currencies involved in illicit transactions.[5]

2.3 Cyber-Physical Systems Security

The CPSSEC program addresses the security concerns for CPSs and the IoT. CPS and IoT play an increasingly important role in critical infrastructure, government, and in everyday life. Automobiles, medical devices, building controls, and the smart grid are examples of CPS. Each includes smart networked systems with embedded sensors, processors, and actuators that sense and interact with the physical world and support real-time, guaranteed performance in safety-critical applications. The closely related area of IoT continues to emerge and expand as costs drop and the confluence of sensors, platforms, and networks increases. Whether referencing the forward collision prevention capability of a car, a medical device's ability to adapt to circumstances in real time, or the latest IoT innovation, these systems are a source of competitive advantage in an innovation economy. At the same time, CPS and IoT also increase cybersecurity risks and attack surfaces. The consequences of unintentional faults or malicious attacks could have severe impact on human lives and the environment.

Advances in networking, computing, sensing, and control systems have enabled a broad range of new devices. Designs are evolving rapidly and standards are only now emerging. Many devices being deployed now have life spans measured in decades, so current design choices will impact the next several decades in transportation, health care, building controls, emergency response, energy, and other sectors.

If security is overlooked, there is an increased risk of unintentional faults or even malicious attacks changing how cars brake, how medical devices adapt, and how buildings and the smart grid respond to events. Cybersecurity only becomes more challenging if billions of devices with security vulnerabilities are added.

The objective of the CPSSEC project is to ensure CPS and IoT security vulnerabilities are identified and addressed before system designs are complete and the resulting devices are widely deployed. In other words, the goal is to build security in rather than bolt on it on later. To accomplish this, the project will have to

- Rapidly develop cyber security technical guidance for critical infrastructure sectors facing CPS and IoT challenges.
- Conduct this effort in collaboration with key government, infrastructure, and industry partners.
- Transition guidance in a sustainable way so that security is an integral part of CPS and IoT designs.
- When appropriate, produce reference implementations and risk-assessment tools to promote the inclusion of security in CPS and IoT devices.

The CPS and IoT space is vast and covers many distinct sectors. The Cyber-Physical Systems Vision Statement from the NITRD Program identifies nine areas of critical importance to government: agriculture, building controls, defense, energy, emergency response, health care, manufacturing and industry, society, and transportation. Further, these areas share crosscutting issues of cybersecurity, economics, interoperability, privacy, safety and reliability, and social aspects. No single agency can tackle these areas alone.[6]

2.4 Data Privacy Technologies

Data Privacy R&D Program helps government program managers with the R&D expertise and resources needed to enhance the security and trustworthiness of their programs. The program investigates architectures, technical approaches, studies, processes, technologies, tools, and proof-of-concepts across the following R&D topic areas:

- Automating control of personal data to minimize cognitive overload and privacy risk.
- Addressing privacy concerns with connected devices, mobile computing, and sensor platforms.
- Addressing privacy concerns with big data and algorithms.
- Managing PII or information deemed sensitive, while protecting individual privacy.
- Privacy respecting anomaly detection and counter-fraud technologies with population scale applicability.

The program regularly engages with agencies and the community to identify needs that cannot be met with current technologies, and to understand the current state of the art and practice in the data privacy domain. As an R&D program a major goal is to ensure that privacy managers are not surprised by the emerging trends or emerging issues in the future. This interaction drives the R&D of the capabilities needed to protect cyberspace in a manner that incorporates both security and privacy.

In cases where technologies do not exist or are immature, the program makes the necessary investments in applied research, advanced development, test and evaluation, and technology transition to ensure their availability to the HSE. Each engagement starts with a discovery process in which DHS works with agencies to understand and identify their need or the problem they are experiencing. Results of the discovery process generally results in one of two possible courses of action:

- A determination that technologies currently available in the marketplace can be used to solve the problem. (If technology meeting the need currently exists in the marketplace agencies are directly connected with potential solution providers.)
- A determination that a capability gap exists between the current state of technologies and what is needed to solve the problem. (If needed technology does not exist in the marketplace DHS performs analysis, proof-of-concepts, and any other activity to develop the capabilities to solve the problem and transition solutions to it using an agencies' existing acquisition mechanisms.)

DHS works with researchers and technology providers that present innovative ideas and technologies that map to the DHS research agenda. In general, DHS interest is focused around the following:

- Technology: developing an understanding and awareness of the current state of the art and practice to ensure that DHS can connect agencies to vetted providers and technologies that can solve their problems.
- Talent: DHS engages with talented researchers and organizations who can work to develop solutions to the complex needs of agencies that cannot be solved with current technologies.
- Transition: DHS lookouts for technology transition partners with the ability to commercialize, or incorporate into their existing product development roadmap, the technologies and solutions that DHS funds and develops.

DHS S&T awards in this area include

- $3.66M for Privacy-Enhancing Technology Research and Development (July 2016)

- International Computer Science Institute $664K for Data Privacy Research and Development (June 2016)
- Raytheon BBN Technologies $1.3M for Data Privacy Research (April 2016)
- Yale University $1.7M For Data Privacy Research (February 2016)[7]

2.5 Distributed Denial of Service Defense

A classic DDoS can disrupt a financial institutions website and temporarily blocks the ability of consumers to conduct online banking. A more strategic attack makes a key resource inaccessible during a critical period. Attacks can and have targeted any system that relies on Internet connectivity. The financial services sector has been a frequent target of large-scale DDoS attacks and continues to face ever-growing attacks. While these incidents are well documented, this segment of the economy is not a special case and some the largest attacks have been directed at security-related sites and services. Over the past five years, the scale of attacks has increased tenfold. It is not clear if the current network infrastructure could withstand future attacks if they continue to increase in scale. The DDoSD project has three complementary objectives:

- Reduce the ability to send forged (spoofed) packets through deployment of existing best practices such as Best Current Practice (BCP) 38.
- Develop Tools for Communication and Collaboration that allow a medium-scale organization to withstand a 1 terabit per second (1 Tbps) DDoS attack.
- Double the capacity of critical system such as 911 and NG911 to handle large telephony-based attacks (Telephony DoS [TDoS]) attacks.

This project addresses three related DDoSD challenges. First, DDoSD is working to increase deployment of best practices that would slow attack scale growth, specifically a technique called Internet BCP 38 that blocks forged packets at or near the source. Second, DDoSD is seeking to defend networks against massive 1 Tbps scale attacks through the development of collaboration tools suitable for medium-scale organizations. Lastly, the project is working to defend emergency management systems, both current 911 and Next Generation 911 systems, from TDoS attacks.

Some DDoS attacks make use of spoofed source addresses. The existing best practices filter out forged addresses at the network periphery. Additional best practices extend this guidance to more complex deployments. The collection of anti-spoofing best practices could help mitigate DDoS attacks that rely on forged addresses. Measurement and analysis tools are required to test whether new anti-spoofing deployments are successful, verify existing anti-spoofing practices are working correctly, and to provide evidence to demonstrate both advantages and limitations when anti-spoofing best practices are deployed in an organization.

The distributed nature of the DDoS attacks provides several advantages to the attacker. An attack often comes from a large number of compromised computers that span multiple organizations. Further, as network bandwidth and computational power increases, the attacker benefits from the increased resources, providing the capability to conduct more powerful attacks. To counter the threat, organizations that make use of network services should invest in resources that keep pace with the increasing significance of the attacks. In addition, organizations that deploy resources carelessly may simply provide the attacker with easily compromised resources that can then be used in future attacks. Even organizations with global scale capability, including those providing security-related services, have faced challenges in keeping pace with vast DDoS attacks.

Novel DDoS attack mitigation and defense techniques research seeks to address new variations of DoS attacks. DoS attack concepts are being directed at a growing range of services. For example, in spring 2013, DHS and the FBI issued warnings for DoS attacks targeting emergency management services, such as 911 systems. Systems including, but not limited to, mobile devices, CPSs, and critical infrastructure components are all potential targets for these attacks. Further, new variations of DoS attacks exploit vulnerabilities, such as overwhelming power supplies, software vulnerabilities, and other features.

Too often the response to new types of attacks and targets is reactive; attackers develop new techniques and/or target new systems and this drives mitigation efforts. Ideally, new techniques and new targets would be anticipated and defenses would be proactively developed before large-scale attacks occur. Therefore, the goal of this thrust area is to identify the potential targets for DDoS that have not been subject to known large-scale DDoS attacks, and to develop DDoS mitigation capabilities that will be able to withstand a DDoS attack that is double in magnitude from the capabilities of the target's DDoSD capability at the beginning of the project. Emergency management systems and CPSs are examples of nontraditional targets that are vulnerable to DoS and most relevant to this topic area.

DHS S&T awards in this area include

- $2.7M to Colorado State University for Cyber Security Research, September 2015
- USC Information Sciences Institute $1.8M Contract for Cyber Security Research, September 2015
- University of California San Diego $1.3M for Cyber Security Research (September 2015)
- Galois, Inc. $1.7M Contract for Cyber Security Research (September 2015)
- Waverley Labs $629K for Cyber Security Research (September 2015)
- University of Houston $2.6M for Cyber Security Research (September 2015)
- University of Delaware $1.9M for Cyber Security Research (September 2015)
- University of Oregon a 1.38M Contract for Cyber Security Research (August 2015)[8]

2.6 Talent Development Research

DHS has several talent development programs in place along with conducting research on talent development methods. The NICE calls for the development of adequate training and education programs to support cybersecurity needs (Priority III). A critical element of a cybersecurity strategy is having the right personnel at every level to identify, build, and staff the defenses and responses. To fulfill these needs, DHS researches and supports cybersecurity competitions.

The Collegiate Cyber Defense Challenge (CCDC) is a capture the flag-style tournament. The nation is divided into nine regions with an additional at-large region, where teams of eight students compete against each other to defend their networks and associated services and the winners of each region advance to the National CCDC. In 2015, more than 200 colleges and universities participated in CCDC events. The CCDC was recognized for its efforts to promote cybersecurity curriculum in institutions of higher learning by the 111th Congress and is mentioned as a model program in the White House's 2009 Cyberspace Policy Review. The CCDC program was also honored with the Visa Leadership in Security Award.

The U.S. Cyber Challenge (USCC) seeks to create a pipeline through which talented youth will be discovered, guided, and enabled to progress toward careers as technical cybersecurity experts. The goal is to deploy and test multiple talent competitions and talent development initiatives to enable high school and college students to develop and demonstrate their cyber skills. USCC organizes multiple events for high school students throughout the year including Cyber Foundations workshops as well as summer camps. Each camp features four days of intense instruction, culminating in a capture the flag-style competition.

One of the exciting aspects of the competitions for both students as well as DHS is the ability to introduce new tools or methodology into the competitions. The students get an opportunity to experiment and investigate novel tools coming out of government cybersecurity R&D programs, while the government development teams have an opportunity to obtain a rich data set that includes a high density of a variety of attacks with different real-time defense approaches. Competitions allow for the development of a new cybersecurity workforce that is already familiar with not only the current technology for cyber defense, but also the novel and emerging technologies that they can apply from their first day on the job.[9]

Research on the development of CSIRT helps to establish best practices and methods for team training and development. A CSIRT is a group of experts that assesses, documents, and responds to a cyber incident so that a network can not only recover quickly, but also avoid future incidents. S&T funds the CSIRT project to help CSIRT organizations at all levels of government and the private sector improve significantly through the development and application of superior approaches to incident response and organizational learning. Research is needed in this space because CSIRT teams are often dynamically formed and temporary in nature and assembled in response to specific incidents. In cyber incident response, teams often respond to problems or incidents that have not been seen before. There is no overarching set of guiding principles and best practices that CSIRTs can look to in terms of organization, training, and execution.

The core research focuses on current best practices from a business organizational psychology perspective to clearly explain how incident response individuals and teams can best work to improve complex cyber incident response to be faster, more efficient, and more adaptive. The work is being done by an academic/industry research team and in collaboration with the U.S. Computer Emergency Readiness Team and the NCCIC and international government partners from the Netherlands and Sweden. This underscores the international applicability of the cybersecurity challenge and its value as a partnership and confidence-building mechanism. The interdisciplinary team working on the project includes a cybersecurity and software engineering researcher, organizational psychologists, economists, and practitioners from a commercial partner with CSIRT expertise.[10]

DECIDE is another program which DHS has put into place. The DHS S&T, with support from the financial sector, including the Financial Services Sector Coordinating Council (FSSCC), is creating a tool to enable private sector entities located within critical infrastructures to conduct collaborative, realistic, fully immersive, scenario-based exercises with response decisions made by subject matter experts. DECIDE exercises are intended to enable participants to war-game stressful scenarios in a closed-loop manner where the consequences of each participant's actions are given as feedback into the exercise. These exercises are designed to help participants understand the systemic ramifications of their actions and those of their industry peers especially scenarios that may induce or exacerbate cascading failures, resource contention, systemic instability, and other unintended consequences. Furthermore, DECIDE exercises allow critical infrastructure operators to identify scenarios where industrywide coordinated response tactics are beneficial, and enable these scenarios to be exercised efficiently.

The tool significantly reduces barriers to exercise participation by encouraging the reuse of time and monetary investments in the exercise setup and planning process. DECIDE exercises insulate and protect each participant's proprietary information, allowing competitive institutions to exercise with confidence. Efficient, cost-effective, high-value, and low-risk, DECIDE exercises encourage participation from a full range of participants.

To be realistic, business continuity exercises in a large complex industry require participation from multiple organizations. This requirement has made industrywide exercises time- and resource intensive both from a planning standpoint and with respect to the level of commitment required from each participant. Moreover, lack of full industry participation often results in exercises that are incomplete or less robust than intended. DECIDE alleviates this requirement by providing artificial intelligence agents. These agents may be plugged into the exercise as needed to provide realistic simulation of nonpresent players. Artificial intelligence agents able to simulate specific industry activities are developed in close conjunction with industry subject matter experts. DECIDE allows these smart agents to be used interchangeably with human players. DECIDE is sponsored by the AFRL in support of DHS S&T.[11]

2.7 Cybersecurity Metrics

DHS is supporting research on *cybersecurity metrics* from several different perspectives. The Enterprise-Level Security Metrics and Usability project is designed to define effective information security metrics which has proven to be difficult in the past. Even though there is general agreement that such metrics could allow measurement of progress in security measures and, at a minimum, rough comparisons of security between systems. Metrics underlie and quantify progress in many other system security areas. As the saying goes, "You cannot manage what you cannot measure." The lack of sound and practical security metrics is severely hampering progress both in research and engineering of secure systems. However, general community agreement on meaningful metrics has been hard to achieve. This is due in part to the rapid evolution of IT, as well as the shifting focus of adversarial action.

Enterprise-level security metrics address the security posture of an organization. Experts, such as system administrators, and nontechnical users alike must be able to use an organization's system while still maintaining security. This project is developing security metrics and the supporting tools and techniques to make them practical and useful as decision aids. This will allow the user to measure security while achieving usability and make informed decisions based on the threat and cost to the organization.[12]

The *Cyber Analytics*, Behavior and Resilience projects go beyond the focus on technical aspects of cybersecurity to investigate aspects of security practice that involve human behavior, address trust of code and networks, and try to measure resilience of individuals and societies to cyber events. In 2013, S&T and the U.K. Home Office signed an Information Sharing Annex to support a joint project called Collaboration on Resiliency and Security (ColoRS). ColoRS is a collaboration between CSD and the U.K. Science and Technology Facilities Council. The purpose of this project is to identify areas of mutual interest related to resilient critical or societal infrastructures, which will lead to further focus and research. This work will focus on three topical areas: Securing Infrastructure from Cyber Disruptions; Modeling and Measuring Societal Resilience during a Cyber Event; and Streaming Analytics for Effective Data Exploitation.

The Visual Analytics for Security Applications (VASA) project is applying visual analytics to disaster prevention and crisis response, with a focus on critical infrastructures in logistics, transportation, food safety, digital networks, and power grids at the national levels. The connectedness and dependency of these critical infrastructures make the problem of monitoring and understanding their functioning and dependencies one of the most complex analytical tasks faced by society.

A number of U.S. universities and the Pacific Northwest National Laboratory (PNNL) are actively engaged in research under VASA focusing on the key aspects of interdependencies of failures, cascading effects, response, resiliency, and holistic risk management across infrastructures.

The Cyber Identity (Cy-identity) seedling project will combine provenance, network security, and identity management in a process that would secure cyber and critical infrastructure networks through high-precision identity attribution. This project complements current protection-focused cybersecurity measures, such as those being investigated in most CSD projects, and offers a method for measuring, quantifying, and expressing the relative security of cyber infrastructures. This seedling will fund an exploratory activity to further develop various approaches for demonstrating this concept.

The Super Identity (SuperID) project merges identity artifacts across the biometric, cyber, psychological, and biographical domains to enable identification and attribution across physical and online environments. The project takes help from cognitive psychologists, social psychologists, cybersecurity experts, forensic anthropologists, biometric engineers, user researchers, and designers to discover connections between the different domains of a person's identity. This project is collaboration between six U.K. universities funded by the Engineering and Physical Sciences Research Council (EPSRC) (Southampton, Leicester, Oxford, Dundee, Bath, Kent) and PNNL. The goal of all research efforts within the SuperID team is to contribute to an integrated model of the cyber, biometric, psychological, and biographical elements of identity. Taking a data-driven approach, a 120-person data collection study was performed in the United Kingdom to identify potential connections among these elements. To organize and annotate all the results from the research, the elements and transforms between them are represented as a graph called the SuperID Model. To bind the problem to realistic applications, use cases were researched through several interviews with law enforcement and intelligence communities.

Spatiotemporal Network Dynamics for Community Detection (SNDCD) project will explore the overall characterization of the social network structure with respect to its relationship with geographic places. The goal of SNDCD is to link information pertaining to real and virtual worlds in order to better manage the uncertainties inherent in establishing human identity. The basic premise is that uncertainty in identifying and characterizing individuals may be managed and understood by (a) exploring and analyzing spatiotemporal profiles of lifestyles and activity patterns; (b) concatenating and conflating detailed but underexploited datasets in the virtual and real domains; and, more speculatively; and (c) seeking and analyzing crowd-sourced volunteered data that link physical and virtual identities. Through these actions, it may be possible to improve the ability to characterize and validate an individual's identity, to devise improved profiles of individuals and groups that bridge the real and virtual domains, and to document and manage the uncertainties inherent in these tasks.[13]

The Cyber Security Assessment and Evaluation Project ensures that cybersecurity technologies developed both inside and outside of the DHS S&T are assessed and evaluated prior to operational deployment within the HSE and also provides an environment where emerging technologies are exposed to a broad range of end users and investors.

Assessments and evaluations are conducted through technical assessment, modeling, vulnerability and risk analysis, and red team evaluations and operational assessments. Performers execute a technology transition process whereby cybersecurity tools developed under sponsorship by DHS can be acquired, evaluated, and transitioned to end users, including owners and operators of U.S. critical infrastructures, private sector entities, and federal, state, and local law enforcement agencies. By leveraging cutting edge tools and technologies, end users have the opportunity to address contemporary cyber threats and enhance their security posture. This project impacts and influences the entire cybersecurity community, both within the federal government and in the private sector, in identifying and assessing cyber threats and vulnerabilities and assisting in the acquisition, evaluation, and deployment of cybersecurity technologies.[14]

The Cyber Economic Incentives Project is designed to measure where and how much should the private sector invest in cybersecurity as well as how can law enforcement alter the behaviors and motives of criminal enterprises investing in cybercrime. Unlike other research efforts, the methods being investigated focus on business aspects rather than technical aspects. By measuring the market or business value of cybersecurity targeted, lower-cost investments can be made that both control the effects of cyber threats and mitigate the risks of cybercrime and cyberattacks. The impact of this work will be realized through the production and use of the following:

- Actual data on the relative value of cybersecurity measures.
- Testable models or mathematical rules for determining where, how much, and on what measures to invest.
- Models for cybercriminal activities and Internet supply chains applicable to financial crimes and Internet trafficking of drugs and humans.
- Affordable and usable information-sharing schemes and networks that enable law enforcement agencies or private organizations to coordinate and prevent crimes or minimize threats.[15]

2.8 Experimental Research Testbed, Experiments, and Pilots

The DETER testbed is used to test and evaluate cybersecurity technologies by more than 220 organizations from more than 40 states and 30 countries, including DHS-funded researchers, the larger cybersecurity research community, government, industry, academia, and educational users. It provides the infrastructure needed to support the development and experimental testing of next-generation cybersecurity technologies. Due to the inherent risks of testing malicious software in operational networks, neither existing research network infrastructures nor the operational Internet meet this need. New security technologies are currently tested and validated in small- to medium-sized private research laboratories, which are not representative of the large operational networks or Internet elements that might be involved in a security attack.

The testbed facilitates scientific experimentation and validation against established baselines of attack behavior and supports innovative approaches that involve breaking the network infrastructure. The testing framework allows researchers to experiment with a variety of parameters representing the network environment, including deployed defense technologies, attack behaviors, and mechanism configurations. Current efforts support larger and more complex experiments with increased usability.[16]

Technology transfer from the lab to the marketplace is a vital aspect of the CSD's R&D efforts. The DHS Office of the Chief Information Officer, Federal Law Enforcement Training Center, National CSD, and other operational components need experimental deployment opportunities to investigate operational capabilities of new technologies. The Cyber Security Experiments and Pilots project provides a platform for experimentation, testing, evaluation, and operational deployment to facilitate technology transfer. Experiments and pilots allow for technologies developed through S&T to be tested and evaluated in operational environments and provide feedback for performers and vendors. Not only does this facilitate technology transfer, but also the feedback allows the DHS components to refine their requirements and ultimately make their infrastructure more secure. Examples of previous successful experiments and pilots include the Cyber Scenario Modeling and Reporting Tool and the Public Regional Information Security Event Management system, which used an S&T-funded botnet detection and mitigation tool.[17]

2.9 Internet Measurement, Attack Modeling, and Cyber Forensics

Research in Internet measurement will address the need for better understanding of connectivity among Internet service providers (ISPs). Associated data analysis, such as geographic mapping, will improve the understanding of peering relationships and thus provide a more complete view of network topology, which will help to identify the infrastructure components in greatest need of protection. In conjunction with this work, research in attack modeling will allow critical infrastructure owners/operators to predict the effects of cyberattacks on their systems, particularly in the areas of malware and botnet attacks, a growing area of concern (ref Conficker and Stuxnet attacks), and situational understanding and attack attribution. Attack protection, Prevention and Pre-emption, and Automated Attack Detection, Warning and Response are documented requirements found in the Federal Plan for CSIA R&D, a report coauthored by S&T and other program participants. Internet Measurement and Attack Modeling program focus areas include resilient systems and networks, modeling of Internet attacks, and network mapping and measurement.

The technical approach for Internet measurement is to improve the system used to collect network traffic information to provide scalable, real-time access to the data as it is being collected from around the globe. This data are being improved by increasing both the number of data collectors and the number of data points being monitored. To build a more complete map of the Internet, the effort will build upon previous research projects, which have built large research platforms capable of Internet measurements from points across the globe. These efforts include the following:

- Internet-scale emulation of observable malware, specifically botnets and worms to help identify weaknesses in the malware code and how it spreads or reacts to outside stimuli.
- New approaches in malware and botnet detection, identification and visualization, and automated binary analysis.
- Malware repository creation and sharing for collaborative detection may involve privacy-preserving security information sharing across independent domains. This may involve sharing malware samples, metadata of a sample, and/or experiences with appropriate access controls.
- Robust security against operating system exploits, such as binary-exploit malware targeting the operating system.
- Remediation of systems infected at levels ranging from the user level down to the root level, possibly including built-in diagnostic instrumentation and virtual machine (VM) introspection providing embedded digital forensics.[18]

In the area of cyber forensics, law enforcement has a significant challenge keeping up with the technology changes. New technology, both hardware and software, is released into the market at a very rapid pace and used in criminal activity almost immediately. The large volume of information contained on digital devices can make the difference in an investigation, and law enforcement investigators require updated tools to address the changing technology.

Since its inception in November 2008, the Cyber Forensics Working Group (CFWG) has provided project requirements. Part of S&T's CSD, CFWG is composed of representatives from federal, state, and local law enforcement agencies. Members meet biannually to provide requirements, discuss capability gaps, and prioritize the areas of most immediate concern to focus technology development and participate as test and evaluation partners of resultant solutions.

The Cyber Forensics Tool Testing Program at the NIST is a project that offers a measure of assurance that the tools used by law enforcement in the investigations of computer-related crimes produce valid results. The implementation of testing based on rigorous procedures provides impetus for vendors to improve their tools to provide consistent and objective test results to law enforcement that will stand up in court. There are also research efforts focused on the capabilities to forensically acquire data from information and entertainment systems found in vehicles seized during law enforcement investigations.[19]

2.10 Mobile Device and Cloud-Based Systems Security

The DHS workforce has become increasingly mobile, driving the need for secure mobility solutions and a coordinated approach and framework to guide the selection and implementation of common enterprise mobility solutions. To promote safe and secure adoption of mobile technology in the federal government, DHS S&T has established the MDS program.

The need for this program is the direct result of mobile threats presenting an increasingly common and more sophisticated threats specific to mobile devices, applications, and data that have grown dramatically in the past few years. A recent analysis of threats highlighted several key developments, including the following:

■ Increased focus of cybercriminals targeting mobile users. McAfee Labs reported seeing 2.4 million unique pieces of malware in the last three months of 2015, a dramatic increase from 300,000 in 2014.
■ Mobile threat sophistication is increasing. Certain malware even has entered the marketplace preinstalled on certain devices, indicating a compromised supply chain. Malware self-defense mechanisms also are gaining sophistication, evading attempts to detect and defeat the application.[20]

Along with an increase in the use of mobile devices cloud computing is rapidly transforming information technology (IT) in the private and public sectors. Cloud-based solutions provide significant scalability, realize significant cost effectiveness, can be quickly deployed and provisioned, and can enable full transparency in managing operational costs. Owing to this, organizations face enormous pressure to incorporate cloud solutions into their operational environment. However, the novel combination of technologies used to implement cloud services introduces new vulnerabilities to malicious attack, which will only increase as more applications and platforms move to cloud environments.

A comprehensive cloud security solution must be resilient in the face of significant node corruption and must incorporate regenerative capabilities that can ensure the continued mission effectiveness of the system. Current solutions to prevent an attacker from stealing a compromised node's data require unacceptably high bandwidth, which can significantly slow systems. These approaches also assume a static architecture, a situation that inherently favors the attacker since it provides them with time to discover the network's architecture and layout and implement an effective attack.

To address these and other challenges, CSD is supporting the R&D of several technologies within the Security for Cloud-based Systems program. This work focuses on developing and deploying cloud investigation and auditing tools and capabilities, technologies that allow for advanced VMs management, methods that provide for secure multiparty computing as well as the development of other technologies to secure the endpoints in a cloud system.[21]

2.11 The Insider Threat Program

Insider threats are the source of many losses in many critical infrastructure industries. An insider threat can be defined as the potential damage to the interests of an organization by a person or persons regarded, inaccurately, as loyally working for or on behalf of the organization, or who inadvertently commits security breaches. To address the growing concern the insider threats project seeks more advanced R&D solutions to provide needed capabilities to address six areas:

- Collect and analyze (monitoring)
- Detect (provide incentives and data)
- Deter (prevention)
- Protect (maintain operations and economics)
- Predict (anticipate threats and attacks)
- React (reduce opportunity, capability, and motivation and morale for the insider)

The beneficiaries of this research range from the national security bodies operating the most sensitive or classified systems, to homeland security officials who need to share sensitive-but-unclassified/controlled unclassified information (CUI) and to healthcare, finance, and many other sectors where sensitive and valuable information is managed. In many systems, such as those operating critical infrastructures, the integrity, availability, and total system survivability are of the highest priority and can be compromised by insiders. Current efforts include the following:

- Monitoring Database Management System (DBMS) Activity for Detecting Data Exfiltration by Insiders: A malicious insider who has the proper credentials to access organizational databases may, over time, send data outside the organization's network through a variety of channels, such as email, file transfer, or web uploads. The existing security tools for detecting cyberattacks focus on protecting the boundary between the organization and the outside world. While data exist throughout the organization, the most harm is done by exfiltration of those massive amounts of data that reside in an organizational DBMS. By studying the patterns of interaction between users and a DBMS, it is possible to detect anomalous activity that is indicative of early signs of exfiltration. An anomaly and misuse detection system that operates at the data source (i.e., the DBMS) prevents data from leaving the source even before it escapes into an organizational network where it is very hard to track.

■ Insider Threat Research Corpus: DHS S&T is developing a corpus of generated synthetic data based on insider threat scenarios to enable a broader group of researchers to more easily test their tools. Generating data is time consuming, so having free access to the generated test data will encourage insider threat research by removing some of the burden associated with testing.

■ Lightweight Media Forensics for Insider Threat Detection: This effort is developing novel methods and capabilities to detect insider threat through disk-level storage behavior (e.g., file types, sensitive data, strings, etc.) and how an individual's behavior diverges from prior behavior and/or that of their organizational peers. Current approaches rely on rules and signatures and look for patterns matching previous insider attacks. Analyzing disk-level storage behavior with a lightweight media forensics agent will provide a more in-depth look at user behavior for insider threat indicators and proactively identify potential insider threats.[22]

2.12 Summary

The DHS S&T CSD focuses on applied R&D, test, evaluation, and transition for technologies to support civilian federal, state, and local governments and private sector unclassified needs to protect the cyber infrastructure. Important characteristics of the CSD research approach include the following:

■ CSD funds cybersecurity R&D projects that result in a deployable solution.

■ Of particular interest to DHS are technologies that can be developed and transitioned to commercial products or used in federal, state, and local government systems.

■ By using a cybersecurity R&D lifecycle process which includes research, development, test, evaluation, and transition to practice these unclassified solutions can be implemented in both public and private sectors.

■ Research planners and decision makers recognize that cybersecurity only becomes more challenging if billions of devices with security vulnerabilities are added to cyber infrastructures and networks. The goal is to build security in rather than bolt on it on later.

■ The CSD program investigates architectures, technical approaches, studies, processes, technologies, tools, and proof-of-concepts across several R&D areas of interest.

- The program regularly engages with agencies and the community to identify needs that cannot be met with current technologies and to understand the current state of the art and practice in each area of need.
- In cases where technologies do not exist or are immature, the program makes the necessary investments in applied research, advanced development, test and evaluation, and technology transition to ensure their availability to the HSE.
- Assessments and evaluations are conducted through technical assessment, modeling, vulnerability and risk analysis, and red team evaluations and operational assessments. Performers execute a technology transition process whereby cybersecurity tools developed under sponsorship by DHS can be acquired, evaluated, and transitioned to end users.
- DHS has several talent development programs in place along with conducting research on talent development methods.

2.13 Seminar Discussion Topics

Discussion topics for graduate or professional-level seminars are the following:

- What experience has seminar participants had working with or utilizing U.S. DHS cybersecurity programs or cybersecurity research efforts? Which areas was that experience with?
- What experience has seminar participants had with private corporations or nongovernmental organizations that have worked on similar research to that being conducted and supported by DHS?
- What areas of U.S. DHS cybersecurity research do seminar participants think are the most important? Why?
- What areas of U.S. DHS cybersecurity research do seminar participants think are the most relevant to the private sector? Why?

Key Terms

anonymous networks: enable users to access the World Wide Web while blocking any tracking or tracing of their identity on the Internet
cryptocurrencies: are digital assets designed to work as a medium of exchange using cryptography to secure the transactions and to control the creation of additional units of the currency
cyber analytics: analytical data generated by specialized tools that enable network security managers to address pressing information security problems
cyber-physical systems: are engineered systems that are built from, and depend upon, the seamless integration of computational algorithms and physical

components that enable capability, adaptability, scalability, resiliency, safety, security, and usability of physical systems through cyber connections

cybersecurity metrics: help organizations verify that cybersecurity controls are in compliance with a policy, process, or procedure and help to identify security strengths and weaknesses

enterprise-level security metrics: measure the security posture of an organization and allow system administrators and nontechnical users alike to use a system while still maintaining security

spatiotemporal network dynamics: is the interaction and activity that occurs in communities on social networks and can provide direct clues as to the nature of an individual's identity and their role within both online and offline communities, allowing for the creation of cyber-geodemographic profiles

virtual currency: are financial systems that usually provide greater anonymity than traditional payment systems and sometimes lack a central intermediary to maintain transaction information and can be accessed globally to make payments and transfer funds across borders

References

1. U.S. Department of Homeland Security. *Science and Technology. Homeland Security Advanced Research Projects Agency.* Retrieved November 13, 2016, https://www.dhs.gov/science-and-technology/hsarpa
2. The Networking and Information Technology Research and Development Program. *Report on Implementing Federal Cybersecurity Research and Development Strategy.* Retrieved November 11, 2016, https://www.nitrd.gov/PUBS/ImplFedCybersecurityRDStrategy-June2014.pdf
3. U.S. Department of Homeland Security. *Science and Technology CSD Projects.* Retrieved November 13, 2016, https://www.dhs.gov/science-and-technology/csd-projects
4. New York State Department of Financial Services. *Notice of Inquiry on Virtual Currencies.* August 12, 2013. Retrieved November 13, 2016, http://www.dfs.ny.gov/about/hearings/vc_01282014/notice_20130812_vc.pdf
5. U.S. Department of Homeland Security. *Science and Technology CSD Projects. Anonymous Networks and Currencies.* Retrieved November 13, 2016, https://www.dhs.gov/CSD-ANC
6. U.S. Department of Homeland Security. *Science and Technology CSD Projects. Cyber Physical Systems Security.* Retrieved November 13, 2016, https://www.dhs.gov/science-and-technology/csd-cpssec
7. U.S. Department of Homeland Security. *Science and Technology CSD Projects. Data Privacy Technologies.* Retrieved November 14, 2016, https://www.dhs.gov/science-and-technology/csd-privacy
8. U.S. Department of Homeland Security. *Science and Technology CSD Projects. Distributed Dental of Service (DDoS).* Retrieved November 14, 2016, https://www.dhs.gov/science-and-technology/csd-ddosd

9. U.S. Department of Homeland Security. *Science and Technology CSD Projects. Cybersecurity Competitions.* Retrieved November 14, 2016, https://www.dhs.gov/science-and-technology/csd-competitions

10. U.S. Department of Homeland Security. *Science and Technology CSD Projects. Cyber Security Incident Response Teams.* Retrieved November 14, 2016, https://www.dhs.gov/science-and-technology/csd-csirt

11. U.S. Department of Homeland Security. *Science and Technology CSD Projects. Distributed Environment for Critical Infrastructure Decision-Making Exercises.* Retrieved November 14, 2016, https://www.dhs.gov/science-and-technology/csd-decide

12. U.S. Department of Homeland Security. *Science and Technology CSD Projects. Enterprise Level Security Metrics and Usability.* Retrieved November 14, 2016, https://www.dhs.gov/science-and-technology/csd-elsmu

13. U.S. Department of Homeland Security. *Science and Technology CSD Projects. Cyber Analytics, Behavior and Resilience.* Retrieved November 14, 2016, https://www.dhs.gov/science-and-technology/csd-analytics

14. U.S. Department of Homeland Security. *Science and Technology CSD Projects. Assessment and Evaluation.* Retrieved November 14, 2016, https://www.dhs.gov/science-and-technology/csd-ae

15. U.S. Department of Homeland Security. *Science and Technology CSD Projects. Cyber Economic Incentives.* Retrieved November 14, 2016, https://www.dhs.gov/science-and-technology/csd-cei

16. U.S. Department of Homeland Security. *Science and Technology CSD Projects. Experimental Research Testbed.* Retrieved November 14, 2016, https://www.dhs.gov/science-and-technology/csd-deter

17. U.S. Department of Homeland Security. *Science and Technology CSD Projects. Experiments and Pilots.* Retrieved November 14, 2016, https://www.dhs.gov/science-and-technology/csd-ep

18. U.S. Department of Homeland Security. *Science and Technology CSD Projects. Internet Measurement and Attack Modeling.* Retrieved November 14, 2016, https://www.dhs.gov/science-and-technology/csd-imam

19. U.S. Department of Homeland Security. *Science and Technology CSD Projects. Cyber Forensics.* Retrieved November 14, 2016, https://www.dhs.gov/science-and-technology/csd-forensics

20. U.S. Department of Homeland Security. *Science and Technology CSD Projects. Mobile Device Security.* Retrieved November 14, 2016, https://www.dhs.gov/csd-mobile

21. U.S. Department of Homeland Security. *Science and Technology CSD Projects. Security of Cloud-Based Systems.* Retrieved November 14, 2016, https://www.dhs.gov/science-and-technology/csd-cloud

22. U.S. Department of Homeland Security. *Science and Technology CSD Projects. Insider Threat.* Retrieved November 14, 2016, https://www.dhs.gov/science-and-technology/csd-insider-threat

Chapter 3

The National Institute for Standards and Technology

The NIST was founded in 1901 and is now part of the U.S. Department of Commerce. NIST is one of the oldest physical science laboratories in the United States. The Congress established the agency to remove a major challenge to U.S. industrial competitiveness at the time which was the country's second-rate measurement infrastructure that lagged behind the capabilities of the United Kingdom, Germany, and other economic rivals. This chapter covers the cybersecurity research activities of NIST.

3.1 The Cybersecurity Role of NIST

Innumerable products and services rely in some way on technology, measurement, and standards provided by the NIST. NIST measurements support the smallest of technologies to the largest and most complex of man-made creations from *nanoscale* devices so tiny that tens of thousands can fit on the tip of a single strand of human hair up to earthquake-resistant skyscrapers and global communication networks.[1]

NIST's cybersecurity program supports the promotion of innovation and industrial competitiveness of the United States by advancing measurement science, standards, and related technology through R&D in ways that enhance economic and national security.[2]

NIST's ITL is a recognized thought leader in cryptography, identity management, key management, mobile security, risk management, security automation, security of networked systems, foundations of measurement science for information systems, secure virtualization, cloud security, trusted roots of hardware, usability and security, and vulnerability management. ITL is composed of six divisions; each has ongoing work that moves the United States toward the end-state vision of the Cybersecurity R&D Strategic Plan. In particular, the NIST SSD works with industry, academia, and other government agencies to increase trust and confidence in deployed software, standards, and testing tools for contemporary software infrastructures and future next-generation software systems, and conformance testing.

In addition, the NIST Computer Security Division (CSD) within ITL leads the efforts in risk management, identity management, key management, security automation, mobile security, trusted roots for hardware, vulnerability management, and cryptography. CSD's activities in key management, multifactor authentication, and identity management strongly contribute to the *Tailored Trustworthy Spaces* theme.

Among its recent priorities, CSD's efforts in information security support the Moving Target Defense theme by developing tools and specifications that maintain ongoing awareness of information security, vulnerabilities, and threats to support organizational risk management decisions. The NIST NCCoE and NSTIC Program Management Office are focused on driving adoption of cybersecurity and identity management standards and best practices to support measurable improvements in the cybersecurity landscape.[3]

President Obama issued EO 13718, Commission on Enhancing National Cybersecurity, in February 2016. The Commission was to make detailed short- and long-term recommendations to strengthen cybersecurity in public and private sectors, while protecting privacy, ensuring public safety and economic and national security, fostering discovery and development of new technical solutions, and bolstering partnerships between federal, state, and local governments and the private sector in the development, promotion, and use of cybersecurity technologies, policies, and best practices.

The Order 13718 directed NIST to provide the Commission with expertise, services, funds, facilities, staff, equipment, and other support services as may be necessary to carry out its mission. The Commission solicited input from the public through workshops and ongoing outreach and NIST took input from the Commission on Enhancing National Cybersecurity.[4] Frankly, the existing programs in NIST were already significantly addressing the issues discussed by the commission.

3.2 The Cybersecurity Framework

President Obama issued EO 13636, Improving *Critical Infrastructure Cybersecurity* in February 2013. The Order directed the NIST to work with stakeholders to develop a voluntary framework based on existing standards, guidelines, and practices for reducing cyber risks to critical infrastructure. The Cybersecurity Enhancement Act of 2014 reinforced NIST's EO 13636 role. NIST has conducted the research and analysis necessary to construct the framework and provide guidance to organizations that use the framework to improve cybersecurity.

Created through collaboration between industry and government, the voluntary framework consists of standards, guidelines, and practices to promote the protection of critical infrastructure. The prioritized, flexible, repeatable, and cost-effective approach of the framework helps owners and operators of critical infrastructure to manage cybersecurity-related risk. The Framework Core and Informative Requirements are available as separate downloads (https://www.nist. gov/cyberframework).[5]

The Framework Core is a set of cybersecurity activities, desired outcomes, and applicable references that are common across critical infrastructure sectors. An example of framework outcome language is, physical devices and systems within the organization are inventoried. The core presents industry standards, guidelines, and practices in a manner that allows for communication of cybersecurity activities and outcomes across the organization from the executive level to the implementation/operations level.

The Framework Core consists of five concurrent and continuous functions: identify, protect, detect, respond, and recover. When considered together, these functions provide a high-level, strategic view of the lifecycle of an organization's management of cybersecurity risk. The Framework Core then identifies the underlying key categories and subcategories for each function, and matches them with examples of Informative References, such as existing standards, guidelines, and practices for each subcategory.

A framework profile represents the cybersecurity outcomes based on business needs that an organization has selected from the framework categories and subcategories. The profile can be characterized as the alignment of standards, guidelines, and practices to the Framework Core in a particular implementation scenario. Profiles can be used to identify opportunities for improving cybersecurity posture by comparing a current profile (the as is state) with a target profile (the to be state). To develop a profile, an organization can review all of the categories and subcategories and, based on business drivers and a risk assessment, determine which are most important. They can also add categories and subcategories as needed to address the organization's risks. The current profile can then be used to support prioritization and measurement of progress toward the target profile, while factoring in other business needs including cost effectiveness and innovation. Profiles can be used to conduct self-assessments and communicate within an organization or between organizations.

Framework Implementation Tiers provide the context on how an organization views cybersecurity risk and the processes in place to manage that risk. Tiers describe the degree to which an organization's cybersecurity risk management practices exhibit the characteristics defined in the framework (e.g., risk and threat aware, repeatable, and adaptive). The tiers characterize an organization's practices over a range, from partial (Tier 1) to adaptive (Tier 4). These tiers reflect a progression from informal, reactive responses to approaches that are agile and risk informed.

During the tier selection process, an organization should consider its current risk management practices, threat environment, legal and regulatory requirements, business/mission objectives, and organizational constraints.

The key tenet of the tiers is to allow organizations to take stock of their current activities from an organization-wide point of view and determine if the current integration of cybersecurity risk management practices is sufficient given their mission, regulatory requirements, and risk appetite. Progression to higher tiers is encouraged when such a change would reduce cybersecurity risk and would be cost effective.

The companion roadmap discusses NIST's next steps with the framework and identifies the key areas of development, alignment, and collaboration. These plans were based on input and feedback received from stakeholders through the framework development process. This list of high-priority areas was not intended to be exhaustive, but were important areas identified by stakeholders that should inform future versions of the framework.[6] The framework is discussed in more depth in Chapter 11, Cybersecurity Research, for the Critical Industry Sectors.

3.3 Advanced Network Technologies Division

The Advanced Network Technologies Division (ANTD) provides expertise in Network Science and Engineering. It develops knowledge about networks to understand their complexity and form their future design. It seeks to discover and understand the common principles and fundamental structures underlying networks and their behaviors. It studies the processes underlying networks evolution and the paradigms for network engineering to enhance their efficiency, reliability, security, and robustness. ANTD remains very active in The Internet Engineering Task Force (IETF) where it participates in the development of network protocols and algorithms, studies system issues in interoperability of communication networks, and actively transitions the lessons learned to industrial partners for commercialization. It responds to national priorities with programs in Internet infrastructure protection, cloud computing, next-generation Internet (NGI), and several joint projects such as smart grid, smart manufacturing, and localization. ANTD has recently extended its NGI program to include software-defined networking and network function virtualization projects, and initiated new programs in information-centric networking, high-performance networking, and IoT.[7] ANTD research programs and opportunities include the following:

▪ Robust Inter-Domain Routing Project seeks researchers/students with interests in global Internet routing security and robustness, *Border Gateway Protocol* (BGP), measurement monitoring and analysis of global BGP behavior, BGP security and performance issues, and next-generation routing architectures. Specific desirable experience includes IETF Resource Public Key Infrastructure (RPKI) or BGP security specifications, analysis of RouteViews/

Réseaux IP Européens (French for "European IP Networks") (RIPE) Routing Information Service (RIS) data, software development on open-source router platforms (Quagga, BIRD, etc.), protocol development in C, and the use of cryptographic libraries and cryptographic accelerators.

■ High-Assurance Domains Project seeks researchers/students with interests in Domain Name System (DNS) technologies, DNS security extensions (DNSSEC) security protocols, IETF DNS-Based Authentication of Named Entities (DANE) technologies to leverage the DNS as a key discovery and management infrastructure, use of DANE and other DNSSEC enabled technologies, X.509/PKIX certificate technologies, Transport Layer Security (TLS)/ Secure Sockets Layer (SSL) implementation, and Secure/Multipurpose Internet Mail Extensions (S/MIME)/Pretty Good Privacy (PGP) email security protocols. Specific desirable experience includes python and java development of network protocols, web development with AJAX, browser extension and plug-in technologies, or email user agent development.

■ Network Anomaly Detection/Traffic Modeling/Synthetic Traffic Generation Project seeks researchers/students with interests in network anomaly detection, network intrusion detection, synthetic traffic generation, statistical modeling of network traffic, machine learning, test, and instrumentation of Network Access Device (NAD)/Network Identification Number (NID) systems. Specific desirable experience includes SiLK traffic analysis tools, NAD/NID design and development, multidimensional statistical analysis of Internet scale network traffic.

■ Network Function Virtualization/Software-Defined Networking (NFV/SDN) Project seeks researchers/students with interests in network virtualization, network service function chaining, software-defined networks, technologies and techniques to address robustness safety and security of virtualized network services, novel applications of NFV/SDN to domains such as network security and intrusion detection, support of machine-to-machine communications, support of advanced mobility and cloud computing. Specific desirable experience includes development with open-source SDN/NFV platforms such as OpenDayLight and Openflow, and simulation and emulation modeling environments for SDN/NFV technologies.

■ Measurement Science of Complex Networks Project seeks researchers/students with interests in R&D of techniques to measure, predict, and control macroscopic emergent behavior in complex information systems; modeling and analysis techniques to characterize Internet-scale networks and distributed system; use of genetic algorithms to search for rare event; and runtime techniques to predict phase transitions in system behavior. Specific desirable experience includes simulation modeling with Simulation Language with Extensibility (SLX), statistical experiment design, and data analysis techniques for large-scale systems, network measurement, and monitoring technologies.

- Advanced DDoS Mitigation Techniques Project seeks guest researchers/students with interests in new techniques and systems to detect and mitigate large-scale DDoS attacks; tractable means to prevent the exchange of spoofed data and control traffic; techniques to address DDoS attacks in virtualized network and computing architectures; and techniques to measure and monitor the effectiveness of DDoS mitigation techniques. Specific desirable experience includes measurement and analysis of IP spoofing mechanisms at Internet scales.

- Networked CPSs seek researchers/students with interests in networked control systems; simulation and design techniques for co-simulation/codesign of cyber and physical components, metrics, and techniques for prediction; validation and understanding of the properties of National Cybersecurity Protection System (NCPS); and the application of emerging network technologies (e.g., software-defined networking, cloud architectures, network virtualization) to NCPS. Specific desirable experience includes simulation and emulation of NCPS, NCPS testbed development, IoT technologies, and NCPS application domains such as smart manufacturing, intelligent transportation, and critical infrastructure protection.

- *NGI Architectures* seeks researchers/students with interests in next-generation network architectures, such as fundamentally new approaches to content delivery, service architectures, management and control, security and privacy, disruption-tolerant networking, and handling of mobility. Particular interest in measurement and modeling techniques enables quantitative comparisons between significant Next-Generation Internet Architectures (NGIA) proposals emerging from the academic research community. Specific desirable experience is simulation and emulation modeling of Information-Centric Networking architectures and other prototype Integrated Computing Network (ICN) systems.[8]

3.4 Computer Security Division

The Computer Security Division (CSD), a division of ITL is responsible for developing cybersecurity standards, guidelines, tests, and metrics for the protection of non-national security federal information systems. CSD's standards, guidelines, tools, and references are developed in an open, transparent, traceable, and collaborative manner that enlists broad expertise from around the world. While developed for federal agency use, these resources are voluntarily adopted by other organizations because they are effective and accepted globally.

The need for cybersecurity standards, best practices, tools, and references that also address interoperability, usability, and privacy continue to be critical. CSD aligns its resources to enable greater development and application of practical, innovative security technologies, and methodologies that enhance the ability to address current and future computer and information security challenges. The foundational research and applied cybersecurity programs continue to advance in many areas, including cryptography, automation, roots of trust, identity and access management, advanced security testing and measurement, IoT, CPSs, and public safety networks.

Trust is crucial to the broad adoption of standards and guidelines, including cryptographic standards and guidelines. To ensure that cryptography resources have been developed according the highest standard of inclusiveness, transparency, and security, NIST conducted an internal and external formal review of cryptographic standards development efforts in 2014. NIST documented and solicited public comment on the principles and rigorous processes NIST uses to engage stakeholders and experts in industry, academia, and government to develop and revise these standards. The final report is now published and serves as a basis for all CSD's cryptographic development efforts.

Increasing the trustworthiness and resilience of the IT infrastructure is a significant undertaking that requires a substantial investment in the architectural design and development of systems and networks. A disciplined and structured set of systems security engineering processes that starts with and builds on well-established international standards provides an important starting point. Draft Special Publication (SP) 800-160, Systems Security Engineering: An Integrated Approach to Building Trustworthy Resilient Systems, which was issued in May 2014, helps organizations to develop a more defensible and survivable IT infrastructure. This resource, coupled with other NIST standards and guidelines, contributes to systems that are more resilient in the face of cyberattacks and other threats.[9]

The Cryptographic Technology Group's (CTG) work in the field of cryptography includes researching, analyzing, and standardizing cryptographic technology, such as hash algorithms, symmetric and asymmetric cryptographic techniques, key management, authentication, and random number generation. The CTG's goal is to identify and promote methods to protect communications and storage through cryptographic technologies, encouraging innovative development, and helping technology users to manage risk. The CTG's cryptographic standards program focuses on cryptographic primitives, algorithms, and schemes; the developed standards and guidelines are specified in NIST SPs and NIST Interagency or Internal Reports (NISTIRs). Such standards and guidelines have been considered or adopted by the IT industry and standards development organizations, such as the International Organization for Standardization (ISO), the IETF, the Institute of Electrical and Electronics Engineers (IEEE), and the Trusted Computing Group (TCG), and have been implemented on a variety of platforms.[10]

The Secure Systems and Applications Group's (SSAG) security research focuses on identifying emerging and high-priority technologies, and on developing security solutions that will have a high impact on U.S. critical infrastructure. The group conducted R&D related to both public and private sector use cases. The research considered many aspects of the system's lifecycle from the earliest stages of technology development through proof-of-concept, reference and prototype implementations, and demonstrations. In addition, the group worked to produce new standards and guidance for federal agencies and the industry and to develop tests, test methodologies, and assurance methods. SSAG investigated security concerns associated with such areas as mobile devices, cloud computing, and virtualization, identity management, access control and authorization management, and software assurance. SSAG's research helps to meet federal information security requirements that may not be fully addressed by existing technology. The group collaborated extensively with government, academia, and private sector entities.[11]

The Security Components and Mechanisms Group (SCMG) focuses on the development and management of foundational building-block security mechanisms and techniques that can be integrated into a wide variety of mission-critical U.S. information systems. The group's work spans the spectrum from near-term hardening and improvement of systems, to the design and analysis of next-generation, leap-ahead security capabilities. Computer security depends fundamentally on the level of trust of computer software and systems. This work, therefore, focuses strongly on assurance-building activities ranging from the analysis of software configuration settings, to advanced trust architectures, and to testing tools that identify the flaws in software modules. This work also focuses significantly on increasing the applicability and effectiveness of automated techniques, wherever feasible. The SCMG conducts collaborative research with government, industry, and academia. Outputs of this research consist of prototype systems, software tools, demonstrations, guidelines, and other documentary resources. Collaborating extensively with government, academia, and the private sector, SCMG works on a variety of topics, such as: specifications for the automated exchange of security information between systems; threat information sharing guidelines; hardware roots of trust for mobile devices; and secure basic input output system (BIOS) layers.[12]

3.5 Federal Agencies Still Need to Implement NIST Standards for High-Impact System Security

NIST researches and develops standards and guidelines that include minimum information security requirements to protect federal systems. NIST has prescribed federal standards for minimum security requirements and guidance on security and privacy controls for high-impact systems, including 83 controls specific to such systems.

The Federal Information Security Modernization Act of 2014 (FISMA 2014) provides a comprehensive framework for ensuring the effectiveness of information security controls over information resources that support federal operations and assets and for ensuring the effective oversight of information security risks, including those throughout civilian, national security, and law enforcement agencies. The law requires each agency to develop, document, and implement an agency-wide information security program to provide risk-based protections for the information and information systems that support the operations and assets of the agency.

NIST Federal Information Processing Standards Publication 199, Standards for Security Categorization of Federal Information and Information Systems (FIPS Pub

199) defines how agencies should determine the security category of their information and information systems. Agencies are to consider the potential impact or magnitude of harm that could occur should there be a loss in the confidentiality, integrity, or availability of the information or information system as low, moderate, or high.

■ Low impact: the loss could be expected to have a limited adverse effect on organizational operations, organizational assets, or individuals. For example, the loss might cause degradation in an organization's mission capability to an extent and duration that the organization is able to perform its functions, but the effectiveness of the functions is noticeably reduced.

■ Moderate impact: the loss could be expected to have a serious adverse effect on organizational operations, organizational assets, or individuals. The loss could significantly reduce the agency's capability to effectively perform its mission and functions, among other things.

■ High impact: the loss could be expected to have a severe or catastrophic adverse effect on organizational operations, organizational assets, or individuals. For example, it might cause the organization to be unable to perform one or more of its primary functions or result in a major financial loss.

A 2016 study conducted by the U.S. General Accountability Office (GAO) found that federal agencies face numerous threats to high-impact systems, with most agencies citing nations as the most serious and most often occurring threat. To help protect against threats, agencies reported existing federal guidance to be useful. In addition, they are in the process of implementing various initiatives, although the level of implementation varies across the agencies. Half of the agencies reported that they wanted an expansion of federal initiatives to help protect their high-impact systems; the Cybersecurity Strategy and Implementation Plan generally recognizes these concerns. However, until OMB issues its plans for shared services and security center best practices, agencies will not have the benefit of the efficiency associated with these services and practices to better protect their computing environments. The GAO determined the following:

■ Selected agencies did not always implement controls for selected systems effectively.

■ Up-to-date patches were not always installed to support selected systems.

■ Selected agencies had contingency plans in place for systems reviewed, but not all plans were comprehensive and appropriate tests were not always conducted.

■ Selected agencies had developed security programs, but had not effectively implemented the key elements.

■ Although agencies had developed security plans, consideration of the security baseline controls for high-impact systems varied.

■ Agencies did not always ensure individuals with significant security responsibilities received specialized training.

- Most agencies had conducted information security control assessments for systems, but not all assessments were comprehensive.
- Agencies had developed remedial action plans, but the plans did not include all the required elements.
- Not all agencies had developed a continuous monitoring strategy.[13]

Although NIST continues to research and improve standards and methods for protecting federal information systems and improve cybersecurity, agencies are often slow to implement standards and update security methods. Over the last several years, the GAO has made about 2,500 recommendations to agencies aimed at improving their implementation of information security controls. Many of those recommendations made to agencies were based on NIST research and standard setting. The recommended actions were intended to correct weaknesses in controls designed to prevent, limit, and detect unauthorized access to computer resources, such as controls for protecting system boundaries, identifying and authenticating users, authorizing users to access systems, encrypting sensitive data, and auditing and monitoring activity on their systems. The GAO has also made recommendations for agencies to protect the privacy of PII held on their systems. However, many agencies continue to have weaknesses in security because many recommendations remain unimplemented. As of September 16, 2016, about 1,000 of the GAO information security-related recommendations had not been implemented.[14]

3.6 NIST Smart Grid Program is a Journey into the Future

The *Smart Grid* Program develops and demonstrates smart grid measurement science advances to improve the efficiency, reliability, resilience, and sustainability of the U.S. electric grid. This NIST-wide program is housed in the Engineering Laboratory and draws on the expertise of the Information Technology and Physical Measurement Laboratories. The program portfolio centers on two interacting components: consensus standards and protocols for smart grid interoperability, and measurement science research for future grid capabilities. The former is pursued in collaboration with community organizations such as the Smart Grid Interoperability Panel (SGIP) (originally launched with NIST assistance and now an independent organization), interagency groups such as the Smart Grid Task Force, and other industrial, academic, and government sector stakeholders.

The NIST Framework and Roadmap for Smart Grid Interoperability, which responds to mandates to NIST from Congress and the Administration, is continuously evolved by the program and provides the anchor for NIST standards efforts. An advanced smart grid testbed provides the focus for measurement science research work. The testbed focuses on future *microgrid* concepts and is both agile, to accommodate a wide range of experimental and testing configurations, and to enable its use in combination with other testbeds across the country and around the world for work at significant scale. The research work supports and informs the standards work and together these components enable NIST to promote the emergence of a smart grid for the nation. Some recent accomplishments for the Smart Grid Program include the following:

- NIST Smart Grid Framework and Roadmap for Smart Grid Interoperability Standards, Release 1.0 (January 2010) and Release 2.0 (February 2012): these authoritative framework documents are the primary NIST output fulfilling its Enterprise Information Security Architecture (EISA) role, providing to the U.S. and world smart grid industry the high-level guidance on architectural and cybersecurity principles, standards, and testing and certification based on consensus industry input supported by a comprehensive public review process.
- New private/public organization: SGIP (established in November 2009 as a public–private partnership; transitioned to an industry-led nonprofit organization in April 2013). With nearly 200 member organizations and significant international participation, the SGIP is recognized as the leading worldwide organization and forum for smart grid standards coordination and testing and certification guidance.
- New or revised smart grid standards and guides: NIST-facilitated output from a variety of standards development organizations and other groups, including as part of priority action plans within the SGIP, have been developed and published, covering areas such as energy usage information, smart meters, electric vehicles, demand response, and guidelines for assessing wireless standards for smart grid applications.
- Cybersecurity guidelines and standards: these are NIST-facilitated or NIST Interagency Report output from NIST, the SGIP Cyber Security Working Group, and other groups. The primary NIST-facilitated contribution, NISTIR 7628 Guidelines for Smart Grid Cyber Security (Volumes 1, 2, and 3), provides an analytical framework that organizations can use to develop effective cybersecurity strategies tailored to their particular combinations of smart grid-related characteristics, risks, and vulnerabilities.
- Testing and certification methods and tools: NIST-facilitated output includes the SGIP-published Interoperability Process Reference Manual (IPRM), Version 2.0, which provides recommendations on processes and best practices that enhance the introduction of interoperable products into smart grid markets.
- Measurement methods and tools: development of these methods and tools results in a variety of publications, guides, and models covering areas including *synchrophasor*, advanced meters, time synchronization, building-to-grid and other testbeds, and system performance models.[15]

3.7 The CPSs Program is Necessary for the Journey

CPSs combine the cyber and physical worlds with technologies that can respond in real time to their environments. CPS and related systems (including the IoT, industrial Internet, and more) include co-engineered interacting networks of physical and computational components. Examples include a smart grid for clean, efficient, and reliable energy; intelligent, wearable medical devices for better health and an improved quality of life; autonomous vehicles that increase safety, decrease congestion, and reduce transportation costs; and interacting CPS systems, such as smart emergency response working cooperatively with smart traffic networks to control traffic flows and enable faster transit of emergency vehicles to incident sites and medical facilities. The CPS Program develops and demonstrates new measurement science and promotes the emergence of consensus standards and protocols for advanced systems that are reliable, resilient, effective, safe, sustainable, secure, and privacy enhancing. NIST-wide program coordination is provided by the Engineering Laboratory (Smart Grid and Cyber-Physical Systems Program Office) and the program also draws on the expertise of the Information Technology and Physical Measurement Laboratories.

Measurement science is lacking to support the design, development, and deployment of *composable*, scalable, and interconnected CPS systems in and across multiple smart domains, including in complex smart city environments. The President's Council of Advisors on Science and Technology has identified CPSs as a national priority for federal R&D. Deployment of next-generation CPS across the transportation, energy, and health sectors alone could boost U.S. productivity growth by as much as 1.5%, according to some estimates. The implementation of new CPSs to achieve just a 1% improvement in efficiency can save $30 billion in aviation sector fuel costs, $66 billion in power generation, $63 billion in health care, and $27 billion in freight rail costs over a 15-year period. The design and engineering of a CPS, from initial concept through successful operation, requires a new systems science and engineering approach. This approach must simultaneously embrace all levels of the CPS architecture, from physical components and their associated sensors and actuators, through control systems and analytics, to the overall optimization and user functionality. Advanced CPSs are so complex that the existing approaches for performance prediction, measurement, and management do not apply. The key technical ideas can be summarized as given below:

- The first measurement science problem is the need for a credible technical architecture suitable to the full range of CPS use cases. The research plan provides for the development of a CPS reference architecture that enables collaboration among stakeholders, discovery of common principles applicable to many CPS implementations, and the identification of critical gaps in standards and metrics.
- The second measurement problem is the need to integrate work and share ideas and solutions across a broad range of disciplines and domains. Development of the CPS framework and its analysis methodology through a public consensus

process creates a sense of community, shared purpose, and teamwork at a level that will be needed to take on the complex challenges inherent in CPSs.

■ The third measurement science problem is the need for a platform for CPS experimentation and validation. The research plan provides for the development of a modular CPS testbed to support NIST measurement science development for CPS. Integration of composability and modularity in the design of the CPS testbed allows its application to evaluating performance of CPS systems in multiple domains, enabling its use by a diversity of communities for a range of applications, and demonstrating its agility and application at large scale through reconfigurable combinations with other testbeds at NIST, across the nation, and around the world.

■ The fourth measurement science problem is the need for NIST to lead in organizing governments/users (cities) and technology innovators (industry and academia) to demonstrate a scalable and reproducible model for incubation and deployment of interoperable, adaptable, and configurable IoT/CPS technologies and solutions in smart communities/cities. The use of challenge initiatives, such as SmartAmerica and Global Cities Teams Challenge, further creates a sense of community and shared purpose, creates new teams of innovators and adopters, mobilizes academic, commercial, and government resources toward shared objectives, facilitates the identification of standards and measurement needs, and highlights NIST's role as a neutral convener and technical expert in the CPS field.

The NIST research plan comprises two elements as follows. The first focuses on new approaches enabling the design and engineering of a CPS from initial concept through successful operation. This requires a new systems science and engineering approach. This approach must simultaneously embrace all levels of the CPS architecture, from physical components and their associated sensors and actuators at the base layers, through middle-layer control systems and analytics, to the overall optimization and user functionality at higher layers.

The research plan applies these principles in two key areas to enable new, scalable CPS design approaches. The first area is the development of a common vocabulary that enables shared progress across current, *siloed* CPS domains. These include a reference architecture, syntax, and *ontologies* that provide the basis for modeling, programming, control, and communications languages that span domains and disciplines. This work provides the essential foundation for the subsequent development of standards for interoperability and composability across architectural layers and between components and systems.

The second area focuses on security and privacy status during operations and includes consensus guidelines and measurement processes for security automation, privacy, and high-confidence networks with assured quality of service (QoS). The results are essential to developing CPS for use in sensitive applications such as health care and assisted living; in safety-critical applications such as remote surgery; in time-critical applications such as the smart grid; and in critical infrastructures for disaster resilience, traffic management, and municipal water systems.

The second element of the research plan focuses on the capabilities required for experimental manipulation, measurement, and evaluation of the performance of the more capable and powerful CPSs enabled by the new design approaches targeted under the first area. In this context, CPS performance metrics include efficiency and sustainability, agility and flexibility, reliability (including time-critical performance), resilience, usability, safety, security, and privacy. Research in this second area focuses on the development of a comprehensive abstraction infrastructure comprising tools, platforms, testbeds, and integrated design environments to enable the application of formal methods and standards to the codesign of heterogeneous, interacting components. Testbeds and research platforms developed under this initiative will be modular, reconfigurable, remotely accessible, and adaptable to multiple domains and applications.[16]

A key challenge to progress in CPSs is the lack of robust platforms for experiment and testing, which NIST is addressing through the development of a modular, composable multi-domain CPS testbed. Currently, many CPS experiments are done either in operational systems or in domain-specific testbeds. The former are limited by the severe constraints required to ensure that experiments and testing do not affect reliability and safety for systems that are providing critical, often life- and health-safety, functions in real time. The latter are limited by the inability to test in constrained environments the general applicability of CPS concepts and technologies intended for implementation across multiple domains and in varied applications. The program is addressing this need through the development of design principles for modular, composable testbeds that are interoperable with facilities across the nation and around the world for varying scale and readily reconfigurable for work across domains and applications, and through development of a cross-sector CPS testbed.[17]

Smart grid cybersecurity must address not only deliberate attacks, such as from disgruntled employees, industrial espionage, and terrorists, but also inadvertent compromises of the information infrastructure due to user errors, equipment failures, and natural disasters. The SGIP Cybersecurity Committee (SGCC), which is led and managed by the NIST ITL, Computer Security Division, is moving forward in to address the critical cybersecurity needs in the areas of advanced metering infrastructure (AMI) security requirements, cloud computing, supply chain, and privacy recommendations related to emerging standards. This project will provide foundational cybersecurity guidance, cybersecurity reviews of standards and requirements, outreach, and foster collaborations in the cross-cutting issue of cybersecurity in the smart grid.[18]

3.8 The National Information Assurance Partnership

The National Information Assurance Partnership (NIAP) oversees a national program to evaluate commercial off-the-shelf (COTS) IT products for conformance to the international common criteria. This program includes the NIAP-managed Common Criteria Evaluation and Validation Scheme (CCEVS or Scheme), a national program for developing protection profiles, evaluation methodologies, and policies, which ensures achievable, repeatable, and testable security requirements.

The CCEVS is a partnership between the public and private sectors to provide COTS IT products that meet consumer needs and to help manufacturers of those products gain acceptance in the global marketplace. Successful evaluations benefit industry product developers/vendors and government procurers by validating that the products meet the security requirements for U.S. national security system procurement. Because NIAP is a member of the international 25-nation Common Criteria Recognition Arrangement (CCRA), NIAP-validated products are also available to procurers in the CCRA member nations.

IT security testing is conducted by NIST-accredited and NIAP-approved commercial testing laboratories. A product vendor chooses an approved laboratory to complete the product evaluation against a selected applicable protection profile. A protection profile is an implementation-independent set of security requirements for a particular technology that enables achievable, repeatable, and testable evaluation activities for each evaluation.

All products evaluated within the scheme must demonstrate exact compliance to the applicable technology protection profile. NIAP assesses the results of the security evaluation conducted by the lab and, if the evaluation is successful, issues a validation certificate and lists the product on the U.S. NIAP Product Compliant List and the International CCRA Certified Products List. U.S. Customers (designated approving authorities, authorizing officials, integrators, etc.) may treat these mutually recognized evaluation results as complying with the Committee on National Security Systems Policy (CNSSP) 11, National Policy Governing the Acquisition of IA, and IA-Enabled Information Technology Products dated June 2013 (https://www.cnss.gov/CNSS/issuances/Policies.cfm).

The entire evaluation process can be completed in as little as 90 days but can take up to six months. NIAP does not charge for the services. IT product vendors/developers contract independently with an approved Common Criteria Testing Laboratory (CCTL) for evaluation services. Vendors are encouraged to shop around for the services that best meet their needs, as the prices vary. Only approved laboratories are authorized to provide product evaluations under the CCEVS and CCRA scheme.[19]

The NIAP serves as the U.S. representative to the CCRA, composed of 27 member nations. The purpose of this arrangement is to ensure IT products evaluated according to the terms of the CCRA are mutually recognized by all member nations, allowing industry to evaluate products once and sell to many nations. The U.S. government and its foreign partners in the arrangement share the following objectives with regard to evaluations of IT products and protection profiles:

■ Ensure evaluation of IT products and protection profiles are performed to high and consistent standards and contribute significantly to confidence in the security of those products and profiles.
■ Increase the availability of evaluated, security-enhanced IT products, and protection profiles for national use.
■ Eliminate duplicate evaluations of IT products and protection profiles.
■ Continuously improve the efficiency and cost effectiveness of security evaluations and the certification/validation process for IT products and protection profiles.[20]

NIAP-approved CCTLs are IT security testing laboratories that are accredited by the NIST National Voluntary Laboratory Accreditation Program (NVLAP) and meet the CCEVS-specific requirements to conduct IT security evaluations for conformance to the Common Criteria for Information Technology Security Evaluation, International Standard ISO/IEC 15408. These laboratories must meet the requirements of the

■ NIST Handbook 150, NVLAP Procedures and General Requirements
■ NIST Handbook 150-20, NVLAP Information Technology Security Testing Common Criteria
■ Specific criteria for IT security evaluations and other requirements of the scheme as defined by the NIAP Validation Body

CCTLs enter into contractual agreements with sponsors to conduct security evaluations of IT products and protection profiles using NIAP-approved test methods derived from the Common Criteria, Common Methodology, and other technology-based sources. The IT security evaluations are carried out in accordance with the policies and procedures of the scheme. CCTLs must observe the highest standards of impartiality, integrity, and commercial confidentiality, and operate within the guidelines established by the scheme.

To become a CCTL, a testing laboratory must go through a series of steps that involve both the NIAP Validation Body and NVLAP. Accreditation by NVLAP is the primary requirement for achieving CCTL status. Scheme requirements that cannot be satisfied by NVLAP accreditation are addressed by the NIAP Validation Body. At present, there are only three scheme-specific requirements imposed by the Validation Body. NIAP-approved CCTLs must

■ Reside within the United States and be a legal entity, duly organized and incorporated, validly existing, and in good standing under the laws of the state where the laboratory intends to do business.
■ Agree to accept the U.S. government technical oversight and validation of evaluation-related activities in accordance with the policies and procedures established by the NIAP Common Criteria Scheme.

- Agree to accept the U.S. government participants in selected Common Criteria evaluations conducted by the laboratory in accordance with the policies and procedures established by the NIAP Common Criteria Scheme.

A testing laboratory becomes a CCTL when the laboratory is approved by the Validation Body and is listed on the NIAP-Approved Laboratories List. To avoid unnecessary expense and delay in becoming an NIAP-approved testing laboratory, it is strongly recommended that the prospective CCTLs ensure that they are able to satisfy the scheme-specific requirements prior to seeking accreditation from NVLAP. This can be accomplished by sending a letter of interest to the NIAP Validation Body prior to entering the NVLAP process.[21]

3.9 Summary

NIST is one of the oldest physical science laboratories in the United States. The Congress established the agency to remove a major challenge to U.S. industrial competitiveness at the time when the country's second-rate measurement infrastructure lagged behind the capabilities of the United Kingdom, Germany, and other economic rivals. NIST cybersecurity research activities include the following:

- NIST's ITL is a recognized thought leader in cryptography, identity management, key management, mobile security, risk management, security automation, security of networked systems, foundations of measurement science for information systems, secure virtualization, cloud security, trusted roots of hardware, usability and security, and vulnerability management.
- The ANTD develops knowledge about networks to understand their complexity and inform their future design. It studies the processes underlying networks evolution and the paradigms for network engineering to enhance their efficiency, reliability, security, and robustness. ANTD remains very active in the IETF where it participates in the development of network protocols and algorithms and studies system issues in the interoperability of communication networks.
- The need for cybersecurity standards, best practices, tools, and references that also address interoperability, usability, and privacy continue to be critical for the United States. CSD aligns its resources to enable greater development and application of practical, innovative security technologies and methodologies that enhance the ability to address current and future computer and information security challenges.
- The Smart Grid Program develops and demonstrates smart grid measurement science advances to improve the efficiency, reliability, resilience, and sustainability of the U.S. electric grid. The program portfolio centers on two interacting components: consensus standards and protocols for smart

grid interoperability, and measurement science research for future grid capabilities.
■ A key challenge to progress in CPSs is the lack of robust platforms for experiment and testing, which the NIST is addressing through the development of a modular, composable multi-domain CPS testbed.

Although NIST continues to research and improve the standards and methods for protecting federal information systems and improve cybersecurity, agencies are often slow to implement standards and update security methods. A 2016 study conducted by the U.S. GAO found that federal agencies face numerous threats to high-impact systems. Over the last several years, the GAO has made about 2,500 recommendations to agencies aimed at improving their implementation of information security controls. As of September 16, 2016, about 1,000 of the GAO information security-related recommendations had not been implemented.

3.10 Seminar Discussion Topics

Discussion topics for graduate or professional level seminars are as follows:

■ What experience has seminar participants had working with or utilizing NIST cybersecurity programs, standards, guidelines, or cybersecurity other research efforts?
■ What experience has seminar participants had with private corporations or nongovernmental organizations that have worked with NIST cybersecurity programs or cybersecurity research efforts?
■ What areas of NIST cybersecurity research do seminar participants think are the most important? Why?
■ What areas of NIST cybersecurity research do seminar participants think are the most relevant to the private sector? Why?
■ What areas of research related to the IoT do seminar participants think are the most relevant to the private sector? Why?

Key Terms

Border Gateway Protocol (BGP): was developed in the late 1980s to exchange routing information and compute routes between the networks that comprise Internet. Over time, BGP has evolved into the fundamental glue that enables the commercial Internet

composable: technologies that are able to exist, happen, or work together

critical infrastructure cybersecurity: is designed to protect the critical infrastructure which includes all technology functions that are required to support the national economy and security

cyber-physical systems (CPS): combine the cyber and physical worlds with technologies that can respond in real time to their environments including the IoT, industrial Internet, and co-engineered interacting networks of physical and computational components

microgrid: is a localized grouping of electricity sources and loads that normally operates connected to and synchronous with the traditional centralized grid (macrogrid), but can be disconnected and function autonomously as physical and/or economic conditions dictate

nanoscale: technology or physical items that have dimensions measured in nanometers which is one billionth of a meter

next generation internet architectures: are those which will support future Internet applications and environments such as the Internet or things and the smart grid

ontology: describes a system of concepts and its associated properties for a specific area often intended to support computer applications and exist on a continuum rather than completely distinct types of artifacts

siloed: separate systems, each with a separate function or environment that are often duplicated rather than integrated into a whole system

smart grid: is the secure and resilient electrical grid that enables support for critical infrastructures and the national economy

synchrophasor: is a sophisticated monitoring device that can measure the instantaneous voltage, current, and frequency at specific locations on the electric grid giving operators a near real-time picture of what is happening on the system, and allows them to make decisions to prevent power outages

tailored trustworthy spaces: a security architecture and strategic federal cybersecurity research theme tailored for the smart grid and other cyber environments that assure that all elements in the space are secure

References

1. The National Institute of Standards and Technology. *About NIST.* Retrieved November 16, 2016, https://www.nist.gov/about-nist
2. The National Institute of Standards and Technology. *Cybersecurity.* Retrieved November 16, 2016, https://www.nist.gov/topics/cybersecurity
3. The Networking and Information Technology Research and Development Program. *Report on Implementing Federal Cybersecurity Research and Development Strategy.* Retrieved November 11, 2016, https://www.nitrd.gov/PUBS/ImplFedCybersecurityRDStrategy-June2014.pdf
4. The National Institute of Standards and Technology. *Commission on Enhancing National Cybersecurity.* Retrieved November 16, 2016, https://www.nist.gov/cybercommission
5. The National Institute of Standards and Technology. *Cybersecurity Framework.* Retrieved November 16, 2016, https://www.nist.gov/cyberframework

6. The National Institute of Standards and Technology. *Cybersecurity Framework FAQs Framework Components*. Retrieved November 16, 2016, https://www.nist.gov/cyberframework/cybersecurity-framework-faqs-framework-components

7. The National Institute of Standards and Technology. *Advanced Network Technologies*. Retrieved November 19, 2016, https://www.nist.gov/itl/antd

8. The National Institute of Standards and Technology. *ANTD Opportunities*. October 19, 2016. Retrieved November 19, 2016, https://www.nist.gov/current-opportunities

9. The National Institute of Standards and Technology. *Computer Security*. Retrieved November 19, 2016, https://www.nist.gov/itl/computer-security-division

10. The National Institute of Standards and Technology. *Cryptographic Technology*. Retrieved November 19, 2016, https://www.nist.gov/itl/computer-security-division/cryptographic-technology

11. The National Institute of Standards and Technology. *Secure Systems and Applications*. Retrieved November 19, 2016, https://www.nist.gov/itl/computer-security-division/secure-systems-and-applications

12. The National Institute of Standards and Technology. *Security Components and Mechanisms*. Retrieved November 19, 2016, https://www.nist.gov/itl/computer-security-division/security-components-and-mechanisms

13. U.S. General Accountability Office (GAO). *Information Security: Agencies Need to Improve Controls over Selected High-Impact Systems*. May 18, 2016. Retrieved November 19, 2016, http://www.gao.gov/products/GAO-16-501

14. U.S. General Accountability Office (GAO). *Testimony before the President's Commission on Enhancing National Cybersecurity. Federal Information Security: Actions Needed to Address Challenges. Statement of Gregory C. Wilshusen, Director, Information Security Issues*. September 19, 2016. Retrieved November 19, 2016, http://www.gao.gov/products/GAO-16-885T

15. The National Institute of Standards and Technology. *Smart Grid Program*. Retrieved November 20, 2016, https://www.nist.gov/programs-projects/smart-grid-program

16. The National Institute of Standards and Technology. *Cyber Physical Systems Program*. Retrieved November 20, 2016, https://www.nist.gov/programs-projects/cyber-physical-systems-program

17. The National Institute of Standards and Technology. *Cyber-Physical Systems Testbed Design Concepts*. Retrieved November 20, 2016, https://www.nist.gov/programs-projects/cyber-physical-systems-testbed-design-concepts

18. The National Institute of Standards and Technology. *Cybersecurity for Smart Grid Systems*. Retrieved November 20, 2016, https://www.nist.gov/programs-projects/cybersecurity-smart-grid-systems

19. The National Information Assurance Partnership (NIAP). Retrieved November 27, 2016, https://www.niap-ccevs.org/Ref/What_is_NIAP.CCEVS.cfm

20. Common Criteria Recognition Arrangement (CCRA). Retrieved November 27, 2016, https://www.niap-ccevs.org/Ref/CCRA.Partners.cfm

21. The National Information Assurance Partnership (NIAP). *Common Criteria Testing Laboratories (CCTL)*. Retrieved November 27, 2016, https://www.niap-ccevs.org/Documents_and_Guidance/cctls.cfm

Chapter 4

The Defense Advanced Research Projects Agency

The DARPA is the principal agency within the DoD for high-risk, high-payoff research, development, and demonstration of new technologies and systems that serve the warfighter and the defense of the United States. DARPA's R&D efforts in cybersecurity strongly support the *Moving Target Defense* and *Tailored Trustworthy Spaces* themes. In particular, DARPA's Information Assurance and Survivability Program draws upon biological and immune systems as inspiration for radically rethinking computer hardware, software, and system designs. Such systems will be able to detect, diagnose, and respond to attacks by using their own innate and adaptive immune systems. Furthermore, in response to attacks, such systems will also be capable of dynamically adapting and improving their defensive capabilities over time. As in biological systems, the cyber systems will dynamically diversify, increasing their resiliency and survivability, and that of their individual, constituent computers.[1] This chapter covers the unclassified cybersecurity research of DARPA.

4.1 The DARPA Organization

DARPA itself dates back to the launch of Sputnik in 1957, and a commitment by the United States that, from that time forward, it would be the initiator and not the victim of strategic technological surprises. Working with innovators inside and outside of government, DARPA has transformed revolutionary concepts and even seeming impossibilities into practical capabilities. The ultimate results have included not only game-changing military capabilities such as precision weapons and stealth technology, but also such icons of modern society such as the Internet, automated voice recognition and language translation, and Global Positioning System (GPS) receivers small enough to embed in myriad consumer devices.

DARPA explicitly reaches for transformational change by working within an *innovation ecosystem* that includes academic, corporate, and governmental partners, with a constant focus on the U.S. Military Services. DARPA has approximately 220 government employees in six technical offices, including nearly 100 program managers, who oversee about 250 R&D programs. Program managers report to DARPA's office directors and their deputies, who are responsible for charting technical directions, hiring program managers, and overseeing program execution. The technical staff is also supported by experts in security, legal and contracting issues, finance, human resources, and communications. DARPA's technical offices are the following:

■ The Biological Technologies Office which works in a variety of areas from programmable microbes to human–machine symbiosis; biological technologies are expanding the definition of technology and redefining how humans interact with and use biology.

■ The Defense Sciences Office (DSO) which identifies and pursues high-risk, high-payoff research initiatives across a broad spectrum of science and engineering disciplines and sometimes reshaping the existing fields or creating entirely new disciplines while transforming these initiatives into new, game-changing technologies for U.S. national security.

■ The Information Innovation Office (I2O) which explores game-changing technologies in the fields of information science and software to anticipate and create rapid shifts in the complex national security landscape. Conflict can occur in traditional domains such as land, sea, air, and space, and in rapidly growing domains such as cyber and other types of irregular warfare. I2O's research portfolio is focused on anticipating new modes of warfare in these emerging areas.

■ The Microsystems Technology Office (MTO) has helped to create and prevent strategic surprise through investments in compact microelectronic components such as microprocessors, micro-electromechanical systems (MEMS), and photonic devices. MTO's revolutionary work applying advanced capabilities in areas such as wide-band gap materials, phased array radars, high-energy lasers, and infrared imaging.

■ The Strategic Technology Office (STO) is focused on technologies that enable fighting as a network to increase military effectiveness, cost leverage, and adaptability.

■ The Tactical Technology Office (DARPA/TTO) provides or prevents strategic and tactical surprise with very high-payoff, high-risk development and demonstration of new platforms in ground systems, maritime (surface and undersea) systems, air systems, and space systems.[2]

4.2 The Cyber Grand Challenge

The need for automated, scalable, machine-speed vulnerability detection and patching is large and growing fast as more and more systems ranging from household appliances to major military platforms get connected to and become dependent on the Internet. The process of finding and countering bugs, hacks, and other cyber infection vectors is still effectively artisanal. Professional bug hunters, security coders, and other security pros work tremendous hours, searching millions of lines of code to find and fix vulnerabilities that could be taken advantage of by users with malicious motives.

To help overcome these challenges, DARPA launched the Cyber Grand Challenge, a competition to create automatic defensive systems capable of reasoning about flaws, formulating patches, and deploying them on a network in real time. By acting at machine speed and scale, these technologies may someday overturn the attacker-dominated status quo. Realizing this vision requires breakthrough approaches in a variety of disciplines, including applied computer security, program analysis, and data visualization. Anticipated future benefits include the following:

- Expert-level software security analysis and remediation, at machine speeds on enterprise scales
- Establishment of a lasting R&D community for automated cyber defense
- Creation of a public, high-fidelity recording of real-time competition between automated cyber defense systems

DARPA hosted the Cyber Grand Challenge Final Event which was the world's first all-machine cyber hacking tournament on August 4, 2016 in Las Vegas. It started with more than 100 teams consisting of some of the top security researchers and hackers in the world. DARPA pit seven teams against each other during the final event. During the competition, each team's cyber reasoning system (CRS) automatically identified software flaws, and scanned a purpose-built, air-gapped network to identify affected hosts. For nearly 12 hours, teams were scored based on how capably their systems protected hosts, scanned the network for vulnerabilities, and maintained the correct function of software. Prizes of $2 million, $1 million, and $750,000 were awarded to the top three finishers.

Computer Grand Challenge (CGC) was the first head-to-head competition between some of the most sophisticated automated bug-hunting systems ever developed. These machines played the classic cybersecurity exercise of Capture the Flag in a specially created computer testbed laden with an array of bugs hidden inside custom, never-before-analyzed software. The machines were challenged to find and patch within seconds the flawed code that was vulnerable to being hacked, and find their opponents' weaknesses before they could defend against them.[3]

The winning computer system, dubbed Mayhem, was created by a team known as ForAllSecure, one of seven teams that competed in the all-day competition, performed in front of 5,000 computer security professionals and others at the Paris Las Vegas Conference Center. The entire event was visualized for attendees on giant monitors and live streamed for remote viewers, with expert sportscasters documenting the historic competition. Details and videos about the competing teams can be found at www.cybergrandchallenge.com

Xandra, a computer system designed by team TECHx of Ithaca, New York and Charlottesville, Virginia, was declared the second-place winner and Mechanical Phish, a system designed by team Shellphish of Santa Barbara, California, was named the third-place winner. Judges spent the night verifying the preliminary results, and winners were officially crowned at an award ceremony Friday morning, immediately before the launch of DEFense readiness CONdition (DEF CON) hacker tournament also being hosted at the Paris Hotel.

The event was very significant considering that the Heartbleed security bug existed in many of the world's computer systems for nearly two-and-a-half years, for example, before it was discovered and a fix circulated in spring 2014. By that time, the bug had rendered an estimated half million of the Internet's secure servers vulnerable to theft and other mischief. Analysts have estimated that, on average, such flaws go unremediated for 10 months before being discovered and patched, giving nefarious actors ample opportunity to wreak havoc in affected systems before they move on to exploit the new terrain.[4]

4.3 Active Authentication

The current standard method for validating a user's identity for authentication on an information system requires humans to do something that is inherently unnatural: create, remember, and manage long, complex passwords. Moreover, as long as the session remains active, typical systems incorporate no mechanisms to verify that the user originally authenticated is the user still in control of the keyboard. Thus, unauthorized individuals may improperly obtain extended access to information system resources if a password is compromised or if a user does not exercise adequate *security vigilance* after initially authenticating at the console. The Active Authentication program seeks to address this problem by developing novel ways of validating the identity of the person at the console that focus on the unique aspects of the individual through the use of software-based *biometrics*.

Biometrics is defined as the characteristics used to uniquely recognize humans based on one or more intrinsic physical or behavioral traits. This program focuses on the behavioral traits that can be observed through how we interact with the world. Just as when you touch something your finger you leave behind a fingerprint, when you interact with technology you do so in a pattern based on how your mind processes information, leaving behind a *cognitive fingerprint*.

The focus of the first phase of the program is researching biometrics that does not require the installation of additional hardware sensors, rather the program will look for research on biometrics that can be captured through the technology we already use looking for aspects of this cognitive fingerprint. These could include, for example, how the user handles the mouse and how the user crafts written language in an email or document. A heavy emphasis is placed on validating any potential new biometrics with empirical tests to ensure they would be effective in large-scale deployments to mitigate security threats.

The later phases of the program focus on developing a solution that integrates any available biometrics using a new authentication platform suitable for deployment on a standard DoD desktop or laptop. The combinatorial approach of using multiple modalities for continuous user identification and authentication is expected to deliver a system that is accurate, robust, and transparent to the user's normal computing experience. The authentication platform is to be developed with open application programming interfaces (APIs) to allow the integration of other software or hardware biometrics available in the future from other sources.[5]

4.4 Active Cyber Defense

The U.S. military, government, and commercial IT networks face constant cyber attacks from both criminal and state-sponsored adversaries. Current IT security response practices to these attacks boil down to four steps: find the invading code, unplug the affected systems, create security patches to thwart particular attacks, and apply those patches network-wide. This reactive engagement model is effective on a case-by-case basis but does not address the key advantages the attackers have such as adversaries easily make small changes to malware that bypass patches and distribute that new malware on a massive scale. To stay ahead of increasingly sophisticated, stealthy and dangerous threats, defenders must move beyond traditional static defenses to exploit the natural advantages of their IT systems and expertise.

DARPA's Active Cyber Defense (ACD) program is designed to help reverse the existing imbalance by providing cyber defenders a home field advantage: the ability to perform defensive operations that involve direct engagement with sophisticated adversaries in DoD-controlled cyberspace. The program seeks to develop a collection of synchronized, real-time capabilities to discover, define, analyze cybersecurity metrics to mitigate cyber threats and vulnerabilities. These new proactive capabilities would enable cyber defenders to more readily disrupt and neutralize cyber attacks as they happen. These capabilities would be solely defensive in nature; the ACD program specifically excludes research into cyber offense capabilities.[6]

4.5 Automated Program Analysis for Cybersecurity

To be effective, DoD cybersecurity solutions require rapid development times. The shelf life of systems and capabilities is sometimes measured in days. Thus, to a greater degree than in other areas of defense, cybersecurity solutions require that the DoD develops the ability to build quickly, at scale, and over a broad range of capabilities.

DoD has made advances in streamlining its technology acquisition process by taking advantage of COTS hardware and software. In particular, the commercial mobile application (apps) marketplace for smartphones and similar *personal technologies* holds great potential as a rapid and adaptable supplier for future military software applications, especially as DoD integrates hardened smartphones into its standard equipment for warfighters. The challenge now becomes validating the security of these apps so that they can be securely and confidently used by warfighters, and doing so on a timeline consistent with operational tempo.

The Automated Program Analysis for Cybersecurity (APAC) program aims to address the challenge of timely and robust security validation of mobile apps by first defining security the properties to be measured against and then developing automated tools to perform the measuring. APAC will draw heavily from the field of formal methods program analysis (theorem proving, logic and machine proofing) to keep malicious code out of DoD Android-based application marketplaces. APAC will apply recent research breakthroughs in this field in an attempt to scale DoD's program analysis capability to a level never before achieved with an automated solution.

For the APAC to succeed, high-level DoD cybersecurity objectives for mobile apps must be translated into properties that are at a sufficiently low level to be proven with automated program analysis tools. As an example, the generic property, "This application contains no malicious code," is too high level to be proven by likely tools. The narrower property, "This Push-to-Talk application is not an eavesdropper," is still too high level. The more limited property, "This Push-to-Talk application only records audio when the 'Talk' button is pressed," may be sufficiently low level to be workable for automated program analysis. The APAC will attempt to define many such low-level properties to come closer to the DoD goal of no malicious code present in its mobile apps marketplaces.

The second challenge APAC aims to address is producing practical, automated tools to demonstrate the cybersecurity properties identified. Successful tools would minimize false alarms, missed detections, and the need for human filtering of results to prove properties.

To validate approaches, APAC plans to examine multiple forms of program analysis, including static analysis and hybrid static–dynamic analyses based on symbolic execution. Performers will be broken into R&D teams to define properties and create tools and Adversarial Challenge (AC) teams to create applications loaded with Trojan horse malicious code using techniques derived from the existing Android malware. Performance will be evaluated on the metrics of: rate of false alarms in identifying malicious code, rate of missed detections in identifying malicious code, and human analysis time required.[7]

4.6 Clean-Slate Design of Resilient, Adaptive, Secure Hosts

The Clean-Slate Design of Resilient, Adaptive, Secure Hosts (CRASH) program will pursue innovative research into the design of new computer systems that are highly resistant to cyber attacks, can adapt after a successful attack to continue rendering useful services, learn from previous attacks how to guard against and cope with future attacks, and can repair themselves after attacks have succeeded. Exploitable vulnerabilities originate from a handful of known sources (e.g., memory safety); they remain because of deficits in tools, languages, and hardware that could address and prevent vulnerabilities in the design, implementation, and execution stages. Often, making a small change in one of these stages can greatly ease the task in another. The CRASH program will encourage such cross-layer codesign and participation from researchers in any relevant area.[8]

4.7 Cyber Fault-Tolerant Attack Recovery

The rapid pace of innovation in software and hardware over the past three decades has produced computational systems that, despite security improvements, remain stubbornly vulnerable to attack. Although clean-sheet design can produce fundamental security improvements that gradually diffuse into the installed base, this process can take years.

The objective of the Cyber Fault-tolerant Attack Recovery (CFAR) program is to produce revolutionary breakthroughs in defensive cyber techniques that can be deployed to protect the existing and planned software systems in both military and civilian contexts without requiring changes to the concept of operations of these systems. To accomplish this, CFAR will exploit and extend several recent developments in computer science and technology:

- The end of frequency scaling has caused CPU manufacturers to shift their focus to new features, particularly multiple cores. Multi-core chips are now common; even smartphones come with four cores. The proliferation of cores may enable a trade of silicon for security.
- Fault-tolerant architectures run multiple subsystems in parallel and constantly cross-check results to rapidly detect, isolate, and mitigate faults, which manifest as differences across the subsystems. Adapting fault-tolerant systems to run multiple variants of a vulnerable software system in parallel present the opportunity to immediately detect and interdict cyberattacks before they gain a foothold.
- Transforming software to create variants of binary executables has the potential to increase the adversary's work factor, because an attack on one variant would likely fail on others. Recent advances in lifting compiled binaries

to intermediate representations suitable for recompilation may enable the application of this approach to systems for which there is no access to source code.

CFAR seeks to enable the DoD to make legacy computer systems more secure by recompiling them. The resulting systems would operate identically to the originals, so there would be no retraining costs and no change to existing operations.[9]

4.8 Edge-Directed Cyber Technologies for Reliable Mission Communication

The U.S. military is heavily dependent on networked communication to fulfill its missions. The wide-area network (WAN) infrastructure that supports this communication is vulnerable to a wide range of failures and cyber attacks that can severely impair connectivity and mission effectiveness at critical junctures. Examples include inadvertent or malicious misconfiguration of network devices, hardware and software failures, extended delays in IP route convergence, DoS flooding attacks, and a variety of control- and data-plane attacks resulting from malicious code embedded within network devices.

The objective of the Edge-Directed Cyber Technologies for Reliable Mission Communication (EdgeCT) program is to bolster the resilience of communication over IP networks solely by instantiating new capabilities in computing devices within user enclaves at the WAN edge. It is envisioned that EdgeCT systems will mitigate WAN failures and attacks on the fly, in a mission-aware manner, by incorporating the following three technical components:

- Real-time network analytics that extract useful information about WAN characteristics and events from enclave-based observation of packet flows into and out of the WAN.
- Holistic decision systems that use knowledge gained from real-time network analytics, as well as configurable information concerning mission plans (including tasks, priorities, and deadlines, if applicable) to determine actions that mitigate network events, in a manner that best serves the mission as a whole.
- Dynamically configurable protocol stacks that implement these decisions by modifying the manner in which information is handled at the network, transport, and application layers of the five-layer protocol stack model of Internet operation.

EdgeCT systems and all of their functionality will be positioned solely within enclaves fronted by one or more in-line military encryption devices. These systems will have no ability to communicate directly with the WAN control or management planes or with the WAN administrator, and will have no knowledge of WAN architecture except for what EdgeCT systems can infer from edge-based observation of packet flows into and out of the WAN. EdgeCT system designs cannot require any changes to the WAN or to the encryption boundaries. Deployed EdgeCT systems may ultimately have to recognize and support robust communication for a variety of user applications including real-time streaming video, real-time audio, file transfer and situational awareness, among others.[10]

4.9 Enhanced Attribution

Malicious actors in cyberspace currently operate with little fear of being caught due to the fact that it is extremely difficult, in some cases perhaps even impossible, to reliably and confidently attribute actions in cyberspace to individuals. The reason cyber attribution is difficult stems at least in part from a lack of end-to-end accountability in the current Internet infrastructure. Cyber campaigns spanning jurisdictions, networks, and devices are only partially observable from the point of view of a defender that operates entirely in friendly cyber territory (e.g., an organization's enterprise network). The identities of malicious cyber operators are largely obstructed by the use of multiple layers of indirection. The current characterization of malicious cyber campaigns based on indicators of compromise, such as file hashes and command-and-control infrastructure identifiers, allows malicious operators to evade the defenders and resume operations simply by superficially changing their tools, as well as aspects of their tactics, techniques, and procedures. The lack of detailed information about the actions and identities of the adversary cyber operators inhibits policymaker considerations and decisions for both cyber and noncyber response options.

The Enhanced Attribution program aims to make currently opaque malicious cyber adversary actions and individual cyber operator attribution transparent by providing high-fidelity visibility into all aspects of malicious cyber operator actions and to increase the government's ability to publicly reveal the actions of individual malicious cyber operators without damaging the sources and methods. The program goal is to develop techniques and tools for generating operationally and tactically relevant information about multiple concurrent independent malicious cyber campaigns, each involving several operators, and the means to share such information with any of a number of interested parties.[11]

4.10 Extreme DDoS Defense

The threat of DDoS attacks has been well recognized in the data networking world for two decades. Such attacks are orchestrated by sets of networked hosts that collectively act to disrupt or deny access to information, communications, or computing capabilities, generally by exhausting critical resources such as bandwidth, processor capacity, or memory of targeted resources. The nature of DDoS attacks can span a wide range. Botnet-induced volumetric attacks, which can generate hundreds of gigabits per second of malicious traffic, are perhaps the best-known form of DDoS. However, low-volume DDoS attacks can be even more pernicious and problematic from a defensive standpoint. Such attacks target specific applications, protocols, or state-machine behaviors while relying on traffic sparseness (or seemingly innocuous message transmission) to evade traditional intrusion detection techniques.

The current art in DDoS defense generally relies on combinations of network-based filtering, traffic diversion, and scrubbing or replication of stored data (or the logical points of connectivity used to access the data) to dilute volumetric attacks and/or to provide diverse access for legitimate users. In general, these existing approaches fall well short of desired capabilities in terms of response times, the ability to identify and to thwart low-volume DDoS, the ability to stop DDoS within encrypted traffic, and the need to defend real-time transactional services such as those associated with cloud computing and military command and control.

To address these shortcomings, the DARPA Extreme DDoS Defense (XD3) program focuses on three broad areas of opportunity to improve resilience against DDoS attacks. The program aims to thwart DDoS attacks by: (1) dispersing cyber assets (physically and/or logically) to complicate adversarial targeting; (2) disguising the characteristics and behaviors of those assets through networked maneuver to confuse or deceive the adversary; and (3) using adaptive mitigation techniques on endpoints (e.g., mission-critical servers) to blunt the effects of attacks that succeed in penetrating other defensive measures. This research program will include formulation of new algorithms, demonstrations, and field exercises with software prototype; development of performance metrics to assess effectiveness; and integration of systems across the three aforementioned areas to maximize overall defensive capabilities.[12]

4.11 High-Assurance Cyber Military Systems

Embedded systems form a ubiquitous, networked, *computing substrate* that underlies much of modern technological society. Such systems range from large supervisory control and data acquisition (SCADA) systems that manage physical infrastructure to medical devices such as pacemakers and insulin pumps, to computer peripherals such as printers and routers, to communication devices such as cell phones and radios, to vehicles such as airplanes and satellites. Such devices have been networked for a variety of reasons, including for their ability to conveniently access diagnostic information, perform software updates, provide innovative features, lower costs, and improve ease of use. Researchers and hackers have shown that these kinds of networked embedded systems are vulnerable to remote attack, and such attacks can cause physical damage while hiding the effects from monitors.

The goal of the High-Assurance Cyber Military Systems (HACMS) program is to create technology for the construction of high-assurance CPSs, where high assurance is defined to mean functionally correct and satisfying appropriate safety and security properties. Achieving this goal requires a fundamentally different approach from what the software community has taken to date. Consequently, HACMS seeks to adopt a clean-slate, formal methods-based approach to enable semiautomated code synthesis from executable, formal specifications. In addition to generating code, HACMS seeks a synthesizer capable of producing a machine-checkable proof that the generated code satisfies functional specifications as well as security and safety policies. A key technical challenge is the developments of techniques to ensure that such proofs are *composable*, allowing the construction of high-assurance systems out of high-assurance components.

Key HACMS technologies include interactive software synthesis systems, verification tools such as theorem provers and model checkers, and specification languages. Recent fundamental advances in the formal methods community, including advances in satisfiability (SAT) and satisfiability modulo theories (SMT) solvers, separation logic, theorem provers, model checkers, domain-specific languages, and code synthesis engines suggest that this approach is feasible. If successful, HACMS will produce a set of publicly available tools integrated into a high-assurance software workbench, which will be widely distributed for use in both commercial and defense software sectors.

HACMS intends to use these tools to (1) generate open-source, high-assurance, and operating system and control system components and (2) use these components to construct high-assurance military vehicles. HACMS will likely transition its technology to both the defense and commercial communities. For the defense sector, HACMS can enable high-assurance military systems ranging from unmanned vehicles (e.g., unmanned aerial vehicles [UAVs], unmanned ground vehicle [UGVs], and unmanned underwater vehicles [UUVs]) to weapons systems, satellites, and command and control devices.[13]

4.12 Integrated Cyber Analysis System

The DoD IT infrastructure is made up of a large, complex network of connected local networks composed of thousands of devices. Cyber defenders must understand and monitor the entire environment to defend it effectively. Toward this end, cyber defenders work to correlate and understand the information contained in log files, executable files, databases of varying formats, directory structures, communication paths, file and message headers, as well as in the volatile and nonvolatile memory of the devices on the network. Meanwhile, adversaries increasingly use targeted attacks that disguise attacks as legitimate actions, making discovery far more difficult. It is within this complicated web of networked systems that cyber defenders must find targeted cyber attacks.

The Integrated Cyber Analysis System (ICAS) program aims to make system information readily useful for attack forensics and tactical cyber defense. ICAS is designed to integrate all sources of network data in a federated database to enable reasoning across the enterprise. If successful, ICAS will provide cyber defenders with a complete, current picture of the IT environment and will reduce the time required to discover targeted attacks.[14]

4.13 Mission-Oriented Resilient Clouds

The February 2011 Federal Cloud Computing Strategy released by the U.S. Chief Information Officer reinforces the U.S. government's plans to move IT away from traditional workstations and toward cloud computing environments. Where compelling incentives to do this exist, security implications of concentrating sensitive data and computation into computing clouds have yet to be fully addressed. The perimeter defense focus of traditional security solutions is not sufficient to secure existing enclaves. It could be further marginalized in cloud environments, where there is a huge concentration of homogeneous hosts on high-speed networks without internal checks, and with implicit trust among hosts within those limited perimeter defenses.

The Mission-Oriented Resilient Clouds (MRC) program aims to address some of these security challenges by developing technologies to detect, diagnose, and respond to attacks in the cloud effectively building a community health system for the cloud. MRC also seeks technologies to enable cloud applications and infrastructure to continue functioning while under attack.

To achieve these goals, the program will research development of innate distributed cloud defenses, construction of shared situational awareness and dynamic trust models, and introduction of manageable and taskable diversity into an otherwise homogeneous cloud, as well as development of mission-aware adaptive networking technologies. MRC also aspires to develop resource allocation and optimization techniques that orchestrate interactions between components that maximize effectiveness while accounting for potential risk from perceived threats.[15]

4.14 Rapid Attack Detection, Isolation, and Characterization Systems

The goal of the Rapid Attack Detection, Isolation, and Characterization Systems (RADICS) program is to develop innovative technologies for detecting and responding to cyber attacks on the U.S. critical infrastructure, especially those parts essential to DoD mission effectiveness. DARPA is interested, specifically, in early warning of impending attacks, situation awareness, network isolation, and threat characterization in response to a widespread and persistent cyberattack on the power grid and its dependent systems. Potentially relevant technologies include anomaly detection, planning and automated reasoning, mapping of conventional and ICSs networks, ad hoc network formation, analysis of ICSs protocols, and rapid forensic characterization of cyber threats in ICS devices.[16]

4.15 Space/Time Analysis for Cybersecurity

As new defensive technologies make old classes of vulnerability difficult to successfully exploit, adversaries move to new classes of vulnerability. Vulnerabilities based on flawed implementations of algorithms have been popular targets for many years. However, once new defensive technologies make vulnerabilities based on flawed implementations less common and more difficult to exploit, adversaries will turn their attention to vulnerabilities inherent in the algorithms themselves.

The Space/Time Analysis for Cybersecurity (STAC) program aims to develop new program analysis techniques and tools for identifying vulnerabilities related to the space and time resource usage behavior of algorithms, specifically, vulnerabilities to algorithmic complexity and side-channel attacks. STAC seeks to enable analysts to identify algorithmic resource usage vulnerabilities in software at levels of scale and speed great enough to support a methodical search for them in the software upon which the U.S. government, military, and economy depend.

Software systems can be vulnerable to algorithmic complexity attacks in situations where an adversary can efficiently construct an input that causes one part of that system to consume superlinear space or time processing the input. The adversary's goal is to deny service to the system's benign users, or to otherwise disable the system by choosing a worst-case input that causes the system to attempt a computation requiring an impractically large amount of space or time.

Side channels are unintended indirect information flows that cause a software system to reveal secrets to an adversary. While the software may prevent the adversary from directly observing the secret, it permits the adversary to observe outputs whose varying space and time characteristics are controlled by computations involving that secret. Given sufficient knowledge of how these computations work, the adversary can deduce the secret by observing some number of outputs.

As algorithmic resource usage vulnerabilities are the consequence of problems inherent in algorithms themselves rather than the consequence of traditional implementation flaws, traditional defensive technologies such as address space layout randomization, data execution prevention, reference count hardening, safe unlinking, and even type-safe programming languages do nothing to mitigate them.

The STAC program seeks advances along two main performance axes: scale and speed. Scale refers to the need for analyses that are capable of considering larger pieces of software, from those that implement network services typically in the range of hundreds of thousands of lines of source code to even larger systems comprising millions or tens of millions of lines of code. Speed refers to the need to increase the rate at which human analysts can analyze software with the help of automated tools, from thousands of lines of code per hour to tens of thousands, hundreds of thousands or millions of lines of code per hour.

The STAC program includes four TAs. TA One (TA1) performers are the R&D teams charged with the development of new program analysis techniques and tools to identify algorithmic resource usage vulnerabilities in software. TA2 performers are the AC teams charged with producing challenge programs with known algorithmic resource usage vulnerabilities for use in testing within the STAC program. To measure technical progress, there will be a series of competitive engagements throughout the STAC program in which R&D teams will attempt to use their techniques and tools to find the algorithmic resource usage vulnerabilities in the challenge programs produced by the AC performers. TA3 is the control team performer charged with applying present-day analysis techniques to the same problems as the R&D teams during engagements in order to provide a baseline for comparison. TA4 is the experimentation lead (EL) performer who will plan each engagement, manage the event, and collect measurements of the results.[17]

4.16 Transparent Computing

Modern computing systems act as black boxes in that they accept inputs and generate outputs but provide little to no visibility of their internal workings. This greatly limits the potential to understand cyber behaviors at the level of detail necessary to detect and counter some of the most important types of cyber threats, particularly APTs. APT adversaries act slowly and deliberately over a long period of time to expand their presence in an enterprise network and achieve their mission goals (e.g., information exfiltration, interference with decision making and denial of capability). Since modern computing systems are opaque, APTs can remain undetected for years if their individual activities can blend with the background noise inherent in any large, complex environment. Beyond the APT problem, a lack of understanding of complex system interactions interferes with (and sometimes completely inhibits) efforts to diagnose and troubleshoot less sophisticated attacks or nonmalicious faulty behavior that spans multiple applications and systems.

The Transparent Computing (TC) program aims to make currently opaque computing systems transparent by providing high-fidelity visibility into component interactions during system operation across all layers of software abstraction, while imposing minimal performance overhead. The program will develop technologies to record and preserve the provenance of all system elements/components (inputs, software modules, processes, etc.); dynamically track the interactions and causal dependencies among cyber system components; assemble these dependencies into end-to-end system behaviors; and reason over these behaviors, both forensically and in real time. By automatically or semiautomatically connecting the dots across multiple activities that are individually legitimate but collectively indicate malice or abnormal behavior, TC has the potential to enable prompt detection of APTs and other cyber threats, and allow complete root cause analysis and damage assessment once adversary activity is identified. In addition, the TC program will integrate its basic cyber reasoning functions in an enterprise-scale cyber monitoring and control construct that enforces security policies at key ingress/exit points, for example, the firewall.

The intent of the TC program is to develop basic technologies that are separable and usable in isolation (e.g., within a given software layer/application environment, such as web middleware), while exploring the best way to integrate multiple TC technologies in an experimental prototype. The program will aim to produce basic technologies and an experimental prototype comprising multilayer data collection architecture and an analysis/enforcement engine that will enable both proactive enforcement of desirable policies (permissible/impermissible interactions) and near real-time intrusion detection and forensic analysis. It is expected that this prototype will provide a starting point for technology transition.[18]

4.17 Vetting Commodity IT Software and Firmware (VET)

Seeking to improve the security of the commodity IT supply chain, DARPA's VET program is developing tools and techniques designed to help ensure a devices' software and firmware are free from hidden malicious functionality.

Government agencies and the military rely upon many kinds of COTS commodity IT devices, including mobile phones, printers, computer workstations, and many other everyday items. Each of these devices is the final product of long supply chains involving many vendors from many nations providing various components and subcomponents, including considerable amounts of software and firmware. Long supply chains provide adversaries with opportunities to insert hidden malicious functionality into this software and firmware that adversaries can exploit to accomplish harmful objectives, including exfiltration of sensitive data and sabotage of critical operations.

Organizations often attempt to manage supply chain risk indirectly by investigating manufacturers and their business relationships. However, there is not a current accurate and cost-effective technical means for large enterprises to directly examine the software and firmware commodity IT vendors provide with every individual new device and update. In fact, a common perception among government and industry alike is that the problem of enterprise-scale vetting of the software and firmware on COTS IT devices is so difficult that it is unapproachable.

DARPA created the Vetting Commodity IT Software and Firmware (VET) program to address the threat of hidden malicious functionality in COTS IT devices. VET's goal is to demonstrate that it is technically feasible to determine that the software and firmware shipped on commodity IT devices is free of broad classes of hidden malicious functionality. The program supports the White House's 2009 CNCI, which specifically named developing a multipronged approach for global supply chain risk management as a key national security goal.

Specific VET program objectives include the following:

■ Enable analysts to anticipate the kinds of malicious functionality adversaries might hide in software and firmware of a given commodity IT device intended for a particular kind of deployment.
■ Enable analysts to efficiently rule out the presence of hidden malicious functionality, accidental-seeming flaws and benign features with seemingly unintended negative consequences.
■ Make it feasible to vet the software and firmware on board each and every individual commodity IT device deployed in a large enterprise, even in cases where an adversary has prepared the devices to deceive diagnostics and appear benign when they are in fact malicious.

These three advances in combination would give government agencies a new capability: the ability to gain confidence in the software and firmware on their commodity IT devices by directly examining the devices themselves, rather than reasoning about their provenance.[19]

4.18 DARPA's Request for Information: CSO R&D

In July 2016 DARPA issued CSO R&D Request for Information (RFI) Solicitation Number: DARPA-SN-16-42. DARPA's basic premise behind this request is that cyberspace is a global domain within the information environment consisting of the interdependent network of IT infrastructures and resident data, including the Internet, telecommunications networks, computer systems, and embedded processors and controllers.

CSO are the employment of cyberspace capabilities where the primary purpose is to achieve objectives in or through cyberspace. Cyberspace superiority is the degree of dominance in cyberspace by one force that permits secure, reliable conduct of operations by that force, and its related land, air, maritime, and space forces at a given time and place without prohibitive interference by an adversary.

The request stated that R&D projects in CSO to achieve cyberspace superiority require specialized knowledge, skills, and experience. Often, these projects are classified and can only be solicited from a limited number of sources. DARPA must maintain up-to-date knowledge on the potential performers to maximize the number of sources that can be solicited for classified, highly specialized, CSO R&D initiatives. DARPA seeks information regarding such potential performers. Ideally, respondents will include both potential performers currently holding security clearances and those who may be granted clearances based on technical capabilities and eligibility.

The DARPA I2O requests information on potential performers for classified CSO R&D. Specifically, this RFI seeks information on potential performers who have the capability to rapidly develop state-of-the-art CSO technologies responsive to current and emerging cyber threats, and who have either of the following:

■ Personnel currently holding security clearances and facilities cleared to receive, store, and process CSO information at multiple levels of classification
■ Personnel and facilities eligible to receive clearances

Additional background information is available in DoD Joint Publications 2-0, 3-0, 3-121, 3-12(R) and 3-13.[20]

4.19 Summary

DARPA's technological approach focuses on radical innovation that addresses future warfighting needs, rather than developing technologies that address current warfighting needs. This approach shapes how the agency defines, pursues, and tracks technology transition. DARPA considers a successful transition to be one where its program, or a portion of its program, influences or introduces new knowledge. This knowledge is often passed through program performers, which DARPA relies on to execute technology development in its programs. Typical performers include commercial enterprises; other DOD entities, such as military service laboratories and research agencies; and academic institutions. Further, DARPA generally does not develop technologies to full maturity. Instead, the agency focuses on demonstrating the feasibility of new technologies, which includes verifying that the concepts behind the technologies have potential for real-life applications. As a result, most DARPA technologies require additional development before they are ready for operational or commercial use.[21]

DARPA is working to assure that the United States has cyberspace superiority that permits secure, reliable conduct of operations by U.S. Military forces, and its related land, air, maritime, and space forces at a given time and place without prohibitive interference by an adversary. DARPA is developing the research capabilities and tools necessary to assure that dominance includes the following:

■ The Cyber Grand Challenge is a research and testing ground as much as it is a competition to create automatic defensive systems capable of reasoning about flaws, formulating patches, and deploying them on a network in real time.
■ The Active Authentication, ACD, and CFAR solutions will all provide greatly improved cybersecurity to protect mission critical and high-value systems.

- Enhanced attribution methods, the in ICAS and the RADICS, will enable defenders to more quickly respond to cyber attacks and to identify and track potential attackers.
- DARPA is far ahead of private technology companies in how it views computing and networking technology and how to defend that technology.
- DARPA's RFI: CSO R&D clearly shows that the agency intends to research and develop technology that can get and keep the U.S. military far ahead on cybersecurity and cyber space capabilities.

4.20 Seminar Discussion Topics

Discussion topics for graduate or professional-level seminars are

- What experience has seminar participants had working with DARPA?
- What experience has seminar participants had with private corporations or nongovernmental organizations that have worked with DARPA cybersecurity programs or cybersecurity research efforts?
- What areas of DARPA cybersecurity research do seminar participants think are the most important? Why?
- What areas of DARPA cybersecurity research do seminar participants think are the most relevant to the private sector? Why?

Key Terms

biometrics: are the characteristics used to uniquely recognize humans based on one or more intrinsic physical or behavioral traits

cognitive fingerprint: is the unique pattern arising from an individual's interaction with existing technology without the need for specific data collection technology and without the need for cooperation from the user

composable: technologies that are able to exist, happen, or work together

computing substrate: is a complex of processors and sensors, or collectors that when combined provide arrays of processing abilities interconnected by a communication channel

cybersecurity metrics: help organizations verify that cybersecurity controls are in compliance with a policy, process, or procedure and help to identify security strengths and weaknesses

innovation ecosystem: multidisciplinary research is key and is often driven by military or industrial needs. Disciplines are brought into the innovation ecosystem from many types of universities, national laboratories, private industry, and military laboratories to perform rapid, efficient innovation that could have a transformative economic impact on an industry or sector

moving target defense: is a rotational environment that runs an application on several different operating system platforms to thwart attacker reconnaissance efforts and improve application resilience to the threat of zero-day exploits

personal technologies: include individually owned devices such as cell phones, tablets, laptops, and digital media

security threats: are conditions, people, or events that can jeopardize the security of a nation, organization, a facility, or any asset belonging to the threatened entity

security vigilance: is a constant attention given to security during day-to-day operations and contributes to security by encouraging the reporting of security violations and makes suggestions on how to improve security when weaknesses are observed

tailored trustworthy spaces: a security architecture and strategic federal cybersecurity research theme tailored for the smart grid and other cyber environments that assure that all elements in the space are secure

References

1. Defense Advanced Research Projects Agency (DARPA). *About DARPA*. Retrieved November 21, 2016, http://www.darpa.mil/about-us/about-darpa
2. Defense Advanced Research Projects Agency (DARPA). *DARPA Offices*. Retrieved November 21, 2016, http://www.darpa.mil/about-us/offices
3. Defense Advanced Research Projects Agency (DARPA). *Cyber Grand Challenge*. Retrieved November 21, 2016, http://www.darpa.mil/program/cyber-grand-challenge
4. Defense Advanced Research Projects Agency (DARPA). *DARPA Celebrates Cyber Grand Challenge Winners*. August 7, 2016. Retrieved November 21, 2016, http://www.darpa.mil/news-events/2016-08-05a
5. Defense Advanced Research Projects Agency (DARPA). *Active Authentication*. Retrieved November 21, 2016, http://www.darpa.mil/program/active-authentication
6. Defense Advanced Research Projects Agency (DARPA). *Active Cyber Defense (ACD)*. Retrieved November 21, 2016, http://www.darpa.mil/program/active-cyber-defense
7. Defense Advanced Research Projects Agency (DARPA). *Automated Program Analysis for Cybersecurity (APAC)*. Retrieved November 21, 2016, http://archive.darpa.mil/cybergrandchallenge/
8. Defense Advanced Research Projects Agency (DARPA). *Clean-Slate Design of Resilient, Adaptive, Secure Hosts (CRASH)*. Retrieved November 21, 2016, http://www.darpa.mil/program/clean-slate-design-of-resilient-adaptive-secure-hosts
9. Defense Advanced Research Projects Agency (DARPA). *Cyber Fault-Tolerant Attack Recovery (CFAR)*. Retrieved November 21, 2016, http://www.darpa.mil/program/cyber-fault-tolerant-attack-recovery
10. Defense Advanced Research Projects Agency (DARPA). *Edge-Directed Cyber Technologies for Reliable Mission Communication (EdgeCT)*. Retrieved November 21, 2016, http://www.darpa.mil/program/edge-directed-cyber-technologies-for-reliable-mission-communication
11. Defense Advanced Research Projects Agency (DARPA). *Enhanced Attribution*. Retrieved November 21, 2016, http://www.darpa.mil/program/enhanced-attribution

12. Defense Advanced Research Projects Agency (DARPA). *Extreme DDoS Defense (XD3)*. Retrieved November 21, 2016, http://www.darpa.mil/program/extreme-ddos-defense

13. Defense Advanced Research Projects Agency (DARPA). *High-Assurance Cyber Military Systems (HACMS)*. Retrieved November 21, 2016, http://www.darpa.mil/program/high-assurance-cyber-military-systems

14. Defense Advanced Research Projects Agency (DARPA). *Integrated Cyber Analysis System (ICAS)*. Retrieved November 21, 2016, http://www.darpa.mil/program/integrated-cyber-analysis-system

15. Defense Advanced Research Projects Agency (DARPA). *Mission-Oriented Resilient Clouds (MRC)*. Retrieved November 21, 2016, http://www.darpa.mil/program/mission-oriented-resilient-clouds

16. Defense Advanced Research Projects Agency (DARPA). *Rapid Attack Detection, Isolation and Characterization Systems (RADICS)*. Retrieved November 21, 2016, http://www.darpa.mil/program/rapid-attack-detection-isolation-and-characterization-systems

17. Defense Advanced Research Projects Agency (DARPA). *Space/Time Analysis for Cybersecurity (STAC)*. Retrieved November 21, 2016, http://www.darpa.mil/program/space-time-analysis-for-cybersecurity

18. Defense Advanced Research Projects Agency (DARPA). *Transparent Computing*. Retrieved November 21, 2016, http://www.darpa.mil/program/transparent-computing

19. Defense Advanced Research Projects Agency (DARPA). *Vetting Commodity IT Software and Firmware (VET)*. Retrieved November 21, 2016, http://www.darpa.mil/program/vetting-commodity-it-software-and-firmware

20. Defense Advanced Research Projects Agency (DARPA). *Request for Information Cyberspace Operations Research and Development*. DARPA-SN-16-42. July 11, 2016. Retrieved November 21, 2016, https://www.fbo.gov/index?tab=documents&tabmode=form&subtab=core&tabid=2f7bca34ba9258beba980cad90c3a0b9

21. GAO. *Defense Advanced Research Projects Agency: Key Factors Drive Transition of Technologies, but Better Training and Data Dissemination Can Increase Success*. GAO-16-5. November 18, 2015. Retrieved December 21, 2016, http://www.gao.gov/products/GAO-16-5

Chapter 5

Intelligence Advanced Research Projects Activity and In-Q-Tel

The IARPA invests in high-risk, high-payoff research programs to tackle some of the most difficult challenges of the agencies and disciplines in the IC. IARPA collaborates across the IC to ensure that research addresses relevant future needs. This cross-community focus ensures the ability to: address cross-agency challenges; leverage both operational and R&D expertise from across the IC; and coordinate transition strategies with agency partners. IARPA does not have an operational mission and does not deploy technologies directly to the field. Instead, IARPA facilitates the transition of research results to IC customers for operational application. In-Q-Tel is investing in R&D projects that are of interest to IC. This chapter covers the unclassified cybersecurity research information provided by IARPA and In-Q-Tel.[1]

5.1 The IARPA Organization

Modeled after the DARPA, IARPA was established in 2006 with the mandate to: conduct *cross-community research*; target new opportunities and innovations; and generate revolutionary capabilities. IARPA was tasked to accomplish these objectives by drawing upon the technical and operational expertise that resides within the intelligence agencies. This ensured that IARPA's programs will be uniquely designed to anticipate the long-term needs of, and provide research and technical capabilities for, the IC.[1] There are four research thrusts within IARPA: analysis, anticipatory intelligence, collections, and operations.

The analysis focuses on maximizing insights from the massive, disparate, unreliable, and dynamic data that are or could be available to analysts, in a timely manner from new sources of information and from existing and novel data through the use of innovative techniques that can be utilized in the processes of the analysis. IARPA programs are in diverse technical disciplines but have common features such as they: involve potential transition partners at all stages, beginning with the definition of success; create technologies that can earn the trust of the analyst user by providing the reasoning for results; and address uncertainty and data provenance explicitly (Figure 5.1).[2]

Current IARPA Research in Analysis	
Program	Description
Janus	Computer vision, image processing, pattern recognition, biometrics, facial recognition, identity intelligence, computer graphics
Finder	Geolocation, localization, geospatial fusion, data fusion, machine learning, big data, image processing, image, photograph, video, multimedia, computer vision, natural language processing
Aladdin Video	Image, photograph, video, multimedia, computer vision, natural language processing, image processing, big data, video analytics, machine learning, speech processing
KRNS	Knowledge discovery, brain, neuroscience, artificial intelligence, cognitive bias, judgment, decision making, behavioral science, human factors, training, tradecraft, data sense making, linguistics, language, semantics, culture
DIVA	Machine learning, deep learning or hierarchical modeling, artificial intelligence, object detection, recognition, person detection and re identification, person action recognition, video activity detection, tracking across multiple nonoverlapping camera viewpoints, 3D reconstruction from video, super-resolution, stabilization, statistics, probability and mathematics
CORE3D	Mulit-view satellite image processing, multi modal information fusion, deep learning, remote sensing, photogrammetry, image segmentation and classification, multispectral imagery processing, and geospatial volumetric 3D data representation methods
Babel	Multilingual/multidialectal speech recognition, keyword search algorithms, speech recognition in noisy environments, low resource languages, rapid adaptation to new languages and environments, machine learning
MATERIAL	Natural language processing, machine translation, cross-lingual information retrieval, domain recognition and adaptation, multilingual ontologies, Multilingual speech recognition, cross-lingual summarization, keyword search algorithms, low resource languages, automatic language identification, machine learning, rapid adaptation to new languages, domains and genres

Figure 5.1   Current IARPA research in analysis. (From Intelligence Advanced Research Projects Activity (IARPA). Analysis. Retrieved November 22, 2016 https://www.iarpa.gov/index.php/about-iarpa/analysis)

Anticipatory intelligence focuses on characterizing and reducing uncertainty by providing decision makers with timely and accurate forecasts of significant global events. This research explores or demonstrates the feasibility of revolutionary concepts that may deliver real-time indications and warning, in context, to support rapid, nuanced understanding by the intelligence consumers. IARPA programs are in diverse technical disciplines but have common features: develops technologies to generate timely forecasts for well-defined events and their characteristics (e.g., who, what, when, where, and how); uses a rigorous, open and on-going test and evaluation process; has metrics that include lead time, accuracy, false positive and false negative rates, and are calculated by comparing forecasts to real-world events; and communicates forecasts in context. The key research areas include forecasting events related to science and technology (S&T); social, political, and economic crises; epidemiology and biosecurity; CI; and cybersecurity (Figure 5.2).[3]

The goal of collections research is to dramatically improve the value of collected data from all sources by developing new sensor and transmission technologies, new collection techniques that more precisely target the desired information, and the means for collecting information from previously inaccessible sources. In addition,

Current IARPA Research in Anticipatory Intelligence	
Program	Description
CAUSE	Cybersecurity, cyber-event forecasting, cyber-actor behavior and cultural understanding, threat intelligence, threat modeling, cyber-event coding, cyber-kinetic event detection
CREATE	Forecasting, logic and critical thinking, human judgment
FUSE	Technical emergence, text analytics, knowledge discovery, big data, social network analysis, natural language processing, forecasting, machine learning
HFC	Forecasting, human judgment, machine learning, decision making, human/machine interfaces, text analysis
Mercury	SIGINT analytics, event forecasting, machine learning, streaming data, data fusion, weapons of mass destruction, chemical/biological warfare, human biomarkers, emerging biotechnologies
SCITE	Engineering enterprises that detect low probability events with low accuracy sensors, innovative research methods to evaluate analytic and forecasting tradecraft, innovative statistical methods to estimate performance of systems addressing complex analysis and forecasting problems, scientific research on organizational lessons-learned methods, evidence-based forecasting methods, inductive logic, probabilistic reasoning and its application to analytic tradecraft

Figure 5.2 Current IARPA research in anticipatory intelligence. (From Advanced Research Projects Activity (IARPA). Anticipatory Intelligence. Retrieved November 22, 2016 https://www.iarpa.gov/index.php/about-iarpa/anticipatory-intelligence)

IARPA pursues new mechanisms for combining information gathered from multiple sources to enhance the quality, reliability, and utility of the collected information. Areas of interest include the following:

1. Innovative methods or tools for identifying and/or creating novel sources of new information
2. Sensor technologies that dramatically improve the reach, sensitivity, size, weight, and power for the collection of broad signal or signature types
3. Methods for combining different measures and/or sensors to improve performance and accuracy of systems
4. Approaches for assessing and quantifying the ecological validity of behavioral, neuroscience, and social science research
5. Secure communication to and from the collection points
6. Innovative approaches to gain access to denied environments
7. Tagging, tracking, and location techniques
8. Electrically small antennas and other advanced radio frequency (RF) concepts
9. Agile architectures that intelligently distill useful information at the point of collection
10. Innovative means and methods to ensure the veracity of data collected from a variety of sources
11. Automated methods for sensor data fusion without predefined interface descriptions
12. Approaches to enable signal collection systems to conduct more effective targeted information acquisition rather than bulk collection
13. Tools to identify and mask signal streams and records that contain personal information to avoid unauthorized collection and dissemination (Figure 5.3)[4]

Operations focus on the IC's ability to operate freely and effectively in an often hostile and increasingly interdependent and resource-constrained environment. The key research focus areas include IA, advanced computing technologies and architectures, quantum information science and technology, and threat detection and mitigation (Figure 5.4).[5]

Several of the research programs listed above may impact cybersecurity research and technology in the future. The current IARPA cybersecurity focused research is spearheaded by its Office of SSO, which aims to counter emerging adversary potential to ensure the U.S. IC's operational effectiveness in a globally interdependent and networked environment. SSO's research portfolio is organized into three areas: computational power, trustworthy components, and safe and secure systems. Objectives within the computational power area include developing revolutionary advances in science and engineering to solve problems intractable with modern computers; focusing on the fundamental elements of quantum computing systems; and exploring the feasibility of a superconducting computer. In the trustworthy components area research programs focus on understanding and manipulating very

Current IARPA Research in Collections	
Program	Description
Fun GCAT	Bioinformatics, DNA sequence screening, functional genomics, systems biology, infectious disease, and synthetic biology
HFGeo	Communication systems, ionosphere, antennas, geolocation, electromagnetics, radio frequency
MOSAIC	Behavioral science, cognitive psychology, human performance, mobile computing, context sensing, signal processing, data fusion, machine learning, data privacy and security
Odin	Biometrics, presentation attack, machine learning, computer vision
SHARP	Cognition, psychometrics, fluid reasoning and intelligence, neuroscience, human performance
SLiCE	Communication systems, geolocation, electromagnetics, radio frequency

Figure 5.3 Current IARPA research collections. (From Advanced Research Projects Activity (IARPA). Collections. Retrieved November 22, 2016 https://www.iarpa.gov/index.php/about-iarpa/collection)

Current IARPA Research in Operations	
Program	Description
C3	Advanced/alternative computing technologies, superconducting microelectronics
LogiQ	Advanced/alternative computing platforms, quantum information sciences, qubit systems
MICrONS	Theoretical neuroscience, computational neuroscience, machine learning, connectomics, brain activity mapping
RAVEN	Microelectronics, nondestructive analysis, nanoscale imaging, hardware assurance
TIC	Cybersecurity and information assurance, hardware assurance, microelectronics
VirtUE	Computer virtualization, operating systems, cyber security, vulnerability analysis, insider threat remediation and detection, active defense, big data analytics, sensor fusion, user interfaces, anomalous event detection

Figure 5.4 Current IARPA research operations. (From Advanced Research Projects Activity (IARPA). Operations. Retrieved November 22, 2016 https://www.iarpa.gov/index.php/about-iarpa/operations)

small-scale electronics, obtaining mission-worthy chips from state-of-the-art, but untrusted fabrication facilities, and gaining functionality from unpedigreed software without placing mission systems at risk. Finally, research in the area of safe and secure systems has a broad objective of safeguarding the integrity of missions in a hostile environment.

Some of the current projects focus on enabling collaboration without wholesale sharing of data through privacy-preserving search techniques. Research in both the trustworthy components and safe and secure systems areas contributes directly to the Tailored Trustworthy Spaces research theme.[6]

5.2 IARPA Cyber-Attack Automated Unconventional Sensor Environment

Cyberattacks evolve in a phased approach. Detection typically occurs in the later phases of an attack, and analysis often occur postmortem to investigate and discover indicators from earlier phases. Observations of earlier attack phases, such as target reconnaissance, planning, and delivery, may enable warning of significant cyber events prior to their most damaging phases.

Cyber-Attack Automated Unconventional Sensor Environment (CAUSE) aims to develop and test new automated methods that forecast and detect cyberattacks significantly earlier than the existing methods. The program is envisioned as a multiyear, multiphase, research effort. Research areas include the following:

■ Cybersecurity
■ Cyber-event forecasting
■ Cyber-actor behavior and cultural understanding
■ Threat intelligence
■ Threat modeling
■ Cyber-event coding
■ Cyber-kinetic event detection[7]

Past research, such as IARPA's Open Source Indicators (OSI) program, shows that combinations of publicly available data sources are useful in the early and accurate detection and forecasting of events, such as disease outbreaks and political crises. In the area of cybersecurity, few have researched methods for a probabilistic warning system that fuses internal sensors (sensors inside the logical boundary of an organization, such as host data) and external sensors (sensors outside the logical and physical boundaries of an organization, such as social media or web search trends).

The CAUSE program seeks multidisciplinary unconventional sensor technology that will complement existing advanced intrusion-detection capabilities. Unconventional sensors will leverage data not typically used in practice today for cybersecurity (at least not in the way the data was originally intended) and may come from nontypical disciplines that can be applied to the cybersecurity domain.

IARPA expects performers to identify and extract novel leading signals from both internal and external sensors (both conventional and unconventional) and use them to generate warnings—probabilistic forecasts and/or detections of cyberattacks. Performers will generate warnings for real cyberattacks against one or more U.S. industry organizations that have agreed to participate in CAUSE.[8]

IARPA expects that offerors will identify, create, and evaluate several novel unconventional signals from novel data sources to develop their sensors. In addition to unconventional sensors, existing data sensors or signals from other disciplines may be evaluated, refined, and expanded for use within the program, provided their inclusion is well documented and justified. It is expected that some of the novel signal concepts described in the offeror's proposal will require additional research and further exploration to determine their applicability and utility to the CAUSE Program's goal of creating new unconventional sensors.

IARPA expects complete approaches to include sensors from many disciplines or domains, such as human/behavioral, cultural, cyber-physical, social, economic, and others. Information extracted from social media has been useful in forecasting noncyber events and is expected to be useful for the cybersecurity domain as well; however, it is expected that an offeror's complete solution will extend its unconventional sensor exploration beyond just social media. Offerors are encouraged to consider the influence of culture on cyber-actor group behavior(s) (e.g., motivation, intent). Offerors must address the challenges involved with the integration of conventional and unconventional sensors due to their differences in structure, accuracy, reliability, and complexity.

CAUSE will rely on data and sensors from external sources that are located outside the logical and physical boundaries of an organization (such as social media and economic events) and internal sources that are located within the logical and physical boundaries of a participating organization (including its logical public interfaces).

External sensor data shall be from publicly available data sources, lawfully obtained data available to any member of the general public, to include by purchase, subscription, or registration. IARPA expects that external data acquisition will require significant resources by each performer, and expects that external data requirements will likely overlap across performers. Offerors are asked to list all data sources required for their proposed approach, to explain how each data source supports their approach, and to include estimates of all external data costs in their cost proposals.

It is expected that the technology developed under the CAUSE Program will have no human in the loop. Experts may help develop, train, and improve the solution systems, but they will not manually generate warnings, guide the system, or filter warnings before they are delivered to the Test and Evaluation (T&E) team. The performer-produced warnings must be machine generated and submitted automatically to the T&E team continuously throughout the program. The T&E team will provide details of the automated warning ingestion and acceptance system used for T&E at program kickoff.

The performer must include an audit trail for all warnings. The goal of this requirement is to make the warning transparent to the end user, by allowing a drill down from warning to sensor data. Since the Audit Trail is dependent on the performers' approach and system, the government team, prior to scored warnings, intends to work with each performer to develop the specific requirements for the audit trail. Ultimately, the audit trail capability would be mapped to a series of user interfaces (UIs) as an integral part of the prototype system and be web enabled so that it can easily be demonstrated to facilitate analysis of tools.

In CAUSE Phases 2 and 3, the performer's prototype interface should provide useful contextual information about warnings in human-readable, text format. To the maximum extent possible, this capability should leverage existing tools for *Natural Language Generation*. The interface should explain in natural language why the warning was sent and why now, by extracting and synthesizing details from the audit trail in a *logical narrative*. The narrative can also include contextual information that relates to other warnings and noncyber events (e.g., economic upheaval, political events, kinetic warfare), influences on actor behaviors and motivations, or historical knowledge that might explain the event (e.g., prior bank cyber-theft patterns).

Replication Test is a test of the warning generation system's ability to repeatedly generate the same warning with a given sensor data input. During site visits, performers will be asked to replicate certain warnings they submitted; therefore, this capability must be built into each system. Version control and proper data management are important to be able to rerun a specific version of the system, on the specific portion of the data that was used to generate a particular warning. During phases 2 and 3 of the program, performers will also be asked to perform *ablation tests* during the planned site visits. Ablation tests are intended to promote the use of multiple feeds, and to gauge how performance degrades as a function of the availability of any particular feed.

Understanding the trade-offs (between recall and false discovery rate [FDR], and between lead time, utility time, and warning quality score) is very important for analysts. How the systems should set these trade-offs varies greatly across analytic requirements. Some analysts may favor recall over FDR, or vice versa, and other analysts may favor utility time over warning quality score, or viceversa.

It is therefore important that the systems formalize and quantify the trade-offs and provide the analyst *dial functionality* (as part of the audit trail UI to manage these trade-offs explicitly). This is a requirement for phases 2 and 3 of the program. Performer teams will design, implement, and demonstrate the dial functionality.

The CAUSE solution/system must be flexible enough to integrate with minimal configuration changes for use in organizations with diverse sets of internal sensors, not relying on organization-specific software/hardware hooks to integrate with an organization. Solutions must adapt to new and/or potentially unavailable internal sensors between disparate organizations. A staged approach to prototype development is expected; each successive prototype will leverage research progress made since the previous prototype. Research goals should be set, and research plans should be made, to take full advantage of the length of the CAUSE Program. Offerors must describe how research advances will be incorporated into successive prototypes.

To address the combination of challenges presented by CAUSE, IARPA anticipates that offeror teams will be multidisciplinary and may include, but need not be limited to, members with expertise in computer science, data science, social and behavioral sciences, mathematics, statistics, and rapid software prototype development. Offeror teams might also include content extraction experts, information theorists, and cybersecurity subject matter experts having applied experience with cyber capabilities. Offerors must demonstrate the completeness of their team in their management plan, and that their team does not lack capabilities necessary for success, that their team is tightly knit with strong management and a single point of contact, and that each team member contributes significantly to the program goals, both depth and diversity will be beneficial.

The following are examples of topics considered out of scope for this program:

■ Solutions that identify specific individuals
■ Solutions based on a single sensor data source or type
■ Development of intrusion-detection capabilities leveraging only internal data from traditional/existing cybersecurity data streams
■ Forecasting warnings about insider threats, insider collusion, or insider trading
■ In-depth development of data visualization tools
■ Extensive advancement of natural language processing (NLP) techniques; off-the-shelf NLP tools should be sufficient for extracting features of interest; offerors must justify limited advanced NLP development

Offerors must demonstrate that their approach is consistent with these restrictions.

IARPA expects offerors to plan for the exploration of a minimum of three new novel sensors in each phase of the program to ensure the CAUSE Program can adapt to emerging technologies, cyberattacks, relevant signals, and data. All sensors must be tested by performers regularly throughout the program. Testing plans for each sensor must identify the required data, appropriate metrics and estimated targets, costs, and technical and programmatic risks. The testing plans must include waypoints and a timeline for execution. Proven sensor concepts are expected to be integrated into the performer's solution. The offeror should also propose regular waypoints that provide evidence that the technical and programmatic risks associated with the proposed approach are being addressed. Such waypoints must be clear and well defined, with a logical connection to enabling offeror decisions and/

or government team decisions. Examples of cyber events to be detected include unauthorized access, DoS malicious code successful installation, scans/probes/attempted access, data theft, and data destruction.[9]

5.3 IARPA Trusted Integrated Chips

The goal of the Trusted Integrated Chips (TIC) Program is to develop and demonstrate split manufacturing, a new approach to chip fabrication where security and intellectual property protection can be assured. The semiconductor industry has been advancing rapidly with aggressive scaling. Extending beyond the Moore's Law of digital processing and storage integrated circuits, this scaling has extended to three dimensions to keep pace. This scaling trend has fostered the integration of diverse analog and digital components to provide high-value systems such as sensors, actuators, and biochips. The key capabilities to fabricate the high-performance integrated circuit components for these high-value systems are in the commercial foundries, which now dominate the world's production of high-performance integrated circuits. It is desirable for the U.S. academic community and the U.S. industrial base to have open and assured access to obtain the highest performance integrated circuits (ICs) and systems-on-chips (SoCs) while ensuring that the components have been securely fabricated according to design and that intellectual property is protected.[10]

The TIC Program aims to develop new approaches to chip fabrication where security and intellectual property concerns would otherwise prohibit the use of offshore manufacturing foundries. Specifically, TIC seeks to address secure foundry manufacturing of chips in several ways:

■ Development of split-manufacturing processes in which a front-end-of line (FEOL) process defines transistor building blocks up to the point of the first or second metallization followed by a back-end-of-line (BEOL) process in which remaining metallizations are carried out in secure, trusted facilities in the United States. Initially, the logistics and compatibility of using more than one fabrication facility at the 130 nm node will be of concern.

■ Chip obfuscation methods whereby the intent of digital and analog functions and their associated building blocks are disguised in their function within the FEOL process.

■ New verification methods that ensure that no malicious circuitry has been added during fabrication. New ideas that are different from those being explored in other federal research programs, such as DARPA's Tools for Recognizing Useful Signals of Trustworthiness (TRUST) and iris programs are encouraged.

■ New approaches to three-dimensional (3D) fabrication at significant semiconductor manufacturing nodes. This includes new transistor/circuit designs and creative stacking methods such as those which may be required for integrated MEMS and III-V-on-Si chips.[11]

It is anticipated that the TIC Program will logically scale its capabilities over a four-year period having started with a core 130 nm-node capability and subsequently moving toward a 22 nm capability at the end of a four-year period. It is expected that the methodologies to be demonstrated will define both high-performance integrated circuits and integrated systems such as MEMS over the next 10 years.

Collaborative efforts and teaming among potential performers will be strongly encouraged. It is anticipated that the teams will be multidisciplinary with capabilities including: circuit design, chip manufacturing, and characterization. The vision of the TIC Program is to ensure that the United States can

- Obtain the highest performance possible in integrated circuits
- Obtain near 100% assurance that designs are safe and secure not compromised with malicious circuitry
- Ensure security of designs, capability, and performance while simultaneously protecting intellectual property
- Realize secure systems combining advanced complementary metal–oxide–semiconductor (CMOS) with other high-value chips[12]

5.4 In-Q-Tel and the U.S. IC R&D Needs

The advances in science and technology provide a unique opportunity to transform intelligence applying expanded analytic, collection, and processing capabilities, and to improve cross-component collaboration through the IC System for Information Sharing. Innovative programs such as In-Q-Tel provide Central Intelligence Agency (CIA) and the IC with effective reach into the cutting-edge creativity of the U.S. private sector.[13]

The CIA has supported the development of technology since the 1960s when it supported the development of lithium-ion batteries because certain operational missions required long-lasting batteries of various shapes and sizes. The lithium-ion battery improved the performance of surveillance equipment and prolonged the operation of reconnaissance satellites. In the early 1970s, the CIA passed the technology to the medical community where it was used in heart pacemakers.

In February 2003, the CIA-funded strategic investor In-Q-Tel made an investment in Keyhole, Inc. Keyhole was a pioneer of interactive 3D earth visualization and creator of the Earth Viewer 3D system. CIA worked closely with other IC organizations to tailor Keyhole's systems to meet operational needs. The technology was also useful with multiple television networks using Earthviewer 3D to fly over Iraqi cities during its news coverage of Operation Iraqi Freedom. The popularity of this technology eventually caught the attention of Google, which acquired Keyhole in 2004. This technology is now known as Google Earth.[14]

To keep up with the boom in innovations in the private sector, especially in IT, the CIA assembled a team of senior staff and outside consultants and lawyers in 1998 to design an entity to partner with industry in accelerated solutions to IT problems facing the IC. After meeting with investment bankers, venture capitalists, entrepreneurs, and members of the Congress and staff, the team conceived what is now known as In-Q-Tel.

In-Q-Tel is a congressionally created, government-funded nonprofit venture capital firm that seeks to accelerate market introduction of products that could benefit U.S. intelligence efforts. In-Q-Tel, was created in 1998 but did not get fully underway until later. In-Q-Tel generally does not get involved in technologies until they are well on their way to development or in the prototype stage. The expanding use of government-funded firms that get equity in private companies could raise questions about the appropriate government role in the financial marketplace. In-Q-Tel started off making investments primarily in the IT area, including Internet security, data integration, imagery analysis, and language translation. These investments have helped government agencies keep up with technology developments in the commercial marketplace, and helped the IC in particular to mold, develop, and deploy crucial technologies in a timely manner.[15]

Small or newer companies often do not to target the U.S. Federal Government market because it can be difficult to target or slow to access. As those companies often need to penetrate their markets quickly to generate cash flow, government customers can miss the chance to influence product development. Moreover, private venture capital firms sometimes discourage small companies they invest in from doing business with the government because the complexity of the procurement process and long lead time on procurement decisions. This means that agencies are often two to three years behind the commercial market for technology, especially in areas like IT where there is rapid innovation.

A Board of Trustees oversees In-Q-Tel's direction, strategy, and policies. In-Q-Tel offers the CIA a mechanism by which to involve industry in solving the specific technology problems faced by its one customer, the IC.[15] In-Q-Tel has funded, in part, several technology companies developing social media mining and monitoring capabilities.

In-Q-Tel's 2015 revenue was $91.8 million and the 2014 revenue was $130.6 million. There were 121 employees in 2014 with a salary expenditure of $30.0 million and net assets were $326.8 million. The CEO in 2014 was paid $1.5 million and the Executive Vice President and managing partner was paid $1.8 million. In-Q-Tel received $93.8 million in government grants in 2014 and held publically traded securities valued at $211 million. Since 1999, In-Q-Tel has invested in more than 250 companies and raised $8.9 billion in private sector funds.[16]

In 2014, In-Q-Tel invested $1.9 million in Platfora a data analytics company which has since been acquired by Workday. Platfora provides several analytic capabilities including the analysis of IT system security attacks. Another $1.5 million was invested in Protonex which develops portable power solutions for the military. Expect Labs, the creator of the MindMeld app, which is intelligent assistant that understands conversations and finds information you need before you have to search for it received a $1.5 million investment from In-Q-Tel in 2014.[14]

In April of 2015 Ash Carter, U.S. Secretary of Defense, said DoD has proposed and In-Q-Tel has accepted a pilot project to provide innovative solutions to DoD's most challenging problems. The department will make a small investment with In-Q-Tel to leverage the nonprofit's proven relationships and apply its approach to DoD.[17]

CIA Director David H. Petraeus stated at the In-Q-Tel CEO Summit (March 1, 2012) that the key applications developed by In-Q-Tel investment companies are focused on technologies that are driving the IoT. These include the following:

- Item identification or devices engaged in tagging
- Sensors and wireless sensor networks—devices that indeed sense and respond
- Embedded systems—those that think and evaluate
- Nanotechnology, allowing these devices to be small enough to function virtually anywhere

Petraeus added that the ocean of big data has implications for both intelligence collection and intelligence analysis. For collection, having access to free and open information on so many topics that used to be denied to the CIA to better focus our human intelligence effort which often involves high costs and risks, while still learning the key secrets that justify those costs and risks. CIA analysts must discern the nonobvious relationships embedded deeply within different types of data: finding connections between a purchase here, a phone call there, a grainy video, customs and immigration information, various embedded metadata, and so on, and then making sense of it. Ultimately, combining the open-source feeds with the increasingly massive volumes of classified data the CIA receives, it is clear that the IC partners require new ways to organize and unify this universe of data and to make data usable, to accelerate automation, and to enable data traceability, relevance, and security.

Cloud computing provides important new capabilities for performing analysis across all data, allowing our analysts and decision makers to ask ad-hoc analytic questions of big data in a quick, precise manner. New cloud computing technologies developed by In-Q-Tel partner companies are driving analytic transformation in the way organizations store, access, and process massive amounts of disparate data via massively parallel and distributed IT systems.

Petraeus said he was very encouraged by what he had seen, in fact, we are excited about it. For example, among the analytic projects underway with In-Q-Tel startups is one that enables collection and analysis of worldwide social media feeds, along with projects that use either cloud computing or other methods to explore and analyze big data.[18]

Science and Technology Directorate has also been engaging with the private sector through its investments in In-Q-Tel. In 1999, the CIA supported the establishment of In-Q-Tel as a not-for-profit strategic investment firm designed to bridge the gap between new advances in commercial technology and the technology needs of the U.S. intelligence and security communities. Most In-Q-Tel investments combine funds from more than one partner agency, allowing S&T to leverage significant investments from the IC. In testimony before the House Committee on Science, Space, and Technology, Dr. Tara O'Toole, Under Secretary for Science and Technology Directorate, DHS, stated that according to In-Q-Tel's figures, $1 of government investment can attract more than $10 in private sector funding. In addition to rapidly delivering innovative technologies to their government customers, In-Q-Tel also supports small businesses that may not normally work with the government. In-Q-Tel estimates that following investments via In-Q-Tel, companies have created more than 10,000 jobs.[19]

5.5 Summary

The IARPA invests in high-risk, high-payoff research programs to tackle some of the most difficult challenges of the agencies and disciplines in the IC. IARPA collaborates across the IC to ensure that research addresses relevant future needs. In-Q-Tel is investing in R&D projects in the private sector that are of interest to IC. Both IARPA and In-Q-Tel are leveraging expertise and funding to equip the IC with new technologies including the following:

- Analytical tools such as geolocation, localization, geospatial fusion, data fusion, machine learning, big data, image processing, image, photograph, video, multimedia, computer vision, NLP.
- Anticipatory intelligence tools to support cybersecurity, cyber-event forecasting, cyber-actor behavior and cultural understanding, threat intelligence, threat modeling, cyber-event coding, cyber-kinetic event detection.
- IARPA pursues new mechanisms for combining information gathered from multiple sources to enhance the quality, reliability, and utility of collected information such as innovative methods or tools for identifying and/or creating novel sources of new information.
- Research in both the trustworthy components and safe and secure systems areas contributes directly to the Tailored Trustworthy Spaces research initiative.
- The CAUSE program is seeking multidisciplinary unconventional sensor technology that will complement existing advanced intrusion-detection capabilities.
- Since 1999, In-Q-Tel has invested in more than 250 companies and raised $8.9 billion in private sector funds.

5.6 Seminar Discussion Topics

Discussion topics for graduate or professional-level seminars are as follows:

■ What experience has seminar participants had working with IARPA or In-Q-Tel?
■ What experience has seminar participants had with private corporations or nongovernmental organizations that have worked with IARPA or In-Q-Tel cybersecurity programs or cybersecurity research efforts?
■ What areas of IARPA or In-Q-Tel cybersecurity research do seminar participants think are the most important? Why?
■ What areas of IARPA or In-Q-Tel cybersecurity research do seminar participants think are the most relevant to the private sector? Why?

Key Terms

ablation tests: are used to determine the impact of a data feed being added or subtracted from an information feed used to generate warnings
cross-community research: is research that serves several related organizations by using expertise from government agencies, private companies, and academic institutions that can provide complementary knowledge and skills
dial functionality: provide the ability to change modes or setting that change the trade-offs between recall and FDR, or between lead time, utility time, or warning quality score
logical narrative: an uncomplicated straightforward explanation or directions.
natural language generation: plain uncomplicated jargon-free language that does not require specialized training to understand
replication test: the repeated duplicate answer derived when analyzing a data set

References

1. Intelligence Advanced Research Projects Activity (IARPA). *About IARPA*. Retrieved November 10, 2016, https://www.iarpa.gov/index.php/about-iarpa
2. Intelligence Advanced Research Projects Activity (IARPA). *Analysis*. Retrieved November 22, 2016, https://www.iarpa.gov/index.php/about-iarpa/analysis
3. Intelligence Advanced Research Projects Activity (IARPA). *Anticipatory Intelligence*. Retrieved November 22, 2016, https://www.iarpa.gov/index.php/about-iarpa/anticipatory-intelligence
4. Intelligence Advanced Research Projects Activity (IARPA). *Collection*. Retrieved November 22, 2016, https://www.iarpa.gov/index.php/about-iarpa/collection

5. Intelligence Advanced Research Projects Activity (IARPA). *Operations*. Retrieved November 22, 2016, https://www.iarpa.gov/index.php/about-iarpa/operations

6. The Networking and Information Technology Research and Development Program. *Report on Implementing Federal Cybersecurity Research and Development Strategy*. Retrieved November 11, 2016, https://www.nitrd.gov/PUBS/ImplFedCybersecurityRDStrategy-June2014.pdf

7. Intelligence Advanced Research Projects Activity (IARPA). *Cyber-Attack Automated Unconventional Sensor Environment (CAUSE)*. Retrieved November 22, 2016, https://www.iarpa.gov/index.php/research-programs/cause

8. Intelligence Advanced Research Projects Activity (IARPA). *Cyber-Attack Automated Unconventional Sensor Environment (CAUSE)*. Retrieved November 22, 2016, https://www.iarpa.gov/index.php/research-programs/cause/cause-baa

9. Cyber-Attack Automated Unconventional Sensor Environment (CAUSE) Program. *Solicitation Number: IARPA-BAA-15-06*. July 17, 2015. Retrieved November 22, 2016, https://www.fbo.gov/index?s=opportunity&mode=form&tab=core&id=22083a23219aca598be19218002a374f

10. Intelligence Advanced Research Projects Activity (IARPA). *Trusted Integrated Chips (TIC)*. Retrieved November 22, 2016, https://www.iarpa.gov/index.php/research-programs/tic

11. Intelligence Advanced Research Projects Activity (IARPA). *Trusted Integrated Chips (TIC)*. Retrieved November 22, 2016, https://www.iarpa.gov/index.php/research-programs/tic/baa

12. Intelligence Advanced Research Projects Activity (IARPA). *Trusted Integrated Chips (TIC) Program. Safe and Secure Operations Office*. IARPA-BAA-11-09, Release Date: October 26, 2011. Retrieved November 22, 2016, https://www.fbo.gov/index?s=opportunity&mode=form&id=36a51487427786930733999edc40f321&tab=core&_cview=0

13. Looking Ahead. *U.S. Central Intelligence Agency*. January 3, 2012. Retrieved November 22, 2016, https://www.cia.gov/library/reports/archived-reports-1/Ann_Rpt_2002/looking.html

14. The CIA and You: CIA's Contributions to Modern Technology. *U.S. Central Intelligence Agency*. February 12, 2014. Retrieved November 22, 2016, https://www.cia.gov/news-information/featured-story-archive/2014-featured-story-archive/the-cia-and-you-cia2019s-contributions-to-modern-technology.html

15. *Should Congress Establish "ARPA-E," The Advanced Research Projects Agency-Energy? Hearing before the Committee on Science House of Representatives One Hundred Ninth Congress Second Session*. March 9, 2006. Retrieved November 22, 2016, http://commdocs.house.gov/committees/science/hsy26480.000/hsy26480_0.HTM

16. *In-Q-Tel IRS Form 990 Return of Organization Exempt from Income Tax 2014*. Retrieved November 22, 2016, http://www.TaxExemptWorld.com

17. Cheryl Pellerin. *DoD News, Defense Media Activity. Carter Seeks Tech-Sector Partnerships for Innovation*. April 23, 2015. Retrieved January 10, 2017, https://www.iqt.org/anomali-secures-strategic-investment-by-in-q-tel/

18. Remarks by Director David H. *Petraeus at In-Q-Tel CEO Summit. Excerpts from Remarks Delivered by Director David H. Petraeus at the In-Q-Tel CEO Summit*. March 1, 2012. Retrieved January 10, 2017, https://www.cia.gov/news-information/speeches-testimony/2012-speeches-testimony/in-q-tel-summit-remarks.html

19. Testimony of the Honorable Dr. Tara O'Toole, Department of Homeland Security under Secretary for Science and Technology Directorate, before the House Committee on Science, Space, and Technology. Release Date: March 14, 2011. Strategy and Goals of the DHS Science and Technology Directorate. Retrieved January 10, 2017, https://www.dhs.gov/news/2011/03/14/testimony-honorable-dr-tara-otoole-under-secretary-science-and-technology

Chapter 6

U.S. Military Cybersecurity Research and Deployment

The U.S. military has several diverse challenges in cybersecurity R&D of cyber capabilities. First are the strategic research needs to develop leap ahead transforming technology to maintain cyber superiority which are largely handled by DARPA and other military research laboratories. Second is the combined strategic and applied research, development, and deployment of the technology required to protect the DoD at the enterprise level. The third is the applied research, development, and deployment of the technology required to enable and protect the missions of the diversity of capabilities provided by the air force, army, navy, and marines. The fourth is the applied research, development, and deployment of the technology required to enable and protect the specific units and missions within the four branches of services. Finally is the tactical and action research required to enable and protect all military forces and missions that are in progress as they face emerging and possibly previously unknown cyber threats. This chapter reviews material that is publically available about how the U.S. military meets these challenges.

6.1 The Military Cybersecurity Cross-Community Innovation Ecosystem

In December 2011, the NSTC released Trustworthy Cyberspace: Strategic Plan for the Federal Cybersecurity Research and Development Program, a framework for a set of coordinated federal strategic priorities and objectives for cybersecurity research. No single agency addresses all the priority areas in the Strategic Plan nor should it. Instead, it is the many different agency efforts comprising the federal cybersecurity R&D enterprise that, with guidance from the Strategic Plan and coordination through NITRD, enables progress toward the plan's goals. The military side of the Strategic Plan taps into the DoD Cybersecurity *Cross-Community Innovation Ecosystem*.

The strategic research needs to develop leap ahead transforming technology to maintain cyber superiority which is largely handled by DARPA and other military research laboratories is accomplished in a sophisticated and diverse research establishment. The military centric research is handled by the OSD, the AFRL, the ONR, the ARL, and the respective R&D units within the research structure of the DoD and military branches and in each of their *Research Ecosystems*.

DARPA is the principal agency within the DoD for high-risk, high-payoff research, development, and demonstration of new technologies and systems that serve the warfighter and the nation's defense. The work of DARPA is covered in Chapter 4 of this book.

The OSD programs emphasize game-changing research over incremental approaches, and enhance the organizational ties and *experimental infrastructure* needed to accelerate transition of new technologies into practice.

The AFRL efforts in cybersecurity aim to create a firm, *trustable foundation in cyberspace*, and then to build assured mission capabilities upon it. New technologies are needed to be aware of missions and threats, compute optimal assurance solutions, and implement protection as needed via mission agility or *infrastructure reinforcement*.

The ARL contributes to a number of the Strategic Plan's objectives with a particular focus on Moving Target technologies within its Cyber Maneuver Initiative. The Cyber Maneuver Initiative aims to improve defense against APTs by creating dynamic attack surfaces for protected systems, and includes research in dynamic operating system maneuverability, application diversity, network agility, cyber deception, predictive cyber threat modeling, and cognitive reasoning and feedback to maximize maneuver effectiveness in tactical environments.

The ONR focuses on long- and medium-term scientific and technology areas that have the potential for delivering significant improvements in the robustness, resiliency, security, and operational effectiveness of cyber environments. ONR's cybersecurity research contributes strongly to the objectives identified in the Moving Target, Tailored Trustworthy Spaces, and Designed-In Security areas. At the Georgia Institute of Technology, ONR-funded researchers investigated the theory and models for botnets, and developed state of the art algorithms, methods, and tools for detecting and tracking botnets and their command and control. Their research has been invaluable for the DoD, as also the tools developed and now in use by the FBI for taking down botnets and tracking down botmasters and individual operators. In addition, ONR promotes underexplored research topics that have promising impacts on cybersecurity. For example, at the University of California,

ONR is supporting a technical investigation of the underground economy that allows botnets to exist.[1]

6.2 DoD Enterprise Cybersecurity Research and Deployment

One of the challenges in cybersecurity R&D in the U.S. military is the combined strategic and applied research, development, and deployment of the technology required to protect the DoD at the enterprise level. The OSD is DoD's cybersecurity S&T leader to accelerate the transition of new technologies into DoD cybersecurity structure. To strengthen its ability to pursue a coordinated set of objectives and a shared vision in cybersecurity, the ASD(R&E) formed the DoD Cyber S&T COI (DoD Cyber COI).

The DoD has specialized needs in cybersecurity due to the nature of its national security and warfighting mission. The DoD Cyber COI was charged with developing a DoD Cyber S&T problem statement, challenge areas that address warfighter requirements, a research framework, priority technology areas, and, in particular, a Cyber S&T Roadmap of current and needed research in cybersecurity.[1]

The DoD complex is seemingly endless with coordinating committees, special units, specific directives, and roadmaps. In July 2016, the OSD issued a memo on Cybersecurity Operational Test and Evaluation Priorities and Improvements that identified areas where the DoD operational test and evaluation community should accelerate development of the tools and techniques necessary to conduct cybersecurity assessments which emulate the full range of potential threats in a consistent and rigorous way. The Secretary of Defense and all of the services had articulated the need to improve DoD's capability to develop cyber-hardened systems and ensure the survivability of the most critical systems. Areas covered include:

- Non Internet protocol data transmission
- Multiple spectrum cyber threats
- System-customized attacks
- Test preparation and execution[2]

Each of the DoD branches of service have developed a cybersecurity strategic plan. The U.S. Air Force Cyberspace Command has declared its mission to provide combat-ready forces trained and equipped to conduct sustained combat operations in and through the electromagnetic spectrum, fully integrated with air and space operations. Cyberspace control is now the foundation for effective operations across strategic, operational, and tactical levels. The capabilities and forces required to achieve effects in cyberspace fall into several broad categories: using the domain (Cyberspace Attack and Force Enhancement); controlling the domain (Cyberspace

Defensive Operations and Cyberspace Offensive Counteractions); and establishing the domain (Global Expeditionary CSO, Command and Control Network and Security Operations, and Cyberspace Civil Support Operations).[3]

The U.S. Fleet Cyber Command, U.S. Tenth Fleet developed a Strategic Plan covering activities from 2015 to 2020. The plan has five strategic goals: operate the network as a warfighting platform; conduct tailored signals intelligence; deliver warfighting effects through cyberspace; create shared cyber situational awareness, and establish and mature navy's cyber mission forces.[4]

The U.S. Army Cyber Command and Second Army directs and conducts integrated electronic warfare, information, and CSO as authorized, or directed, to ensure freedom of action in and through cyberspace and the information environment, and to deny the same to our adversaries. In October 2010, the U.S. Army Cyber Command was established as an operational-level army force, reporting directly to Headquarters, Department of the Army. The command is charged with pulling together existing cyberspace resources, creating synergy that does not currently exist, and synchronizing warfighting effects to defend the information security environment. U.S. Strategic Command (USSTRATCOM) supports national security throughout the spectrum of conflict by

- Deterring strategic attack against the United States; providing assurance to allies
- Providing a safe, secure, effective, and ready nuclear deterrent force
- Delivering comprehensive warfighting solutions
- Addressing challenges in space and cyberspace with capability, capacity, and resilience[5]

U.S. Army cyberspace research priorities are risks, detection, agility, and human dimensions:

- Risk: theories and models that relate fundamental properties of dynamic risk assessment to cyber threats of the army's networks and defensive mechanisms.
- Detection: theories and models that relate properties and capabilities of cyber threat detection and recognition to properties of malicious activity.
- Agility: theories and models to support planning and control of cyber maneuvers in network characteristics and topologies.
- Human dimensions: theoretical understanding of the socio-cognitive factors that impact the decision making of the user, defender, and adversary.[6]

The U.S. Marines Corps IT strategy focuses on quality assurance and the ability to deploy IT support where and when it is needed. Cyberspace transcends both the physical domain and the information environment and thus the entire IT structure exists within cyberspace. The Marine Corps Cyberspace Concept calls for improved capabilities to operate within this domain:

- The ability to operate in the cyber domain with the same skill as on land, sea, or air is critical to the Marine Corps' future operational success. Without mastery of computerized technology, many weapon and C2 systems will not work.
- Intelligence, surveillance, and reconnaissance will be ineffective; and sensitive information will be at risk of compromise. Adversaries recognize that much of the United States' economic and military dominance is heavily tied to technology, communications, and automated systems that are enabled by cyberspace and they constantly seek to get a competitive advantage within this domain.

The strategy recognizes that intelligence helps the commander assess the *strategic environment* by providing tailored products and assessments that improve awareness, understanding, and decision making. Within cyberspace, intelligence regarding the cyber threat to IT components is of strategic consequence. Thus, the Marine Corps must leverage superior intelligence to forecast threats and rapidly mitigate and counter their effect on the enterprise. In addition, the Marine Corps must ensure intelligence is produced and used holistically to enhance our ability to conduct CSO. Cyberspace intelligence must ensure a shared awareness of network health, network vulnerabilities, and emerging or imminent network threats. In addition, cyberspace intelligence must incorporate and use tactical computer forensics to ensure a more complete picture of the threat environment. The employment of cyber capabilities purpose is to achieve objectives in or through cyberspace. Such operations include computer network operations and activities to operate and defend the *Global Information Grid (GIG).*[7]

Marine Corps Systems Command is tackling cyber acquisition head-on with enhanced oversight and governance, and new streamlined processes to better respond to the needs of the force. The command's cyber acquisition experts are working with the Marine Corps Cyber Task Force as it creates courses of action to address manpower, organizational, acquisition, and other challenges for CSO. This update to the Corps' approach to cyber warfare is in response to the Commandant's vision to modernize offensive and defensive cyber operations (DCO) in a volatile and complex operating environment. Established in 2015, the Cyber Acquisition Team (CAT) is tasked with developing a rapid cyber acquisition process to address urgent and emergency cyber requirements.

The CAT will lead acquisition and fielding efforts for emergency requirements (<30 calendar days from statement of need to fielding) and assist program management offices, as needed, with urgent cyber requirements (30 to 180 calendar days from statement of need to fielding).

The end goal is to provide speed to the Corps' cyber warfighting capability while maintaining the discipline necessary for a unified, standardized, and configuration-controlled Marine Corps Enterprise Network. These improvements will provide more responsive and effective support to the operational force.[8]

A discussion and description of the various DoD and service branch organization and unit functionality can go on for weeks. The focus here is to provide enough background on the DoD units to provide a context for the cybersecurity research the U.S. military is pursuing.

The DoD Multidisciplinary University Research Initiative (MURI), one element of the University Research Initiative (URI), is sponsored by the DoD research offices. Those offices include the ONR, the Army Research Office (ARO), and the Air Force Office of Scientific Research (AFOSR) (collectively referred to as DoD agencies).

DOD's MURI program addresses high-risk basic research and attempts to understand or achieve something that has never been done before. The program was initiated more than 25 years ago and it has regularly produced significant scientific breakthroughs with far reaching consequences to the fields of science, economic growth, and revolutionary new military technologies. Key to the program's success is the close management of the MURI projects by service program officers and their active role in providing research guidance.[9]

The following sections will cover samples of actual BAA Other Transaction (OT) Agreements, and Sources Sought Notices related to cybersecurity that have been issued by DoD component organizations.

6.3 Cyber Deception through Active Leverage of Adversaries' Cognition Process

The U.S. ARO BAA for Basic and Applied Research MURI (W911NF-07-R-0003-04) included a request for research proposals on Cyber Deception through Active Leverage of Adversaries' Cognition Process.

Recent advances based on applying control theory to stochastically adapt cyber systems has resulted in creation of new methods that significantly improve cyber security. These passive defense methods rely on the cyber system's ability to dynamically change and augment its internal state faster than attackers can probe and adapt, so attackers never develop a sufficiently clear picture of the system to make an attack successful. In general terms, the more computational resources (e.g., memory, CPU cycles) that are used to provide security, the more secure a cyber system can be made. Current trends indicate that the desire for improved security will eventually drive systems to use increasingly excessive amounts of overhead for protection. We seek a new way forward, based on active defense methods, one that potentially exploits new breakthroughs in the Theory of Intent (ToI) to build a cognitive model of the attackers, then uses the mathematical model to actively control and reshape the attacker–defender interactions for the desired benefit of the defender.

Recent honey pots and decoy experiences provide initial insight on how to engage adversaries through deceptive cyber artifacts, but a clear understanding of the dynamics (especially cognitive interactions) between attackers and defenders is missing. Carefully designed multilevel interactive honey schemes could allow us to actively probe and conjecture an adversary's intent, reasoning process, and next action, providing the critical data necessary for constructing an attacker–defender model. Using these data, the recent work of Dennett on ToI has laid the foundation for building a formal mathematical attack–defender framework, one that predicts human agent actions based on belief, desire, reasoning, and prior actions. Despite this progress, there remain significant challenges in expanding Dennett's work to include the adversarial setting, creating metrics that link information content to drive cognitive state changes, and rigorously model the human decision-making process (e.g., cognitive model). Overcoming these challenges will require the focused efforts of a multidisciplinary team drawing from experts in psychology, social-cognitive sciences, dynamic game theory, machine learning, statistics, and computer science.

The objective is to establish a scientific foundation for modeling adversarial cognitive states and decision-making processes, identify information metrics for driving cognitive state change by deception, and create an integrated framework of information composition and projection to manipulate adversaries' cognitive state and decision-making process that provides a future basis for ACD.

Multidisciplinary participation is expected from Subject Matter Experts (SMEs) in psychology, social-cognitive sciences, dynamic game theory, machine learning, statistics, and computer science. Potential topics include but are not limited to

- Psychological and social–cultural adversarial cognitive models that can be used to estimate and predict adversarial cognitive states and decision processes
- Adversary observation/learning schemes through both active multilevel honey bait systems and passive observation, in conjunction with active learning and reasoning to deal with partial information and uncertainties
- Metrics for quantifying deception effectiveness in driving adversary cognitive state and in determining optimized deception information composition and projection
- Theoretical formulation for a one-shot or multiple rounds of attacker/ defender interaction models that can fully capture the rich dynamics of cyber deception
- Identification of social/cultural factors in cognitive state estimation and decision-making leverage process
- Formulation of deception information and projection based on cognitive models and effective metrics

It is anticipated that awards under this topic will be no more than an average of $1.25M per year for five years, supporting no more than six funded faculty researchers. Exceptions warranted by specific proposal approaches should be discussed with the topic chief during the white paper phase of the solicitation.[9]

6.4 ONR Long Range BAA for Navy and Marine Corps Science and Technology

The Long Range BAA for Navy and Marine Corps Science and Technology (ONR BAA Announcement #N00014-17-S-B001) is intended to solicit proposals related to basic research, applied research, or advanced technology development and that part of development not related to the development of a specific system or hardware procurement. Descriptions of the cybersecurity aspects of this BAA include the following.

Command, Control, Computers, and Communication (C4) Technology Area seeks to provide future small unit naval expeditionary warfighters with the precise information they need, when they need it, in highly contested environments. The portfolio seeks to develop and mature those technologies enabling real-time manipulation of the electromagnetic and cyberspace domains, providing both offensive and defensive capabilities. The desire is to provide a non-fixed-infrastructure communications, networking, and information architecture that enable expeditionary warfighters to exchange vital information between the sea base and maneuvering forces ashore beyond line of sight. The solutions must enable operations in contested electromagnetic and cyberspace domains. Potential proposers are encouraged to consider the unique environments in which expeditionary forces operate constrain possible S&T solutions and differ considerably from the commercial environment. To fulfill this vision, ONR is interested in: authentication of users and establishing secure communications sessions in an opportunistic (ad hoc) manner without the use of controlled cryptographic items; and offensive cyber, cyberphysical, RF-cyber, and electronic attack (EA) capabilities.

DoD was seeking the opportunity to invest in areas of science and their applications such as data science, mathematical and computational science, computer and information sciences, quantum information sciences, cybersecurity, electronics, command and control and combat systems, communications, cyber operations, electronic warfare, sensing and surveillance, and precision timing and navigation. Specific thrusts and focused research areas are: mathematics, computer and information sciences, which sponsors basic and applied research, and advanced technology development efforts in mathematics and computer and information sciences that address navy and DoD needs in computation, information processing, information operation, IA and cybersecurity, decision tools, and command and control with a specific focus on enabling rapid, accurate decision making. Specific scientific and TAs include cybersecurity and complex software systems.

The Marine Corps Warfighting Lab (MCWL) utilizes concept-based experimentation as a primary means to explore both material and nonmaterial solutions enabling warfighting concepts. The concept-based experimentation process provides the unique opportunity to assess the utility of experimental technologies employed in operational scenarios and environments. MCWL leverages ONR's S&T efforts to inform and support the concept-based experimentation process. Because ONR and

MCWL focus on technologies of different maturity levels (Technology Readiness Level [TRL]), offerors responding to ONR Code 30 thrusts and research areas are encouraged to submit white papers to both organizations for wider consideration. Focus areas for MCWL experimentation include: CSO technologies to defend networks, evade/react to attacks and counter or exploit enemy networks; protection of networks and detection of intrusion/disruption; secure handheld devices; and capabilities to exploit network activities, attacks, and threats.[10]

6.5 OT Agreements for Prototype Projects

One way that DoD organizations move projects forward is to post OT Agreements for Prototype Projects. The Army Contracting Command at Aberdeen Proving Ground, Research Triangle Park (RTP) Division, on behalf of the U.S. ARL, released a special notice to inform interested parties about ARL's interest in establishing one or more OT Agreements for Prototype Projects in accordance with Section 815 of the National Defense Authorization Act for FY 2016, 10 USC § 2371b. The purpose of an OT is to engage, collaborate, and do business with an entity or group of entities, to include industry, institutions of higher education, and nonprofit, partners that have expertise in the human information interaction (HII), cybersecurity, and electromagnetic spectrum technology areas. ARL was considering a number of business models to include

- Award of OT(s) to a single entity for effort
- Award of an OT to a managing entity (most likely a nonprofit entity) who will seek out partners as appropriate to perform the effort
- Award to a consortium of entities with a managing entity (most likely a nonprofit entity) to perform the effort

Industry involvement is expected to include nontraditional defense contractor participants. The RFI was seeking information from those who are interested in potentially partnering and participating under an OT in any of the business models or technology areas discussed above.

The general intent behind releasing the notice is to communicate that ARL is committed to being a more innovative and effective defense laboratory that can be adaptive and responsive to the future challenges of national security through technological advantage. Secretary Ashton Carter stated on April 23, 2015, "Start-ups are the leading edge of commercial innovation, and right now, DoD researchers don't have enough promising ways to transition technologies that they came up with to application." The use of an OT will give ARL access to technologies, and technological-based companies, that advance so rapidly that the DoD finds it difficult to contractually engage, collaborate, and do business with them. The goal of this OT Agreement is to

- Provide a method to combine public and private resources to focus research, prototype development, and commercialization on specific shared military technology needs
- Facilitate the negotiation of flexible operations, collaborations, and competitive project awards that are not subject to the Federal Acquisition Regulation (FAR) and the 2 C.F.R. 200 and DoD Grant and Agreement Regulations policies and procedures
- Attract small businesses and nontraditional contractors
- Provide access to information concerning government technology requirements
- Provide a forum for conducting emerging technology discussions

The HII technology area has also been described as human–machine interaction and human–computer interaction (HCI). The focus of this area is the interaction of humans and information (machines/agents) for decision making. R&D goals are to apply fundamental principles of HII across domains, including complex information systems, human–agent teams, cybersecurity, communication, and organizational social networks. Concepts will be pursued to provide situation understanding and relevant actionable information to users at the point of need by engaging the greater HII community. HII R&D prototype projects could be in the following areas:

- Naturalistic and mixed reality human interfaces developed through the use of balanced bidirectional human–human and human–agent communications and decision-making approaches. Prototype projects in tool and model development to transition deep insights into human states and intentions and how hybrid interface concepts join the strengths of naturalistic and mixed reality interface concepts.
- Joint human–agent decision making developed through effective teaming of human and autonomous, intelligent agents. This area will develop tools and model human and autonomous agents in order to accentuate strengths and mitigate weaknesses and enable heterogeneous teams to make decisions faster and more effectively than homogeneous teams.
- Context-aware analytics and resource management addressed through the development of models that deliver actionable information to the point of need and allow enhanced decision making.

Projects in these areas could include the development of human-in-the-loop systems, human–robot communication, improved Processing Exploitation Dissemination (PED) through development of 3D—common operating picture (COP), generation of 3D scene rendering using video sensor, development of smart sensor systems, development of image and video analytics, design and development of 3D viewers for mission planning, and design and development of video annotation and retrieval.

The cybersecurity technology area focuses on developing and fielding secure devices, systems, and networks which will be able to execute commander and warfighter mission objectives. As technology evolves, namely wireless communications technology, and as more and more commercial wireless technology becomes integrated into our warfighter networks, the lines of delineation between cyber exploitation/attacks and electronic warfare attacks will continue to become more indistinct. In addition, the cybersecurity technology area concentrates on understanding and exploiting interactions of information with cyber attackers. These interactions involve friendly operations against adversary information systems and networks, defense of friendly information systems and networks, and assurance of persistent information support to users even when parts of the friendly systems and networks are compromised. ARL's areas of interest include Defeat of Cyber Threats and Cyber Resilience. Threat defeat projects in cybersecurity seek to develop models that relate properties and capabilities of cyber threat detection, recognition, and defeat processes/mechanisms to properties of a malicious activity, and of properties of army networks.

The electromagnetic spectrum technology area is proliferated with the use of emerging commercial communications technologies, and the threat derivatives of these technologies are quickly becoming a significant impediment to the operation of all U.S. weapons, sensors, communication, and position navigation and timing (PNT) systems operating in the electromagnetic environment (EME). This is significantly different than in the past several decades, where the EME was relatively sparsely populated with spurious RF signals and noise. Objectives are to develop methodologies and tools to analyze, assess, and evaluate the effects of this new RF clutter on systems operating in this environment. In addition, we seek to develop underpinning technologies that will provide a high degree of situational understanding against ground and airborne threats while operating in complex environments. Objectives are to develop the necessary models, signal processing, prototype sensors and subsystems to support the next generation of route clearance, air defense, and tactical sensing RAdio Detection And Ranging (RADAR) technologies.

It is important to note that such special notices are for information and planning purposes only and shall not be construed as an invitation for bid, request for quotation, request for proposal, or a commitment by the U.S. government.[11]

6.6 DCO Research and Supporting Elements

The U.S. Department of the Army also posts Sources Sought Notices. They are not a request for proposal, but rather a survey to locate potential sources. They are for market research purposes only. In November 2016, the U.S. Department of the Army posted a Sources Sought Notice to gain knowledge of interest, capabilities, and qualifications of various businesses in advance of a planned solicitation for R&D and technical services needed to support the cybersecurity service provider (CSSP) (DCO Research and Supporting Elements Solicitation Number: W911QX-17-R-0006). The government wanted to ensure there was adequate competition among the potential pool of responsible contractors. The ARL intends to use information gathered from these responses to gain awareness of capabilities, determine interested parties, and to support formulation of an acquisition strategy.

The focus of the effort is defense against the sophisticated cyber adversaries of ARL, the army, DoD, and the U.S. government. This effort strives to improve the state of the art in cyber defense. Cyber defense R&D is reliant on raw data from real-world networks that contain vital evidence of the threats being perpetrated by hostiles against the network. Analysis of the data and the ability to improve attack detection accuracy and timeliness is intrinsically coupled with the agile development of new tools and techniques to combat adversaries. This ARL cyber defense effort partners with many organizations; some of which use the ARL CSSP services to provide primary or supplementary network defense services. Some are research partners using ARL-developed cyber defense tools and test-beds, and others are intelligence and law enforcement organizations that leverage ARL technology and share vital information about current threats. The extensive network view is a key enabler to the cyber research and technology enhancement mission. This effort's initiative is particularly focused on improving capabilities to combat sophisticated cyber adversaries as well as investigating the next generation of Defensive Cyber Operational Tools, Techniques, and Procedures (TTP), tactical network security, exploring prospective sensor capabilities, executing components of the ISCM strategy, risk measurement and monitoring, improving adversary attribution, and insider threat analysis. The ARL cyber mission uniquely derives its strength from the close synergistic bond between research and the technical services answering operational necessities. These activities demand skilled, forward-thinking staff at every position. The objective is to research and develop a fundamental understanding of the dynamic cyber domain while providing 24x7 Cyber Defense Operations and Services within the environment of the DoD.

In addition, this Sources Sought was to inform interested parties of an upcoming Industry Day. The Industry Day allows for one-on-one meetings with the first 10 responding prospective offerors. Each one-on-one meeting is limited to 30 minutes. The intent of the one-on-one meetings is the opportunity to discuss technical capabilities. It is recommended that at least one technical representative from prospective offerors attend. Due to the high interest, the maximum number of attendees is limited to three representatives per contractor.

Offerors for this type of work must have a valid U.S. facility clearance of Top Secret, secret storage capability, and have technical personnel with Top Secret/Special Compartmented Information (SCI) Clearance in order to have access to details under this draft and/or formal solicitation process.[12]

6.7 Summary

Each military branch has developed cybersecurity goals and strategies which help to guide the type of research which is conducted internally or for which contracts are initiated with research partners. The BAA, OT Agreements, and Sources Sought Notices reviewed in this chapter are examples of how the DoD approaches the cybersecurity process. Significant aspects of the DoD cybersecurity research efforts include

- DoD approaches research on cybersecurity from several different perspectives.
- DoD has been working to expand the pool of potential offerors. Secretary Ashton Carter stated on April 23, 2015, "Start-ups are the leading edge of commercial innovation, and right now, DoD researchers don't have enough promising ways to transition technologies that they came up with to application."
- The strategic research needs to develop leap ahead transforming technology to maintain cyber superiority which is largely handled by DARPA.
- The operational centric research is handled by the OSD, the AFRL, the ONR, ARL, and the respective R&D units within the research structure of the DoD and the military branches in each of their research ecosystems.
- The DoD Cyber COI was charged with developing a DoD Cyber S&T problem statement, challenge areas that address warfighter requirements, a research framework, priority technology areas, and, in particular, a Cyber S&T Roadmap of current and needed research in cybersecurity.
- One way that DoD organizations move projects forward is to post OT Agreements for Prototype Projects.
- The DoD also posts Sources Sought Notices that are not a request for a proposal, but rather a survey to locate potential sources and are for market research purposes only.

6.8 Seminar Discussion Topics

Discussion topics for graduate or professional-level seminars are

- What aspects of DoD cybersecurity research do seminar participants think are the most important? Why?
- What areas of DoD cybersecurity research do seminar participants think are the most relevant to the private sector? Why?
- What experience has seminar participants had with private corporations or nongovernment organizations that have worked with DoD cybersecurity programs or cybersecurity research efforts?

Key Terms

cross-community research: is research than serves several related organizations by employing expertise from government agencies, private companies, and academic institutions that can provide complementary knowledge and skills

experimental infrastructure: is the established ability to conduct experimental cutting edge research on extraordinary and previously unexplored areas of S&T

Global Information Grid (GIG): is the communications system necessary to accomplish mission and theater superiority anywhere in the world as and when needed

infrastructure reinforcement: is the physical and logical technological and human capability required to create and maintain the necessary organizational ability and resources to meet mission needs

innovation ecosystem: multidisciplinary research is intrinsic and is driven by military or industrial needs. Disciplines are brought into the innovation ecosystem from many types of universities, national laboratories, private industry, and military laboratories to perform rapid, efficient innovation that could have a transformative economic impact on an industry or sector

research ecosystems: research capabilities and resources are brought into a research ecosystem from many types of universities, national laboratories, private industry, and military laboratories to perform complex and effective research with each organization contributing their specific expertise and organizational capabilities

strategic environment: the environment that military branches must be capable of establishing, maintaining, and adapting in order to achieve the mission at hand

trustable foundation in cyberspace: is a basic underlying structure that is reliable, defensible, and available when and where needed to protect national and economic security

References

1. The Networking and Information Technology Research and Development Program. *Report on Implementing Federal Cybersecurity Research and Development Strategy.* Retrieved November 11, 2016, https://www.nitrd.gov/PUBS/ImplFedCybersecurityRDStrategy-June2014.pdf
2. Office of the Secretary of Defense. *Cybersecurity Operational Test and Evaluation Priorities and Improvements.* July 27, 2016. Retrieved November 21, 2016, http://www.dote.osd.mil/pub/policies/2016/20160727_Cybersec_OTE_Priorities_and_Improvements(11093).pdf
3. Air Force Cyber Command. *Air Force Cyber Command Strategic Vision.* February 2008. Retrieved November 22, 2016, www.dtic.mil/cgi-bin/GetTRDoc?AD=ADA479060

4. U.S. Fleet Cyber Command, U.S. *Tenth Fleet. Strategic Plan 2015 to 2020.* Retrieved November 22, 2016, www.navy.mil/strategic/FCC-C10F%20Strategic%20Plan%202015-2020.pdf

5. U.S. Army Cyber Command and Second Army. Retrieved November 22, 2016, http://www.arcyber.army.mil/Pages/ArcyberHome.aspx

6. U.S. Army Research Laboratory. *Cyber Security Research Focus.* February 2014. Retrieved November 23, 2016, www.arl.army.mil/www/pages/1417/03.Cyber.CRA.overview_2014_02_18%20Swami_final.pdf

7. Marine Corps Information Enterprise (MICENT) Strategy. December 2010. Retrieved November 23, 2016, http://www.hqmc.marines.mil/Portals/156/Newsfeeds/SV%20Documents/Marine_Corps_Information_Enterprise_Strategy%20(MCIENT)%20V1.0.pdf

8. Marine Corps rolls out tailored cyber acquisition strategy. *By Emily Greene, MCSC Office of Public Affairs and Communication Marine Corps Systems Command,* March 10, 2016. Retrieved November 23, 2016, http://www.marcorsyscom.marines.mil/News/Press-Release-Article-Display/Article/690480/marine-corps-rolls-out-tailored-cyber-acquisition-strategy/

9. U.S. Army Research Office. *W911NF-07-R-0003-04; BAA for Basic and Applied Research Multidisciplinary University Research Initiative (MURI).* Retrieved November 23, 2016, http://www.arl.army.mil/www/pages/8/2017%20MURI%20FOA%20FINAL.pdf

10. Office of Naval Research. *Long Range Broad Agency Announcement (BAA) for Navy and Marine Corps Science and Technology. ONR BAA Announcement #N00014-17-S-B001.*

11. U.S. Army Contracting Command. *Request for Information (RFI): Seeking Information from Those interested in Partnering with the Army Research Laboratory in the Areas of Human Information Interaction, Cybersecurity, and Electromagnetic Spectrum through an Other Transaction (OT) Agreement. Solicitation Number: W911NF-16-R-0037.* September 30, 2016. Retrieved November 23, 2016, https://www.fbo.gov/index?s=opportunity&mode=form&id=9d0f3a4fa33589255b19a2cf8b9034d7&tab=core&_cview=0

12. U.S. Department of the Army. *Sources Sought Synopsis: Defensive Cyber Operations (DCO) Research and Supporting Elements. Solicitation Number: W911QX-17-R-0006.* November 14, 2016. Retrieved November 25, 2016, https://www.fbo.gov/index?s=opportunity&mode=form&id=6b03b64d275d7358e47ce89b9577b740&tab=core&_cview=1

Chapter 7

The National Security Agency

The National Security Agency (NSA) has several research efforts exploring the Tailored Trustworthy Spaces theme, including exploration of risk through behavioral analytics and large-scale data analysis, a novel means to detect modifications to computing systems and network analytics, and efforts to customize system controls. NSA is also exploring Moving Target technologies. By conducting a full scope analysis of the Moving Target problem and solution space, NSA plans to develop movement prototypes and evaluate several critical enabling functions. In partnership with the DoD, the agency produced a survey of current Moving Target techniques, thereby enabling a cost-benefit analysis that will take into account different approaches and technologies, the potential impact Moving Target protections may have on mission operations, the costs and overheads associated with implementation, and the overall effectiveness of the movement response. In addition, NSA is supporting activities that foster an interdisciplinary collaborative community around the SoS, including a virtual organization and four university-based multidisciplinary research centers. The nature of NSA is such that most things will happen in secret. However, NSA does do considerable unclassified cybersecurity research which is applied in the development of advisories, guidance, and standards. Selected areas of NSA research are covered in this chapter.

7.1 NSA and the SoS

In a world where commercial product vendors hype their cybersecurity solutions consumers and businesses are often left with very little trustworthy research and guidance as to improving their own cybersecurity. NSA has long been a reliable source of cybersecurity guidance for both government and industry. NSA applies rigor and thoroughness when in the development of advisories, guidance, and standards. To continue this legacy NSA sponsors the *SoS* initiative for the promotion of a foundational cybersecurity science that is needed to mature the cybersecurity discipline and to underpin advances in cyber defense. The SoS initiative works in several ways:

- Engage the academic community for foundational research
- Promote rigorous scientific principles
- Grow the SoS community

The SoS initiative, together with academia, industry, and other government partners is making a strong effort to create a research community dedicated to building security science. NSA seeks to discover formal underpinnings for the design of trusted systems which include contributions from the disciplines of computer science, mathematics, behavioral science, economics, and physics. The research work addresses both the establishment of pieces of security science as well as how security science is created.

The NSA position is that the creation of a security science is seen as an evolving long-term research endeavor. It is not assumed that a holistic body of knowledge that scientifically addresses all aspects of security: economics, behavioral science, computer science, physics, etc. will be successful. There is not one assured path that will create security science. It will require building both the theory of how to create the science and specific artifacts of security science work. The infancy of this work will be directed at experiments seeking to explore methods to create possible pieces that enable this science, as well as creating a large collaborating community leveraging the cutting-edge research necessary to push new bounds in security. Some of NSA's efforts in the area of security science are

- The SoS virtual organization provides a focal point for security science-related work as well as a collaborative environment the community can use to further advance security science.
- Research Lablets stimulates basic research to create scientific underpinnings for security; advocates for scientific rigor in security research; creates and broadens a SoS community and culture in the IC; and identifies hard problems in security that require science as a community focus and measurement of progress.
- The best scientific cybersecurity paper competition offers a yearly award that highlights papers which display scientific rigor in the multidisciplined area of security research.
- The Intel International Science and Engineering Fair award sponsors an award in cybersecurity recognizing the need for scientific measures in cybersecurity, and takes place annually.

NSA contends that hard problems in security require science as a community to focus and measure their progress. Following are the hard problems requiring such focus and measurement:

- The scalability and composability challenge is to develop methods to enable the construction of secure systems with known security properties from components with known security properties, without a requirement to fully reanalyze the constituent components.
- *Policy-Governed Secure Collaboration* projects are designed to develop the methods to express and enforce normative requirements and policies for handling data with differing usage needs and among users in different authority domains.
- Security-metrics-driven evaluation, design, development, and deployment projects are focused on developing *security metrics* and models capable of predicting that a given cyber system preserves a given set of security properties (deterministically or probabilistically), in a given context.
- Resilient architectures projects develop the means to design and analyze system architectures that deliver the required service in the face of compromised components.
- Understanding and Accounting for Human Behavior projects develop models of human behavior (of both users and adversaries) that enable the design, modeling, and analysis of systems with specified security properties.[1]

The basic principles of security science are

- Security science is taken to mean a body of knowledge containing laws, axioms, and provable theories relating to some aspect of system security.
- Security science should provide an understanding of the limits of what is possible in some security domain, by providing objective and qualitative or quantifiable descriptions of security properties and behaviors.
- The notions embodied in security science should have broad applicability that transcends specific systems, attacks, and defensive mechanisms.
- The individual elements contained within security science should contribute to a general framework that supports the principled design of systems that are trustworthy, they do what people expect it to do and not something else, despite environmental disruption, human user and operator errors, and attacks by hostile parties.
- Trustworthy systems design may include contributions from a diverse set of disciplines including computer science, systems science, behavioral science, economics, biology, physics, and others.[2]

7.2 The NSA IA Research

NSA's Trusted Systems Research Group, formerly the National Information Assurance Research Laboratory, is the U.S. government's premier IA research and design center. NSA IA experts conduct and sponsor research in the technologies and techniques which will secure future information systems. The major areas of areas of NSA research are Security Enhanced Linux, IA, Mathematical Sciences, Computer and Analytic Sciences, and Technology Transfer.[3]

Built upon a foundation of five decades of experience designing methods to fight against threats, the IA Lab's extensive in-house research program covers a wide range of areas. These include cryptographic algorithms to photonics, from operating systems like SELinux to advanced intrusion detection tools. The experience of the NSA workforce has close and creative partnerships in high-technology-with industry, academia, government, and with colleagues scattered around the globe. The Trusted Systems Research Group conducts in-house research in the following focus areas:

- Cryptography
- Cryptographic infrastructure and standards
- High-confidence software and systems (HCSS)
- Authentication
- High-speed security solutions
- Secure wireless multimedia
- Technical security
- Attack, sensing, warning, and response
- Research integration
- Trusted computing[3]

7.3 Information for IT Decision Makers, Staff, and Software/Hardware Developers

The IA programs at NSA deliver mission enhancing IA technologies, products, and services that enable organizations to secure operational information and information systems. NSA Capability Packages provide product-neutral information for a given operational requirement, which helps organizations successfully implement their own solutions. A *Capability Package* identifies critical architectural components, while also describing the role each component plays in protecting data. These publications also identify approved Commercial Solutions for Classified (CSfC) products and share guidance for administrators and testers. Capability Packages are typically unclassified and are geared toward a wide audience. Among the IA's most popular packages are those for mobility and multi-site virtual private networks. Published guidance on IA security solutions provide a unique and deep understanding of risks, vulnerabilities, mitigations, and threats. These documents include: secure configuration guides, frameworks, security tips, technical briefs, and more.

IA publishes Information Assurance Advisories (IAA) and alerts for stakeholders, clients, and partners. Advisories and alerts warn of risks and offer specific information about vulnerabilities, mitigation guidance, products, services, and ways to harden security architectures. Site content of special interest to IT decision makers, staff, and software/hardware developers includes

- IA advisories and alerts
- IA guidance
- Guidance archive
- Defense in depth
- Algorithm guidance
- IA standards
- Secure architecture
- Trusted engineering solutions
- Security configuration guidance
- Industrial control systems
- Networks
- Operating systems
- Hardening authentication
- Host intrusion prevention systems
- Cloud security considerations
- Identity theft threat and mitigations
- Adversary mitigations
- Mitigating insider threats[4]

7.4 NSA Office of Research and Technology Applications Technology Transfer Program

The NSA Technology Transfer Program (TTP) transfers NSA-developed technology to industry, academia, and other research organizations. The program has an extensive portfolio of patented technologies across multiple technology areas. A full listing of technologies is available in a catalog (https://www.nsa.gov/what-we-do/research/technology-transfer/assets/files/nsa-technology-transfer-program.pdf).

NSA scientists and engineers have developed cutting-edge, cost-saving technologies. Through Patent License Agreements (PLA), Cooperative Research and Development Agreements (CRADA), Open Source Software Releases, Education Partnership Agreements (EPA), and Technology Transfer Sharing Agreements (TTSA), these technical advances have contributed to the creation and improvement of dual-use products both for government and the commercial marketplace. The economic value of NSA patent license agreements is $346 million.

The NSA TTP offers business and industry streamlined access to NSA technology. The program identifies technologies and research capabilities, providing a single point-of-contact for drafting, negotiating, and brokering both licensing and R&D agreements. Recent high interest NSA technologies include

- Data port protection and tamper detection
- Dynamic network traffic rerouting
- Identifying connected data in a relational database
- Local administrative privileges
- Detecting SIM card removal and reinsertion
- Measuring similarity between data sets

The NSA TTP facilitates a variety of partnerships through the following agreement vehicles:

- PLA Title 35 USC, Sections 207 to 209, gives NSA the authority to grant licenses on its domestic and foreign patents and patent applications. This authority is implemented through PLAs. The goal of these licenses is to provide the private sector with the opportunity to commercially develop federally funded research to promote economic growth and global competitiveness.
- CRADA is one of the most valuable technology transfer mechanisms for obtaining long-term value. Title 15 USC, Section 3710, gives NSA the authority to enter into CRADAs to foster collaborative relationships with industry, local and state governments, and academia to obtain valuable technology transfer goals and benefits.
- EPA formalizes the relationship between a federal lab and an educational institution. Title 10 USC, Section 2194, allows NSA to share its unique experience by providing training to personnel in the science and technology fields at all education levels using EPAs.
- TTSA protects NSA's right to seek commercialization of technologies it owns and to effectively track the transfer of these technologies.
- Open Source Software Releases (OSS) is a collaborative model for technology transfer, inviting cooperative development of technology and encouraging broad use and adoption. The public can benefit by adopting the code, enhancing it, adapting it, or taking it into the commercial marketplace. The government can gain from the open source community's shared enhancements and advances.[5]

7.5 NSA Cybersecurity Publications

NSA has published several digital publications related to cybersecurity topics. The Next Wave: The National Security Agency's Review of Emerging Technology. Volume 19 Number 4 2012, for example, had an introduction by General Alexander on the federal cybersecurity R&D strategic plan. It also covered NSA initiatives in cybersecurity science and barriers to achieving a science of cybersecurity as well as funding research for a science of cybersecurity.

The Next Wave: Building a science of cybersecurity: The next move. Volume 21 Number 1 2015 covered resilient and secure CPSs, improving power grid cybersecurity, analyzing the cost of securing control systems as well as build it, break it, fix it: competing to build secure systems and the social engineering behind phishing.[6]
NSA research papers and technical reports include

- Understanding the damping of a quantum harmonic oscillator coupled to a two-level system using analogies to classical friction. February 2012. Author(s): M. Bhattacharya, M. J. A. Stoutimore, K. D. Osborn, and Ari Mizel.
- Closed-form Maker fringe formulas for poled polymer thin films in multilayer structures. January 2012. Author(s): Dong Hun Park and Warren N. Herman.
- The sliding shortest path algorithm. September 2010. Author(s): Ramesh Bhandari, PhD.
- The Optical networking for quantum key distribution and quantum communications. March 2009. Author(s): N. A. Peters, P. Toliver, T. E. Chapuran, R. J. Runser, S. R. McNown, C. G. Peterson, N. Dallmann, R. J. Hughes, K. P. McCabe, J. E. Nordholt, K. T. Tyagi, J. Jackel, M. S. Goodman, L. Mercer, and H. Dardy.
- Using the flask security architecture to facilitate risk adaptable access controls. 2007. Author(s): Machon Gregory and Peter Loscocco.
- Configuring the SELinux Policy. February 2005 (Revised). Author(s): Stephen Smalley.
- Meeting critical security objectives with security-enhanced linux. July 2001. Author(s): Peter Loscocco and Stephen Smalley.[7]

7.6 National CAE-CD

NSA and DHS jointly sponsor the National CAE-CD program. The goal of the program is to reduce vulnerability in national information infrastructure by promoting higher education and research in cyber defense and producing professionals with cyber defense expertise. The CAE-CD program comprises the following designations:

- Four-Year Baccalaureate or Graduate Education (CAE-CDE)
- Two-Year Education (CAE2Y)
- Research (CAE-R)

All regionally accredited two-year, four-year, and graduate-level institutions in the United States are eligible to apply. Prospective schools are designated after meeting stringent CAE criteria and mapping curricula to a core set of cyber defense knowledge units. Schools may also elect to map their curricula to specialized focus areas. CAE-CD institutions receive formal recognition from the U.S. government as well as opportunities for prestige and publicity for their role in securing important information systems. Designation as a center does not carry a commitment of funding from NSA or DHS. Funding opportunities may become available periodically from other sources such as the NSF.

The initial National CAE in Information Assurance Education (CAE-IAE) program was started by NSA in 1998, with DHS joining as a partner in 2004. The CAE in IA Research component was added in 2008 to encourage universities and students to pursue higher-level doctoral research in cybersecurity. In 2010, the CAE2Y component was established to afford two-year institutions, technical schools, and government training centers the opportunity to receive such designation.

Complimentary in nature, the CAE-Cyber Operations program focuses on technologies and techniques related to specialized cyber operations (e.g., collection, exploitation, and response) to enhance the national security posture.[8] A current list of designated centers is available at https://www.iad.gov/nietp/reports/current_cae_designated_institutions.cfm

7.7 Summary

NSA has several research efforts exploring the Tailored Trustworthy Spaces theme, including exploration of risk through behavioral analytics and large-scale data analysis, novel means to detect modifications to computing systems and network analytics, and efforts to customize system controls. Areas of NSA research include Security Enhanced Linux, IA, Mathematical Sciences, and Computer and Analytic Sciences. NSA also supports an active technology transfer program. Recent NSA research activity includes

■ NSA plans to develop movement prototypes and evaluate several critical enabling functions by conducting a full scope analysis of the Moving Target problem and solution space.
■ NSA is supporting activities that foster an interdisciplinary collaborative community around the SoS, including a virtual organization and four university-based multidisciplinary research centers.
■ NSA sponsors the SoS Initiative for the promotion of a foundational cybersecurity science that is needed to mature the cybersecurity discipline and to underpin advances in cyber defense.
■ The NSA has long been a reliable source of cybersecurity guidance for both government and industry applying rigor and thoroughness in the development of advisories, guidance, and standards.

- NSA IA experts conduct and sponsor research in the technologies and techniques which will secure future information systems.
- NSA and DHS jointly sponsor the National CAE-CD program which is designed to reduce vulnerability in the national information infrastructure by promoting higher education and research in cyber defense and producing professionals with cyber defense expertise.

7.8 Seminar Discussion Topics

Discussion topics for graduate or professional-level seminars are

- What experience have seminar participants had with the NSA technology transfer program? What are participant's opinions on the technology transfer program?
- What experience have seminar participants had with NSA guidance and advisory publications? What are participant's opinions on the publications?
- What areas of NSA cybersecurity research do seminar participants think are the most important? Why?

Key Terms

capability package: identifies critical architectural components, while describing the role each component plays in protecting data and also identifies approved CSfC products

policy-governed secure collaboration: is the process of providing a collaborative platform, normative requirements, and standard policies for handling data with differing usage needs and among users in different authority domains

science of security (SoS): is science that is needed to mature the broad range of cybersecurity disciplines necessary to establish a foundation to achieve advances in cyber defense

security-metrics: are the necessary standardized measures that are rigorously tested and universally applied to evaluation, design, development, and deployment so security solutions

References

1. U.S. National Security Agency. *Science of Security.* June 21, 2016. Retrieved November 28, 2016, https://www.nsa.gov/what-we-do/research/science-of-security/index.shtml
2. This Science of Security Virtual Organization. *About Science.* June 21, 2016. Retrieved November 28, 2016, http://cps-vo.org/group/SoS/about

3. U.S. National Security Agency. *Research*. May 3, 2016. Retrieved November 28, 2016, https://www.nsa.gov/what-we-do/research/ia-research/
4. U.S. National Security Agency. *Information for IT Decision Makers, Staff, and Software/Hardware Developers*. Retrieved November 28, 2016, https://www.iad.gov/iad/help/faq/information-for-it-professionals.cfm
5. NSA Office of Research and Technology Applications Technology Transfer Program. November 18, 2016. Retrieved November 28, 2016, https://www.nsa.gov/what-we-do/research/technology-transfer/
6. The Next Wave Building a science of cybersecurity: The next move. Vol. 21 No. 1 2015. Retrieved November 28, 2016, https://www.nsa.gov/resources/everyone/digital-media-center/publications/the-next-wave/index.shtml
7. U.S. National Security Agency. *Research Papers & Technical Reports*. May 3, 2016. Retrieved November 28, 2016, https://www.nsa.gov/resources/everyone/digital-media-center/publications/research-papers/
8. U.S. National Security Agency. *National Centers of Academic Excellence in Cyber Defense*. May 3, 2016. Retrieved November 28, 2016, https://www.nsa.gov/resources/educators/centers-academic-excellence/cyber-defense/

Chapter 8

The National Science Foundation

NSF invests in cybersecurity research through several programs, including the Directorate of Engineering (ENG) programs in CCSS and EPAS. A major program in cybersecurity is spearheaded by the NSF Directorate of CISE, in collaboration with the Directorates of EHR, Engineering (ENG), MPS, and SBE Sciences. NSF's solicitation for the SaTC Program provides funding to university investigators for research activities with an explicit option for transition to practice projects. NSF provides funding for projects related to cybersecurity education, as well as SBE perspectives on cybersecurity. Another major program is CyberCorps SFS led by the EHR Directorate. This program supports cybersecurity education and workforce development. NSF's program is distinguished from other agency efforts by its comprehensive nature, and by the strong role of research on cybersecurity foundations.[1] This chapter highlights some of NSF's cybersecurity research activities.

8.1 NSF Overview

NSF is an independent federal agency created by Congress in 1950 to promote the progress of science; to advance national health, prosperity, and welfare; and to secure national defense. NSF supports basic research and people to create knowledge that transforms the future. With an annual budget of $7.5 billion (FY 2016), NSF is the funding source for approximately 24% of all federally supported basic research conducted by U.S. colleges and universities. In many fields such as mathematics, computer science, and the social sciences, NSF is the major source of federal backing. There are about 12,000 new awards per year, with an average duration of three years. Most of these awards go to individuals or small groups of investigators. Others provide funding for research centers, instruments, and facilities that allow scientists, engineers, and students to work at the outermost frontiers of knowledge.

NSF's goals of discovery, learning, research infrastructure, and stewardship provide an integrated strategy to advance the frontiers of knowledge, cultivate a world-class, broadly inclusive science and engineering workforce and expand the scientific literacy of all citizens, build research capability through investments in advanced instrumentation and facilities, and support excellence in science and engineering research and education through a capable and responsive organization.

Many of the discoveries and technological advances have been truly revolutionary. In the past few decades, NSF-funded researchers have won some 223 Nobel Prizes as well as other honors too numerous to list. These pioneers have included the scientists or teams that discovered many of the fundamental particles of matter, analyzed the cosmic microwaves left over from the earliest epoch of the universe, developed carbon-14 dating of ancient artifacts, decoded the genetics of viruses, and created an entirely new state of matter called the *Bose–Einstein condensate*.

NSF also funds equipment that is needed by scientists and engineers but is often too expensive for any one group or researcher to afford. Examples of such major research equipment include giant optical and radio telescopes, Antarctic research sites, high-end computer facilities and ultra-high-speed connections, ships for ocean research, sensitive detectors of very subtle physical phenomena, and gravitational wave observatories. Another essential element in NSF's mission is support for science and engineering education, from pre-K through graduate school and beyond. The NSF's organic legislation authorizes it to engage in the following activities:

■ Initiate and support, through grants and contracts, scientific and engineering research and programs to strengthen scientific and engineering research potential, and education programs at all levels, and appraise the impact of research upon industrial development and general welfare.
■ Award graduate fellowships in the sciences and in engineering.
■ Foster the interchange of scientific information among scientists and engineers in the United States and foreign countries.
■ Foster and support the development and use of computers and other scientific methods and technologies, primarily for research and education in the sciences.
■ Evaluate the status and needs of the various sciences and engineering and take into consideration the results of this evaluation in correlating our research and educational programs with other federal and nonfederal programs.
■ Provide a central clearinghouse for the collection, interpretation, and analysis of data on scientific and technical resources in the United States, and provide a source of information for policy formulation by other federal agencies.
■ Determine the total amount of federal money received by universities and appropriate organizations for the conduct of scientific and engineering

research, including both basic and applied, and construction of facilities where such research is conducted, but excluding development, and report annually thereon to the President and the Congress.

■ Initiate and support specific scientific and engineering activities in connection with matters relating to international cooperation and national security and the effects of scientific and technological applications upon society.

■ Initiate and support scientific and engineering research, including applied research, at academic and other nonprofit institutions and, at the direction of the President, support applied research at other organizations.

■ Recommend and encourage the pursuit of national policies for the promotion of basic research and education in the sciences and engineering. Strengthen research and education innovation in the sciences and engineering, including independent research by individuals, throughout the United States.

■ Support activities designed to increase the participation of women and minorities and others underrepresented in science and technology.[2]

8.2 NSF Cybersecurity Research Activities

NSF has long supported cybersecurity research to protect the frontiers of cyberspace through investments in basic research that have resulted in innovative ways to secure information and ensure privacy on the Internet with the development of algorithms that form the basis for electronic commerce, software security bug detection, and spam filtering. NSF awarded $160 million in cybersecurity research and education across the agency in FY 2015 including grants through the NSF SaTC program.

The SaTC program supports research that addresses vulnerabilities in hardware, software, and networking technologies. It also supports research exploring the human components of cybersecurity, as well as efforts to enhance cybersecurity workforce education and development.

In total, the SaTC investments included a portfolio of 257 new projects to researchers in 37 states. The projects support early-career investigators and early-concept grants, as well as multi-institutional, broad-scope research. The largest, multi-institutional awards include research to better understand and offer reliability to new forms of digital currency known as *cryptocurrencies*, which use encryption for security; invent new technology to broadly scan large swaths of the Internet and automate the detection and patching of vulnerabilities; and establish the science of censorship resistance by developing accurate models of the capabilities of censors including

■ The science and applications of crypto-currency
■ Internet-wide vulnerability measurement, assessment, and notification
■ Toward a science of *censorship resistance*

That round of awards also included 11 grants with a particular focus on addressing cybersecurity educational and workforce development needs. These included the creation of new training and education programs and the development of effective cybersecurity pedagogy. Among the projects in this track were cybersecurity training for workers in hospitals, virtual environments in which students can experiment with and learn about cybersecurity practices, and competitions and challenges to enhance and broaden cybersecurity education.

Because many aspects of cybersecurity can be implemented by industry, the program supports both a Secure, Trustworthy, *Assured and Resilient Semiconductors* and Systems (STARSS) perspective focused on hardware research in partnership with the Semiconductor Research Corporation (SRC), and a Transition to Practice (TTP) track focused exclusively on transitioning existing research into practice.[3]

The goals of the SaTC program are aligned with the Federal Cybersecurity RDSP and the National Privacy Research Strategy (NPRS) to protect and preserve the growing social and economic benefits of cyber systems while ensuring security and privacy. The RDSP identified six areas critical to successful cybersecurity R&D:

- Scientific foundations
- Risk management
- Human aspects
- Transitioning successful research into practice
- Workforce development
- Enhancing the research infrastructure

The NPRS, which complements the RDSP, identifies a framework for privacy research, anchored in characterizing privacy expectations, understanding privacy violations, engineering privacy-protecting systems, and recovering from privacy violations. In alignment with the objectives of both strategic plans, the SaTC program takes an interdisciplinary, comprehensive, and holistic approach to cybersecurity research, development, and education, and encourages the transition of promising research ideas into practice.[4]

8.3 NSF Cybersecurity Research Grants

NSF funds research and education in most fields of science and engineering. It does this through grants, and cooperative agreements to more than 2,000 colleges, universities, K-12 school systems, businesses, informal science organizations, and other research organizations throughout the United States. NSF accounts for about one-fourth of federal support to academic institutions for basic research.

NSF receives approximately 40,000 proposals each year for research, education, and training projects, of which approximately 11,000 are funded. In addition, NSF receives several thousand applications for graduate and postdoctoral fellowships.

NSF operates no laboratories itself but does support National Research Centers, user facilities, certain oceanographic vessels, and Antarctic research stations. NSF also supports cooperative research between universities and industry, U.S. participation in international scientific and engineering efforts, and educational activities at every academic level.[5]

Through its merit review process, NSF ensures that proposals submitted are reviewed in a fair, competitive, transparent, and in-depth manner. The merit review process is described in detail in Part I of the NSF Proposal and Award Policies and Procedures Guide (PAPPG): the Grant Proposal Guide (GPG). The GPG provides guidance for the preparation and submission of proposals to NSF.[5] Several recent research awards are briefly described below.

Security as an Everyday Practical Concern explores how people resolve the tension between these two realities and the practices that people have adopted to balance competing demands upon them. The goal is to understand how people manage security online, in two ways. The first is in the sense of engaging in technical fixes for potential problems and the second is how they come to terms with the potential risks and develop strategies, accommodations, and justifications for particular ways of working online. Using techniques from anthropology and sociology, this project sets out to understand online security as part of people's everyday lives. The research will have two major outcomes. The first is to document the conditions of contemporary digital life, as a contribution to ongoing studies of the impact of digital technology. The second is to provide the basis on which new technologies can more adequately protect people's privacy and security online, and more easily integrate with people's online and offline practices.[6]

Online Safety for the Ages (OSA): Generational Differences in Motivations to Use Security Protections in an online banking context examines generational differences in motivations to use risky online services and self-protective measures in the context of online banking. An influx of older adults attracted to the Internet by social media but at times unfamiliar with dealing with the hazards of online life, as well as younger users who are sometimes oblivious to those dangers, pose distinct challenges to the preservation of online safety. A partnership with the Michigan State University Federal Credit Union provides access to both users and nonusers of online banking services of various ages to explore these issues. OSA will work from group interviews and observations of users in their homes to understand the risks that ordinary users perceive when attempting to use online banking, how they cope with risks currently, and the gaps that they see in their own abilities to bank safely online. In-depth analysis of surveys administered to credit union customers will reveal the factors that drive and the barriers that prevent the adoption of online banking and online consumer safety measures. OSA will contribute new knowledge about how to motivate average users to play their part in making the Internet safer for their own use. The project focuses on a vulnerable group of older Americans whose lives can be improved through secure access to financial services. Older Americans, however, are also vulnerable to online scammers and are too often uninformed about online dangers and inexperienced with effective protections.[7]

The Building Public Cyber Health: Designing and Testing the Efficacy of a School-Focused, Gamification Approach to Create a Secure Computing Environment project was designed to examine the use of online incentives as an effective tool for enhancing an individual's engagement with a task. This project explores the use of online incentives and social networking to improve an organization's *cyber health* by coalescing the micro cyber behaviors of individuals within the organization to create a more secure computing environment. Schools represent an ideal setting in which to test such a new model for cybersecurity. Teachers, faculty, and parents are motivated to keep students safe and secure. This project approaches the school as a system in which cybersecurity is improved and maintained through the use of digitally mediated interventions that combine online psychological incentives for student engagement and social networking to reinforce social and authority figure influences. In short, the project broadly aims to build cybersecurity in by engaging multiple stakeholders to help build a more robust public cyber health system. The effectiveness of incentives in building collective cybersecurity awareness and reinforcing positive cyber behaviors is being explored through intervention experiments that are implemented in the following three student populations:

- Elementary school students who are being exposed to supervised use of digital devices, both in a school environment and at home, for the first time
- Middle school students who are experimental users of digital devices and have limited awareness of cybersecurity concepts
- College students who have been shown to demonstrate risky cyber behaviors that often put them and other university stakeholders at risk

Furthermore, this research will explore whether interventions delivered through digital devices can be successful in both changing an individual's current risky behavior and introducing new safer behaviors at various ages. To assess the impact of the interventions, data will be collected on individuals' cybersecurity knowledge, perceptions, and behaviors using surveys and by monitoring intervention experiments throughout the study. If successful, the novel public cyber health interventions developed in this project will provide benefits that cascade over the long-term to businesses that hire participating students, additional organizations that adopt the intervention techniques, and the broader cyber community. In the near term, this project will directly benefit student participants, as well as teachers and parents, by improving their cybersecurity knowledge, perceptions, and behaviors, thus reducing their risks.

Thereafter, the techniques developed as results of the research will be made widely available for use by other schools and organizations, as individuals become more secure. The project's impacts have the potential to be further amplified by participants' security behaviors outside of the organizational environment. Specific at-risk groups are being targeted in the study with two of the student populations participating providing unique challenges to the research as well as unique rewards if the research is successful. The elementary school population will be drawn from a charter school composed exclusively of minority youth in North Carolina that face significant social, economic, and educational challenges. The middle school partner, located in rural, economically challenged eastern North Carolina, is struggling to provide the technical skills that its students need to succeed in the wider global economy.[8]

The Pocket Security Smartphone Cybercrime in the Wild project is a significant study because most of the world's internet access occurs through mobile devices such as smart phones and tablets. While these devices are convenient, they also enable crimes that intersect the physical world and cyberspace. For example, a thief who steals a smartphone can gain access to a person's sensitive email, or someone using a banking app on the train may reveal account numbers to someone looking over her shoulder. This research will study how, when, and where people use smartphones and the relationship between these usage patterns and the likelihood of being a victim of cybercrime. This research is the first step to a better scientific understanding how the physical world surrounding smartphone use enables cybercrime. Tired users may be less cautious in browsing to unsafe websites, or distracted users may miss a critical pop-up that a virus has been detected. This research collects sensor data from the smartphones of 160 volunteers such as GPS location, call frequency, and app usage. The smartphone sensor data are combined with questionnaires, demographic data from the U.S. Census, and neighborhood condition data from Google Street view. This research also provides a baseline of smartphone security threats stemming from behavioral and social factors, and applies new methods for social science research using mobile sensor data to unobtrusively observe the daily activities of subjects.[9]

The Value-Function Handoffs in Human–Machine Compositions that are under Design for the IoT project is an interdisciplinary effort that brings together social scientists, computer scientists, engineers, and designers to engage in a collaborative research project. The goal of the project is to obtain a better understanding of value handoffs in complex systems that involve interconnected social and technological agents. The social agents may include humans and organizations, the technological agents may include devices and infrastructures. An example of such a system is the Internet, a global communication network that allows almost all users of computers worldwide to connect and exchange information. When there are interactions between agents in such systems, there is a handoff of functions. With regard to the Internet, one such function is the preservation of information content; that handoff involves others that represent specific values such as reliability and trustworthiness. This project focuses on the IoT, an extension of the Internet to include physical devices (such as vehicles, buildings, and sensing devices) that are monitored and controlled remotely across that network. The research team will develop three case studies in this broader domain: bio-sensing, smart homes, and visual data processing. The research team has developed a preliminary model for value handoffs. In each of the three case studies, they will collaborate with an identified technical researcher to use the model to shape the technology, and to gain insights from the technology to refine their model. The version of the model that results from numerous feedback processes that are to occur through the sequence of cases is expected to be applicable to a broad range of socio-technical systems. The results of this project will serve to meet an urgent need to foster rigorous thinking about humans and machines in relation to one another, to making things work well across society, in concert with human need, and in service of societal values. Among the values potentially under consideration in this project are security, privacy, trustworthiness, accountability, transparency, autonomy, intellectual property, freedoms of speech and association, justice, and fairness. Failures to protect value handoffs are likely to pose barriers to technical adoption, and to impose burdens on the least privileged in society. This indicates that models to guide decisions about value handoffs are likely to be of critical importance.[10]

The Technological Con-Artistry: An Analysis of Social Engineering study focuses on one of the most serious threats in the world today to the security of cyberspace which is social engineering. The social engineering process is used to get people with access to critical information regarding information systems security to surrender such information to unauthorized persons, thereby allowing them access to otherwise secure systems. This research will examine who social engineers are, why they engage in social engineering, the processes they use to conceive of and implement social engineering projects, and how they view information privacy and security and justify their behavior. Further, to understand how organizations affected by social engineering cope with the threat it poses, this research also examines the perspectives on social engineering of IT professionals who oversee organizational computer systems and the security of potentially sensitive information. This study uses a cross-sectional, non-experimental research design that employs both qualitative and quantitative data. The qualitative component involves semi-structured interviews of social engineers in the wild, security auditors, and IT professionals. Open-ended interview questions will be used to elicit this data. In addition, these interviews will be used to gather quantitative data to measure demographics, computer use, and other social characteristics of social engineers. A set of structured survey questions will be administered by the interviewer as part of the interview process.[11]

Understanding the Cyber Attackers and Attacks via Social Media Analytics is a study of cyber attacker communities designed to learn more about cyber attacker behaviors, emerging threats, and the cybercriminal supply chain. Many cyber attacker communities take careful measures to hide themselves by employing anti-crawling measures. For these reasons, research studying hacker communities is needed, as well as research that advances the capacity to understand and investigate content from such communities. Specifically, the development of automated tools and analyses increases the potential for more cybersecurity research. Web mining and machine learning technologies can be used in tandem with social science methodologies to help answer many questions related to hacker behaviors and culture, illegal markets and covert networks, cybercriminal supply chain, malware analysis, emerging security threats, and other matters. In this research, important questions about hacker behaviors, markets, community structure, community contents, artifacts, and cultural differences are explored. Automated techniques to collect and analyze data from forums, Internet Relay Chat, and honeypots will be developed. Better understanding of hacker communities across multiple geopolitical regions will support a better understanding of cybercriminal behavior and improved and safer practices for security researchers and practitioners. Knowing more about cyber criminals, hackers, and their illegal black markets can help policy makers and security professionals make better decisions about how to prevent or respond to attacks.[12]

Brain Hacking: Assessing Psychological and Computational Vulnerabilities in Brain-based Biometrics evaluates the strengths and weaknesses of brain biometrics. Brain biometrics are more difficult to steal than fingerprints, since the current technology for collecting brain biometrics is impossible to use without a person's knowledge and consent. Brain biometrics, importantly, can also be cancelled if stolen. This is because there are vast networks of the brain that generate unique activity, meaning that if a person's brainprint is stolen, they can generate a new one by tapping into a different brain network. This investigation holds the potential to transform existing authentication systems into more secure and attack-resistant brain biometric solutions; critical for high-security applications. Brain biometrics has recently been shown to be 100% accurate in identifying people, in a pool of 50 users and across a period of up to a year. This research project will systematically evaluate the potential vulnerabilities of brainprint biometrics, with the goals of demonstrating the resistance and robustness of brainprints to the most likely attacks and developing a comprehensive protection plan addressed at the most vulnerable aspects of this method. In particular, the interdisciplinary team plans to investigate psychological and computational attacks. Psychological attacks consist of attempting to force a user to provide their brainprints under duress, or attempting to impersonate a target brainprint through a biofeedback entrainment process. Computational attacks consist of attempting to circumvent brainprint authentication system through presenting a counterfeit or stolen brainprint, with varying levels of obfuscation, such as the addition of noise, and attacking the stimuli database. This project will examine potential vulnerabilities in brain biometrics at an unprecedented level of detail, and convert the resulting knowledge into recommendations for the implementation of brain biometrics to guard an increasingly vulnerable cyberspace.[13]

A Socio-Technical Approach to Privacy in a Camera-Rich World is a project is designed to gain a deeper understanding of the privacy implications of camera technologies from both a social and a technical perspective. Cameras are now pervasive on consumer devices, including smartphones, laptops, tablets, and new wearable devices like Google Glass and the Narrative Clip life logging camera. The ubiquity of these cameras will soon create a new era of visual sensing applications, for example, devices that collect photos and videos of our daily lives, augmented reality applications that help us understand and navigate the world around us, and community-oriented applications, for example, where cameras close to a crisis are tasked with obtaining a real-time million-eye view of the scene to guide first responders in an emergency. These technologies raise significant implications for individuals and society, including both potential benefits for individuals and communities, but also significant hazards including privacy invasion for individuals, and, if unchecked, for society, as surveillance causes a chilling effect in the public square. The proposed research has the potential for profound and positive societal impact by laying a foundation for privacy-sensitive visual sensing techniques for a society where cameras are ubiquitous.[14]

Security and Privacy for Wearable and Continuous Sensing Platforms is a research project focused on security and privacy for wearable devices. This includes how to empower users and enable them to control how apps on wearable devices can access audio and video resources, how to use privilege separation and the least-privilege principle to mitigate risks associated with third-party applications that run on wearable devices, how operating systems for wearable devices can be architected to prevent applications from collecting extraneous data, and new threats from wearable computing and how each of these threats could be countered with secure platform designs. Wearable computing is poised to become widely deployed throughout society. These devices offer many benefits to end users in terms of real-time access to information and the augmentation of human memory, but are also likely to introduce new and complex privacy and security problems. To protect privacy, the researchers are conducting user studies to improve the understanding of what data users find most sensitive; the findings from these user studies is helping the researchers design techniques to prevent applications from accessing sensitive data inappropriately.[15]

Knowing Your Enemy: Understanding and Counteracting Web Malvertising research endeavors to gain a holistic, in-depth understanding about the scope and magnitude of malicious display, search and contextual advertising, features of their infrastructures and ad content, behavior of malicious ad-related parties, and economics of this underground business. With the Internet becoming the dominant channel for marketing and promotion, online advertisements (ad for short) are also increasingly used for propagating malware, committing scams, click frauds, and other illegal activities. These activities, which we call *malvertising*, systematically deliver malicious ad content and victimize visitors through an infrastructure, which includes malicious advertisers, ad networks, redirection servers, exploit servers, and others. Our preliminary study shows that most of such malvertising activities are missed by popular detection services such as Google Safe Browsing and Microsoft Forefront. This points to a disturbing lack of understanding of such web malvertising activities, which renders existing countermeasures less effective, and an urgent need to study the features of this threat to better prepares us to defend against it.[16]

8.4 Summary

NSF invests in cybersecurity research through several programs. A major program in cybersecurity is spearheaded by the NSF Directorate of CISE, in collaboration with the Directorates of EHR, Engineering (ENG), MPS, and SBE Sciences. Another major program is CyberCorps SFS led by the EHR Directorate.[1] NSF cybersecurity research activities include

- NSF awarded $160 million in cybersecurity research and education across the agency in FY 2015 including grants through the NSF SaTC program.
- The RDSP identified six areas critical to successful cybersecurity R&D: (1) scientific foundations; (2) risk management; (3) human aspects; (4) transitioning successful research into practice; (5) workforce development; and (6) enhancing the research infrastructure.
- NSF receives approximately 40,000 proposals each year for research, education, and training projects, of which approximately 11,000 are funded. In addition, NSF receives several thousand applications for graduate and post-doctoral fellowships.
- The wide variety of NSF-funded cybersecurity research will impact all aspects of cybersecurity and the social and business use of the Internet.
- Research such as Brain Hacking: Assessing Psychological and Computational Vulnerabilities in Brain-based Biometrics that evaluates the strengths and weaknesses of brain biometrics can help set the foundation for a new area of biometrics to open in the future.
- Projects like The Technological Con-Artistry: An Analysis of Social Engineering will help security professionals and law enforcement officers gain insight into cyberspace-based criminal enterprises and provide an advantage when working to stop or investigate crime.

8.5 Seminar Discussion Topics

Discussion topics for graduate or professional-level seminars are

- What experience have seminar participants had working with NSF grants?
- What experience have seminar participants had with research organizations that have worked with NSF cybersecurity programs or cybersecurity research efforts?
- What areas of NSF cybersecurity research do seminar participants think are the most important? Why?
- What areas of NSF cybersecurity research do seminar participants think are the most relevant to the private sector? Why?

Key Terms

assured and resilient semiconductors: are semiconductors that are free of any malicious code that can compromise cyber operations or cybersecurity

Bose–Einstein condensate: Eric A. Cornell of the NIST and Carl E. Wieman of the University of Colorado at Boulder led a team of physicists at JILA, a joint institute of NIST and CU-Boulder, in a research effort that culminated in 1995 with the creation of the world's first Bose–Einstein condensate—a new form of matter. Predicted in 1924 by Albert Einstein, who built on the work of Satyendra Nath Bose, the condensation occurs when individual atoms meld into a superatom behaving as a single entity at just a few hundred billionths of a degree above absolute zero

censorship resistance: is the ability of a digital publishing tool to overcome the capabilities of censors and the censorship resistance tools that researchers develop that can serve the needs of citizens who require them to communicate

cryptocurrencies: are digital assets designed to work as a medium of exchange using cryptography to secure transactions and to control the creation of additional units of the currency

cyber health: is the state of the ability of cyber-human systems to be resilient in the face of attacks, the level that the systems will not be compromised by attacks or human error, and will provide access and availability as, when, and where needed

malvertising: is the undisclosed and often unauthorized insertion of advertising or misleading content in social media posts, webpage content, and email messages

References

1. The Networking and Information Technology Research and Development Program. *Report on Implementing Federal Cybersecurity Research and Development Strategy.* Retrieved November 11, 2016, https://www.nitrd.gov/PUBS/ImplFedCybersecurityRDStrategy-June2014.pdf
2. NSF. *At a Glance.* Retrieved November 28, 2016, https://www.nsf.gov/about/glance.jsp
3. NSF. *Awards $74.5 Million to Support Interdisciplinary Cybersecurity Research.* October 7, 2015. Retrieved November 29, 2016, https://nsf.gov/news/news_summ.jsp?cntn_id=136481&org=NSF&from=news
4. NSF. *Secure and Trustworthy Cyberspace (SaTC).* Retrieved November 29, 2016, https://nsf.gov/funding/pgm_summ.jsp?pims_id=504709
5. NSF. *About Funding.*
6. NSF. *Security as An Everyday Practical Concern. Award Abstract #1525861.* August 21, 2015. Retrieved November 29, 2016, https://www.nsf.gov/awardsearch/showAward?AWD_ID=1525861

7. NSF. *Safety for the Ages: Generational Differences in Motivations to Use Security Protections in An Online Banking Context. Award Abstract 1318885*. June 2, 2015. Retrieved November 29, 2016, https://www.nsf.gov/awardsearch/showAward?AWD_ID=1318885

8. NSF. *Building Public Cyber Health—Designing and Testing the Efficacy of a School-Focused, Gamification Approach to Create a Secure Computing Environment. Award Abstract #1319045*. September 6, 2013. Retrieved November 29, 2016, https://www.nsf.gov/awardsearch/showAward?AWD_ID=1319045

9. NSF. *Pocket Security—Smartphone Cybercrime in the Wild. Award Abstract # 1619084*. September 12, 2016. Retrieved November 29, 2016, https://www.nsf.gov/awardsearch/showAward?AWD_ID=1619084

10. NSF. *Value-Function Handoffs in Human–Machine Compositions That Are under Design for the Internet of Things. Award Abstract # 1650589*. September 13, 2016. Retrieved November 29, 2016, https://www.nsf.gov/awardsearch/showAward?AWD_ID=1650589

11. NSF Technological Con-Artistry: An Analysis of Social Engineering. *Award Abstract #1616804*. September 6, 2016. Retrieved November 29, 2016, https://www.nsf.gov/awardsearch/showAward?AWD_ID=1616804

12. NSF Securing Cyber Space: Understanding the Cyber Attackers and Attacks via Social Media Analytics. *Award Abstract #1314631*. March 4, 2016. Retrieved November 29, 2016, https://www.nsf.gov/awardsearch/showAward?AWD_ID=1314631

13. NS. *Brain Hacking: Assessing Psychological and Computational Vulnerabilities in Brain-Based Biometrics. Award Abstract #1564104*. August 22, 2016. Retrieved November 30, 2016, https://www.nsf.gov/awardsearch/showAward?AWD_ID=1564104

14. NSF. *A Socio-Technical Approach to Privacy in a Camera-Rich World. Award Abstract #1408730*. August 26, 2014. Retrieved November 30, 2016, https://www.nsf.gov/awardsearch/showAward?AWD_ID=1408730

15. NSF. *Security and Privacy for Wearable and Continuous Sensing Platforms. Award Abstract #1513584*. January 25, 2016. Retrieved November 30, 2016, https://www.nsf.gov/awardsearch/showAward?AWD_ID=1513584

16. NSF. *Knowing Your Enemy: Understanding and Counteracting Web Malvertising. Award Abstract #1223477*. August 16, 2012. Retrieved November 30, 2016, https://www.nsf.gov/awardsearch/showAward?AWD_ID=1223477

Chapter 9

Federally Funded Research and Development Centers

Federally Funded Research and Development Centers (FFRDCs) are government-funded entities that have long-term relationships with one or more federal agencies to perform R&D and related tasks. FFRDCs are typically entirely federally funded, or nearly so, but they are operated by contractors or other nongovernmental organizations.[1] FFRDCs sponsored by the DOE are covered in Chapter 10. This chapter covers FFRDCs that are sponsored by the DoD and other agencies.

9.1 FFRDCs Overview

FFRDCs are government-funded entities that have long-term relationships with one or more federal agencies to perform R&D and related tasks. FFRDCs are typically entirely federally funded, or nearly so, but they are operated by contractors or other nongovernmental organizations. The NSF has reported that federal agencies provide billions of dollars each year for R&D activities at FFRDCs. Federal agencies sponsor FFRDCs by establishing contracts or other agreements with nonprofit, university-affiliated, or private industry organizations, which in turn operate the FFRDCs. As described in the FAR, FFRDCs are intended to meet special, long-term research or development needs of the sponsoring agencies that are integral to their missions and cannot be met as effectively by existing federal or non-FFRDC contractor resources.

The agencies that sponsor FFRDCs are subject to various laws and regulations concerning the management and performance of their activities. These laws and regulations guide the sponsors' oversight activities and shape the relationship between sponsors and the FFRDC contractors. Federal law caps the total allowable compensation for certain contractor positions for which federal agencies may reimburse contractors. In addition, the FAR provides criteria for agencies and contractors to use to determine what costs may comprise the compensation charged to the government. The FAR also describes characteristics of FFRDCs operated by contract and includes requirements for their establishment, use, and review. Among other things, the FAR encourages long-term relationships between the federal government and FFRDCs to provide continuity and to attract high-quality personnel to the FFRDCs. Because FFRDCs are contractor operated, sponsoring agencies do not directly determine pay or non-pay benefits for contractor employees.

The GAO studied the budgets of 30 FFRDCs sponsored by the DOE, DOD, and NSF that received nearly $84 billion in total funding for FYs 2008 through 2012. Of these 30 centers, the 16 sponsored by the DOE received about 79% of this funding according to GAO's analysis of sponsoring agencies' responses to a GAO survey on FFRDC funding and compensation. During this time, the DOE obligated about 34% of its budget to the FFRDCs it sponsored, and the DOD and NSF devoted less than 1% and 4% of their budgets, respectively. FFRDCs sponsored by these agencies received approximately $15 billion of their total funding from sources other than the sponsoring agency, specifically other federal agencies, nonfederal entities such as state or local governments, and private entities.[1]

R&D laboratories fill voids where in-house and private sector R&D centers are unable to meet agency core area needs. Specific objectives for these FFRDCs are to

- Maintain over the long-term a competency in technology areas where the government cannot rely on in-house or private sector capabilities
- Develop and transfer important new technology to the private sector so the government can benefit from a wider, broader base of expertise

R&D laboratories engage in research programs that emphasize the evolution and demonstration of advanced concepts and technology, and the *transfer or transition of technology*. Figure 9.1 shows the list of federally funded R&D laboratories. The cybersecurity research activities of selected laboratories are covered later in this chapter and national laboratories funded by the DOE are covered in the following chapter.

Study and analysis centers deliver independent and objective analyses and advise in core areas important to their sponsors in support of policy development, decision making, alternative approaches, and new ideas on issues of significance. Figure 9.2 shows the list of federally funded study and analysis centers.

System engineering and integration centers provide required support in core areas not available from sponsor's in-house technical and engineering capabilities to

Federally Funded Research and Development Laboratories

Ames Laboratory (DOE)
Argonne National Laboratory
Brookhaven National Laboratory
Center for Advanced Aviation System Development
Center for Communications and Computing
Fermi National Accelerator Laboratory
Frederick National Laboratory for Cancer Research
Idaho National Laboratory
Jet Propulsion Laboratory
Lawrence Berkeley National Laboratory
Lawrence Livermore National Laboratory
Lincoln Laboratory
Los Alamos National Laboratory
National Center for Atmospheric Research
National Optical Astronomy Observatory
National Radio Astronomy Observatory
National Renewable Energy Laboratory
National Solar Observatory
Oak Ridge National Laboratory
Pacific Northwest National Laboratory
Princeton Plasma Physics Laboratory
Sandia National Laboratories
Savannah River National Laboratory
Software Engineering Institute
Thomas Jefferson National Accelerator Facility

Figure 9.1   Federally funded R&D laboratories.

Federally Funded Study and Analysis Centers

Arroyo Center
CMS Alliance to Modernize Healthcare
Center for Naval Analyses
Center for Nuclear Waste Regulatory Analyses
Homeland Security Studies and Analysis Institute
National Biodefense Analysis and Countermeasures Center
National Defense Research Institute
Project Air Force
Science and Technology Policy Institute
Systems and Analyses Center

Figure 9.2   Federally funded study and analysis centers.

Federally Funded Systems Engineering and Integration Centers
Aerospace Federally Funded Research and Development Center for Enterprise Modernization Homeland Security Systems Engineering and Development Institute Judiciary Engineering and Modernization Center National Cybersecurity Center of Excellence National Security Engineering Center

Figure 9.3   Federally funded systems engineering and integration centers.

ensure that complex systems meet operational requirements. The centers assist with the creation and choice of system concepts and architectures, specification of technical system and subsystem requirements and interfaces, development and acquisition of system hardware and software, testing and verification of performance, integration of new capabilities, and continuous improvement of system operations and logistics. They often play a critical role in assisting their sponsors in technically formulating, initiating, and evaluating programs and activities undertaken by firms in the for-profit sector.[2] Figure 9.3 shows the list of systems engineering and integration centers.

9.2 The National Cybersecurity FFRDC

NIST, with the active support of the state of Maryland and Montgomery County, Maryland established the NCCoE in October 2014. This was the first FFRDC dedicated to cybersecurity to support the NCCoE mission. The FFRDC functions as the only national laboratory dedicated solely to cybersecurity, providing research, development, technology and engineering expertise in support of NIST and the rest of the federal government. The FFRDC also provides access to expertise across the University of Maryland system and nine other university affiliates around the country.

The NCCoE turns standards and best practices into practical solutions to address some of the nation's most intractable cybersecurity challenges. As a key component of the NIST cybersecurity program, the center collaborates with experts from industry, academia, and government to identify common problems. Then, using commercially available products, the NCCoE and its partners create and promote real-world cybersecurity solutions in the form of practical technical guides. The NCCoE has 22 core partners, from Fortune 50 market leaders to smaller companies specializing in IT security, that have pledged to support the center with hardware, software, and expertise. (For an up-to-date list, see https://nccoe.nist.gov/partners)[3] Areas of focus include the following:

Data integrity: the NCCoE in collaboration with members of the business community and vendors of cybersecurity solutions is creating an example solution to address these complex data integrity challenges. Multiple systems need to work together to prevent, detect, notify, and recover from events that corrupt data. This project explores methods to effectively recover operating systems, databases, user files, applications, and software/system configurations. It will also explore issues of auditing and reporting (user activity monitoring, file system monitoring, database monitoring, scanning backups and snapshots for malware, and rapid recovery solutions) to support recovery and investigations. To address real-world business challenges around data integrity, the resulting example solution will be composed of open-source and commercially available components. The goal of this building block effort is to help organizations confidently identify

■ Altered data, as well as the date and time of alteration
■ The identities of those who alter data
■ Other events that coincide with data alteration
■ Any impact of the data alteration
■ The correct backup version (free of malicious code and corrupted data) for data restoral[4]

Derived personal identity verification (PIV) credentials: In 2005, PIV credentialing focused on authentication through traditional computing devices, such as desktops and laptops, where a PIV card would provide a common authentication through integrated smart card readers. Currently, the proliferation of mobile devices that do not have integrated smart card readers complicates PIV credentials and authentication. Derived PIV credentials will help businesses authenticate individuals who use mobile devices and need access to controlled facilities, information systems, and applications. The goal of the building block effort is to demonstrate a feasible security platform based on federal PIV standards that can support operations in federal (PIV), nonfederal critical infrastructure (PIV-interoperable or PIV-I), and general business (PIV-compatible or PIV-C) environments.[5]

MDS: a compromised mobile device may allow remote access to sensitive on-premise organizational data, or any other data that the user has entrusted to the device. Ensuring the confidentiality, integrity, and availability of the information that a mobile device accesses, stores, and processes is a difficult cybersecurity challenge with no easy solution. This is especially true in light of the growing mobile environment, with multiple parties developing complex systems and software that must securely coexist on the same device in order to keep data safe. Unfortunately, security controls have not kept pace with the risks posed by mobile devices. Enterprises are under pressure to accept these risks due to several factors, such as anticipated cost savings and employees' demand for more convenience, sometimes without the ability to employ defensive mitigations.

Mobile devices pose a unique set of threats to enterprises. Typical enterprise protections, such as isolated enterprise sandboxes and the ability to remote wipe a device, may fail to fully mitigate the security challenges associated with these complex mobile information systems. With this in mind, a set of security controls and countermeasures that address mobile threats in a holistic manner must be identified, necessitating a broader view of the entire mobile security ecosystem. This view must go beyond devices to include, as an example, the cellular networks and cloud infrastructure used to support mobile applications and native mobile services.

The Mobile Threat Catalogue identifies threats to mobile devices and associated mobile infrastructure to support development and implementation of mobile security capabilities, best practices, and security solutions to better protect enterprise IT. Threats are divided into broad categories, primarily focused upon mobile applications and software, the network stack and associated infrastructure, mobile device and software supply chain, and the greater mobile ecosystem. Each threat identified is catalogued alongside explanatory and vulnerability information where possible, and alongside applicable mitigation strategies.[6]

Privacy-enhanced identity federation: As enterprises move more services online, many have given customers the option to use third-party credentials to access their services, rather than asking them to create and manage new accounts. For example, you can use your social media account login to access your fitness tracker account. In effect, the social media company is vouching that the same person is logging in each time they access the tracker website. Allowing third-party credentials are beneficial to businesses because it saves them time and resources in managing identities. For users, the benefit comes from not having another username, password, or a second-factor credential to manage and remember.

While these arrangements are becoming more common, organizations are finding it a time-consuming task to manage each relationship, or third-party integration. The dominant solution is a service called brokered identity management in which identity brokers manage the integration relationships between organizations and credential providers. Organizations can use an identity broker to manage multiple third-party credentialing options instead of having to manage each separately. However, for users, there is a concern that these connections create the opportunity for a breach, or exposure of personal information, as well as for the broker to track a user's online activity. The privacy-enhanced identity brokers project is examining how privacy-enhancing technologies, leveraging market-dominant standards, can be integrated into identity broker solutions to meet the privacy objectives of users and organizations. This project is a joint effort between the NCCoE and the NSTIC National Program Office (NSTIC NPO).[7]

Trusted *geolocation* in the cloud: while cloud computing offers businesses and other organizations cost savings and flexibility, these shared resources can introduce security and privacy challenges. Enterprises that use cloud services want to be assured that

■ The cloud compute platform hosting their workload has not been modified or tampered with

- Sensitive workloads on a multi-tenancy cloud platform are isolated within a logically defined environment from the workloads of competing companies
- Workload migration occurs only between trusted clusters and within trusted data centers
- Cloud servers are located in their preferred regions or home countries so that the cloud provider is subject to the same data security and privacy laws

Unfortunately, traditional geolocation, the process for asserting the integrity of the cloud computer hardware and enforcing the physical location of an object, is based on operational security control but the method is not secure and does not lend itself to automation and scaling of the cloud computing platform.

To meet these business needs and help accelerate the adoption of cost-saving cloud technologies, the NCCoE is collaborating with Intel, RSA, and HyTrust on the Trusted Geolocation in the Cloud building block. This automated hardware root of trust determines the integrity of the computer hardware and restricts the workloads to cloud servers within a location. The hardware root of trust is a tamper-proof combination of hardware and firmware deployed by a cloud service provider, business, or organization using cloud services with a unique identifier for the cloud server host and metadata about the server platform. Using secure protocols, a business can access this information to find out if the platform is still as it was when first deployed, determine the location of the cloud server, and enforce geolocation-based restrictions. The Trusted Geolocation in the Cloud implementation has been published, in a final report, as NIST Interagency Report 7904.[8]

9.3 Jet Propulsion Laboratory

The Jet Propulsion Laboratory (JPL) is a unique national research facility that carries out robotic space and Earth science missions. JPL helped open the Space Age by developing America's first Earth-orbiting science satellite, creating the first successful interplanetary spacecraft, and sending robotic missions to study all the planets in the solar system as well as asteroids, comets, and Earth's moon. In addition to its missions, JPL developed and manages NASA's Deep Space Network, a worldwide system of antennas that communicates with interplanetary spacecraft.

JPL is a federally funded R&D center managed for NASA by Caltech. From the long history of leaders drawn from the university's faculty to joint programs and appointments, JPL's intellectual environment and identity are profoundly shaped by its role as part of Caltech. JPL continues its world-leading innovation, implementing programs in planetary exploration, Earth science, space-based astronomy and technology development, while applying its capabilities to technical and scientific problems of national significance. JPL technology developed to enable new missions is also applied on Earth.[9]

The Cyber Security Visualization project at JPL that addresses the spectra of cyberattacks on aerospace systems is important because many of the components and vulnerabilities that have been successfully exploited by the adversary on other infrastructures are the same as those deployed and used within the aerospace environment. An important consideration with respect to the mission/safety critical infrastructure supporting space operations is that an appropriate defensive response to an attack has the goal to preserve critical mission objectives in the presence of adversarial activity which invariably involves the need for high precision and accuracy, because an incorrect response can trigger unacceptable losses involving lives and/or significant financial damage.

A highly precise defensive response, considering the typical complexity of aerospace environments, requires a detailed and well-founded understanding of the underlying system. To capture this detailed and rigorous understanding, a structured approach for modeling aerospace systems has been developed. The approach includes physical elements, network topology, software applications, system functions, and usage scenarios. JPL leverages model-based systems engineering methodology by utilizing the Object Management Group's Systems Modeling Language to represent the system being analyzed and also utilize model transformations to provide relevant aspects of the model to specialized analyses. A novel visualization approach is utilized to visualize the entire model as a 3D graph, allowing easier interaction with subject matter experts. The model provides a unifying structure for analyzing the impact of a particular attack or a particular type of attack. A graph-based propagation analysis based on edge and node labels is used to analyze the model.[10]

9.4 Cybersecurity Research at Other Federally Funded R&D Centers

A review of the websites of FFRDCs that are not covered above or those of the DOE covered in Chapter 10 did not yield a great deal of usable information regarding their cybersecurity research activities. Several stated that they have cybersecurity capabilities but do not explain or elaborate on their activities related to cybersecurity research. This may just be a transparency issue or it is also possible they are doing very little to pursue cybersecurity research. This gap in information leaves doubts about their activities even if they report having capabilities. In addition, the DoD sponsored FFRDCs generally provided little information about any activity. They may not feel the need for transparency because they have a guaranteed funding stream from the DoD but DoD management of the FFRDCs have raised concerns in the past.

In 1996, the GAO found that there were issues as to whether the DOD limits FFRDCs to performing appropriate work, adequately safeguards the objectivity of FFRDCs, oversees FFRDCs effectively, and adequately considers cost-effective alternatives to using FFRDCs. In addition, the DOD Inspector General's office and others have raised concerns that FFRDC mission statements are too broad and do not clearly identify the specialized tasks that FFRDCs should perform. Congress and others have repeatedly raised questions about the adequacy of DOD policy guidance and oversight as well as concerns regarding whether DOD policy guidance ensures that sponsors adequately justify awarding noncompetitive contracts for the operation of the FFRDCs.[11]

The GAO reported that in 2006, the federal government spent $13 billion (14% of its R&D expenditures) to enable 38 federally funded R&D centers (FFRDCs) to meet special research needs. FFRDCs including laboratories, studies and analyses centers, and systems engineering centers conduct research in military space programs, nanotechnology, microelectronics, nuclear warfare, and biodefense countermeasures, among other areas.

Federal agencies GAO reviewed use cost-reimbursement contracts with the organizations that operate FFRDCs, and three of the agencies generally use full and open competition to award the contracts. Only DOD consistently awards its FFRDC contracts on a sole-source basis, as permitted by law and regulation when properly justified. FFRDCs receive funding for individual projects from customers that require the FFRDCs' specialized research capabilities. Because FFRDCs have a special relationship with their sponsoring agencies and may be given access to sensitive or proprietary data, regulations require that FFRDCs be free from organizational conflicts of interest. The DOD and DOE also have policies that prescribe specific areas that FFRDC contractors must address to ensure their employees are free from personal conflicts of interest. In a May 2008 report, GAO recognized the importance of implementing such safeguards for contractor employees. Currently, although DHS and U.S. Department of Health and Human Services (HHS) have policies that require their FFRDC contractors to implement conflicts-of-interest safeguards, these policies lack the specificity needed to ensure their FFRDC contractors will consistently address employees' personal conflicts of interest. Sponsoring agencies use various approaches in their oversight of FFRDC contractors, including

■ Review and approval of work assigned to FFRDCs, or conducted for other agencies or entities, to determine consistency with the FFRDC's purpose, capacity, and special competency. In this process, only the DOD must abide by congressionally imposed annual workload limits for its FFRDCs.
■ Conduct performance reviews and audits of contractor costs, finances, and internal controls.
■ Conduct a comprehensive review before a contract is renewed to assess the continuing need for the FFRDC and if the contractor can meet that need, based on annual assessments of contractor performance.

Some agencies have adopted other agencies' FFRDC oversight and management practices. For example, DHS mirrored most of the DOD's FFRDC Management

Plan which is an internal DOD guidance document in developing an approach to FFRDC oversight, and DHS officials told the GAO that they learned from the DOE's experience in selecting and overseeing contractors for laboratory FFRDCs. In addition, HHS planned to implement certain DOE practices, including rewarding innovation and excellence in performance through various contract incentives. While agency officials have acknowledged the potential benefits from sharing best practices, there was currently no formal cross-agency forum or other established mechanism for doing so.[12]

It is interesting to note that FFRDCs do come and go out of existence or have their status changed from active FFRDCs. DoD-related FFRDCs that have changed include

- Analytic Services, Inc. Department of the Air Force. Removed from list of FFRDCs in FY 1977.
- Applied Physics Laboratory. Department of the Navy. Removed from list of FFRDCs in FY 1978.
- Center for Research in Social Systems. Department of the Army. Phased out as FFRDC at end of FY 1970.
- Institute for Advanced Technologies. Department of the Army. Phased out as FFRDC November 1993.
- Logistics Management Institute. OSD. Decertified as FFRDC September 1998.
- Research Analysis Corporation. Department of the Army. Phased out as FFRDC September 1972.[2]

9.5 Summary

FFRDCs are government-funded entities that have long-term relationships with one or more federal agencies to perform R&D and related tasks. FFRDCs are typically entirely federally funded, or nearly so, but they are operated by contractors or other nongovernmental organizations. Key points covered in this chapter about FFRDCs include

- As described in the FAR, FFRDCs are intended to meet special, long-term research or development needs of the sponsoring agencies that are integral to their missions and cannot be met as effectively by existing federal or non-FFRDC contractor resources.
- R&D laboratories engage in research programs that emphasize the evolution and demonstration of advanced concepts and technology, and the transfer or transition of technology.
- The NCCoE's goal of accelerating the adoption of secure technologies to address today's most pressing cybersecurity challenges.

- The Cyber Security Visualization project at JPL that addresses the spectre of cyberattacks on aerospace systems is important because many of the components and vulnerabilities that have been successfully exploited by the adversary on other infrastructures are the same as those deployed and used within the aerospace environment.
- A review of the websites of FFRDCs that are not covered above or those of the DOE covered in Chapter 10 did not yield a great deal of usable information regarding their cybersecurity research activities.
- Federally Funded Study and Analysis Centers were among those FFRDCs that provide little if any information about cybersecurity research they may be performing.
- The DOD Inspector General's office and others have raised concerns that FFRDC mission statements are too broad and do not clearly identify the specialized tasks that FFRDCs should perform. Congress and others have repeatedly raised questions about the adequacy of DOD oversight of the FFRDCs it sponsors.

9.6 Seminar Discussion Topics

Discussion topics for graduate or professional-level seminars are

- What experience have seminar participants had working with any FFRDC?
- What do the seminar participants think about the lack of transparency that many of the FFRDCs have?
- What role do the seminar participants think the FFRDCs should have in cybersecurity research?
- What areas of FFRDC cybersecurity research do seminar participants think are the most important? Why?

Key Terms

geolocation: is the location of a user's wireless device or computer location via a GPS chip or triangulation of nearby wireless network towers. The user's device then transmits this information when the website or content provider asks for it. Other geolocation services obtain information from the user's device that does not immediately identify the user's location such as an IP address; they then consult external databases that associate that data with location information such as country and state and pass this information on to website

transfer or transition of technology: is the process of moving technology from one of the national laboratories into use in the private sector or in another organization other than the laboratory

References

1. United States Government Accountability Office. *Federally Funded Research Centers*. August 2014. Retrieved December 1, 2016, http://www.gao.gov/products/GAO-14-593

2. NSF. *Master Government List of Federally Funded R&D Centers*. Retrieved December 4, 2016, https://www.nsf.gov/statistics/ffrdclist/#activity

3. NIST. *About the National Cybersecurity Center of Excellence*. Retrieved December 4, 2016, https://nccoe.nist.gov/sites/default/files/library/fact-sheets/nccoe-fact-sheet.pdf

4. NCCoE. *Data Integrity*. Retrieved December 4, 2016, http://nccoe.nist.gov/projects/building_blocks/data_integrity

5. NCCoE. *Derived PIV Credentials*. Retrieved December 4, 2016, http://nccoe.nist.gov/projects/building_blocks/piv_credentials

6. NCCoE. *Mobile Device Security*. Retrieved December 4, 2016, http://nccoe.nist.gov/projects/building_blocks/mobile_device_security

7. NCCoE. *Privacy-Enhanced Identity Federation*. Retrieved December 4, 2016, http://nccoe.nist.gov/projects/building_blocks/privacy-enhanced-identity-brokers

8. NCCoE. *Trusted Geolocation in the Cloud*. Retrieved December 4, 2016, nccoe.nist.gov/projects/building_blocks/trusted_geolocation_in_the_cloud

9. JPL. *About*. Retrieved December 4, 2016, http://www.jpl.nasa.gov/about/

10. JPL. *Cyber Security Visualization*. Retrieved December 4, 2016, https://www-robotics.jpl.nasa.gov/tasks/showTask.cfm?FuseAction=ShowTask&TaskID=294&tdaID=700098

11. GAO. *Federally Funded R&D Centers: Issues Relating to the Management of DOD-Sponsored Centers*. NSIAD-96-112. August 6, 1996. Retrieved December 5, 2016, http://www.gao.gov/products/GAO/NSIAD-96-112

12. GAO. *Opportunities Exist to Improve the Management and Oversight of Federally Funded Research and Development Centers*. GAO-09-15. October 8, 2008. Retrieved December 5, 2016, http://www.gao.gov/products/GAO-09-15

Chapter 10

DOE-Funded Research and Development Centers

Founded during the time of immense investment in scientific research in the period preceding World War II, the National Laboratories have served as the leading institutions for scientific innovation in the United States for more than 60 years. The Energy Department's National Labs address large scale, complex research and development challenges with a multidisciplinary approach that places an emphasis on translating basic science to innovation. This chapter provides a background on FFRDCs and examines the cybersecurity research activities of the DOE-funded national laboratories.

10.1 Cybersecurity Research Activities of the DOE Research and Development Laboratories

A key mission of the DOE Office of Electricity Delivery and Energy Reliability (OE) is to enhance the reliability and resiliency of the energy infrastructure. Within DOE OE's CEDS Program, cybersecurity R&D is tailored to the unique performance requirements, designs, and operational environments of EDS. The Strategic Plan research themes, particularly Designed-In Security and Tailored Trustworthy Spaces are strongly supported by the strategies and milestones outlined in the CEDS Program. Other elements of DOE also perform related cybersecurity research. The ASCR Program, which is part of the Office of Science, sponsors research to support DOE's leadership in scientific computation. Security of networks and middleware is a critical element in the ASCR Next Generation Networking research program.

The NNSA within DOE also sponsors cybersecurity research to support its unique mission requirements.

The CEDS Program operates with the goal that, by 2020, resilient EDS are designed, installed, operated, and maintained to survive cyber-incidents while sustaining critical functions. To help achieve this vision, OE fosters and actively engages in collaborations among energy stakeholders, utilities, vendors, national labs, and academic institutions. Through these collaborations, OE seeks to solve hand-in-hand with industry the right problems, and to transition next-generation research from the national labs and academia into commercial products operating in the energy sector.[1]

The Cybersecurity and Emerging Threats Research and Development (CET R&D) Division advances the R&D of innovative technologies, tools, and techniques to reduce risks to the critical energy infrastructure posed by cyber and other emerging threats. Continuing to increase the security, reliability, and resiliency of the electricity delivery system will help ensure the success of grid modernization and transformation of the energy systems. CET R&D activities include the ongoing support of research, development, and demonstration of advanced cybersecurity solutions, acceleration of information sharing to enhance situational awareness, and technical assistance in the development and adoption of best practices.[2]

The DOE launched the Grid Modernization Laboratory Consortium, a strategic partnership between DOE headquarters and the DOE National Laboratories to bring together leading experts and resources to collaborate on the goal of modernizing the nation's grid. The Consortium employs an integrated approach to ensure that DOE-funded studies and R&D are efficiently coordinated to reap the greatest return for the taxpayer dollar. It will also allow DOE to become a resource and convener for the diverse and fragmented set of stakeholders across industry, the scientific community, and all levels of government.

One of the many undertakings of the Grid Modernization Laboratory Consortium is to develop a multiyear program plan for grid modernization. The plan will outline an integrated systems approach to transforming the nation's grid by incorporating numerous program activities within DOE as well as activities undertaken by national stakeholders. As a first step, the leaders of the Consortium are focused on coordinating all of DOE's grid-related activities to ensure connectivity, avoid redundancies, and identify gaps in R&D needs of a modern grid.

The Grid Modernization Laboratory Consortium forms a united front employing the department's leading policy and technical experts to work toward transforming the grid for the future. By coupling headquarters collaboration with the strengths of the labs in areas including their computational abilities, knowledge of cybersecurity systems, integration of renewable and energy efficient technologies, and command of sensing and control technologies the Consortium will tackle the challenges associated with achieving a modern grid that will make a clean energy future possible.[3] A special emphasis has been placed on the development of advanced security *cyber-physical system* solutions and real-time incident response capabilities for emerging technologies and systems.[4]

10.2 Argonne National Laboratory

The DOE Argonne National Laboratory, located in Argonne, Illinois, is home to the Cyber Operations, Analysis, and Research (COAR) team. This cybersecurity team works to strengthen and defend critical infrastructure by analyzing, developing, and implementing novel cyber solutions that penetrate three key areas: cyber intelligence, cyber physical, and cyber resilience.[5]

10.3 Idaho National Laboratory

The DOE Idaho National Laboratory (INL), Idaho Falls, Idaho, addresses issues with the interdependencies of systems such as communications, power distribution, and transportation infrastructure to deal with potential vulnerabilities and mitigations to protect critical infrastructure. INL focuses on power grid vulnerabilities that can be exploited by manmade and natural events.

The work in control systems cybersecurity focuses on innovations that provide intelligent sensors and wireless communications to enhance the resilience and security of the Smart Grid, secure control systems to reduce the threat of cyberattack, and physical devices and barriers to protect substations and transformers from geomagnetic disturbance and ballistic attacks.

INL's Critical Infrastructure Test Range allows for scalable physical and cyber performance testing to be conducted on industry-scale infrastructure systems. It includes an Electric Grid Test Bed and a Cybersecurity Test Bed. The Test Range allows organizations to visualize, analyze, and test their infrastructure systems in a domain that is more realistic than computer simulations, yet safe and secure. INL operates its own electrical power transmission and distribution system and performs full-scale, end-to-end grid reliability testing for industry and government.

INL facilities are spread across 890 square miles in clusters similar to modern cities and other environments. It is a 61-mile 138 kV dual-fed power loop complete with seven substations and a control center all linked with state-of-the-art communications and instrumentation capabilities. Portions of the power loop can be isolated and reconfigured for independent, specialized testing.

In addition to conducting vulnerability assessments in Idaho, INL engineers and cyber specialists perform on-site assessments at transmission and generation control centers and at substation automation installations throughout the United States.

In collaboration with the DOD, cyber and electric grid reliability researchers at INL have acquired and are using the physics-based real time digital simulator

(RTDS) to enhance the security of the nation's electric power grid and related control systems including SCADA systems. It allows engineers to visualize the effects of power grid failures. With 15 racks, INL has the largest installation of RTDS in the national lab system.

The ability to simulate real-time power grid information is a key factor in detecting previously unknown vulnerabilities and providing infrastructure owners and operators with a path forward for responding to grid failures. The simulator allows critical infrastructure protection specialists to predict, plan, and prepare for catastrophic events.

Instrumentation, Control, and Intelligent Systems (ICIS) research is centered on developing components, programs, systems, and individuals for any application that requires monitoring, control, and human interaction. External peer review and advisory committees made up of academic, R&D, and customer organizations provide independent and ongoing review of the strategy within the signature and the focus or research funds.[6]

Resilience has emerged in the national dialog; the concept centers on the notion of a complex system being able to recover and continue operating through disruptive, manmade or natural, events. INL research leads the security by design effort to incorporate resilience into critical control system components. INL is focused on the nexus of cyber controls and wireless communications, and our differentiating science-based, full-scale assets uniquely position INL to lead technology and solution development to secure ICSs.

INL experts employ their real-world control system knowledge to advance the physical and cybersecurity protection of ICSs. The lab has developed the capabilities and multidisciplinary teams to provide analysis and deployable solutions to meet the complex and evolving national challenges of cyber-physical integration, infrastructure resilience, and critical support for the lifeline sectors. INL's wireless and cybersecurity capabilities and expertise enable industry, academia, government, and public safety to conduct:

- Real-time spectrum and network research associated with spectrum use and allocation
- Encryption and authentication studies for secure communications adoption and deployment
- Wireless signal propagation modeling, testing, and analysis
- Technology application studies and the development of appropriate concepts of operation

INL's Wireless National User Facility (WNUF) provides industrial, commercial, and academic users access to the full capacity of INL's wireless resources. With suitable sponsorship, academic institutions interested in openly published work may perform research, experimentation, and testing at minimal cost. INL has also developed an early warning system for the threat of radioactive contamination being intentionally dispersed by terrorists: the CellRAD system is a wireless advanced nuclear radiation detection software that runs on a cellphone.[7]

10.4 Lawrence Berkeley National Laboratory

The Berkeley Lab Data Science and Technology Department is an active participant in a number of projects in the arena of CEDS. Projects include collaborations with academic, vendor, and utility partners. Lawrence Berkeley National Laboratory's (LBNL's) work in this space emphasizes both its historical role in developing, deploying, and testing the Bro Network Security Monitor, as well as novel research ideas that leverage physical limitations, physical sensor output, and insight into commands sent to control systems to help monitor and protect networked energy system devices under control.[8]

The project, Threat Detection and Response with Data Analytics, is part of a $220 million, three-year Grid Modernization Initiative launched in January 2016 by the DOE to support R&D in power grid modernization. The goal of this project is to develop technologies and methodologies to protect the grid from advanced cyber threats through the collection of data from a range of sources and then use advanced analytics to identify threats and how best to respond to them. Specifically, the project team will be able to distinguish between power grid failures caused by cyberattacks and failures caused by other means, including natural disasters, normal equipment failures, and even physical attacks.

In addition to LLNL and Berkeley Lab, DOE's Idaho, Oak Ridge, Pacific Northwest, and Sandia national laboratories are also participating in the project. To make the scientific results more realistic and more usable by the power industry, the group is also partnering with the Electric Power Board (EPB) and the National Rural Electric Cooperative Association (NRECA), which will help provide data and collaborate in transferring the technology to the power industry.[9] LBNL is located in Berkeley, California.

10.5 Los Alamos National Laboratory

The Los Alamos National Laboratory, located in Los Alamos, New Mexico has a heightened focus on worker safety and security awareness. A variety of research programs directly and indirectly support the laboratory's basic mission: maintaining the safety, security, and reliability of the nuclear deterrent without the need to return to underground testing. With a national security focus, the laboratory also works on nuclear nonproliferation and border security, energy and infrastructure security, and countermeasures to nuclear and biological terrorist threats.[10]

The Los Alamos National Laboratory is focused on national security threats to the nation's cyber infrastructure. The laboratory develops innovative technologies for detection, response, and predictive vulnerability analysis. These technologies are designed to defeat intrusions into both government and critical infrastructure systems as well as to predict and prepare for potential attacks in times of conflict. This includes

- New methods to instrument computers and networks and detect the activities of cyber insiders be they humans or malicious software.
- Malware detection, classification through the analysis of dynamic instruction traces of malware using the VERA visualization tool, statistical models, and machine learning methods.
- Scalable cyber data science and the development of systems that enable graph analytics while enabling privacy, parallelism, and streaming.
- Resilient cyber command and control systems using EpiCom to improve the resilience, security, and performance of distributed systems addressing vulnerabilities inherent in centralized management and detection systems and use predictive analysis to reason about distributed system security.
- Communications systems modeling and simulation using the multi-scale integrated information and telecommunications system (MIITS) that supports Internet, public switched telephone network (PSTN), wireless, and botnet models which can be combined with other transportation, activity, demand, and social network models.
- The development of methods and tools for creating, disrupting, and detecting covert and *steganographic channels* enable undetected communications in a network.
- Quantum-enabled security which uses quantum (single-photon) communications integrated with optical communications to provide a strong, innate security foundation at the photonic layer for optical fiber networks.
- Work on Optimization and Control Theory for Smart Grids which develops new understanding on how the electrical power grid can be made more robust to attack and failure.[11]
- Los Alamos physicists developed a quantum random number generator and a quantum communication system, both of which exploit the weird and immutable laws of quantum physics to improve cybersecurity.[12]

The Los Alamos National Laboratory also hosted an information security exercise dubbed Eventide that put more than 100 participants from around the complex into a virtual maelstrom of bad news and worse events, as the simulation spewed sensitive data and cracked network security out into the wilderness of the Internet. The participants had to assess what was happening and how to respond, as their systems were progressively compromised, sensitive data appeared on hostile web sites, and invisible bad guys revealed their nefarious plans.[13]

In 2015, Los Alamos National Laboratory partnered with two private sector companies to bring cybersecurity technology developed by the lab to market. The first partnership, with Whitewood Encryption Systems, Inc., developed a quantum random number generator in an effort to address a key fundamental flaw in all cryptosystems: predictability. The security of electronic messages depends on the unpredictability of the random numbers used to scramble the data. Modern data centers have very limited access to true random numbers because computers do not generally do unpredictable things and to provide truly secure data communications, systems need a reliable source of unpredictable numbers that are not generated by a set of mathematical operations.

From the physicist's point of view, the only true unpredictability comes from quantum mechanics. These physical laws state that events at the subatomic level cannot be predicted; random quantum events lie at the root of the universe. From that starting point, Los Alamos developed a revolutionary method to generate unpredictable, theoretically unhackable random numbers. Quantum mechanics itself guards the secret. Unlike current math-based encryption keys, which are derived from random numbers generated by a potentially knowable algorithm, a quantum key cannot be determined through calculation, no matter how powerful a computer one uses.

Quantum random number generation technology, commercialized by Whitewood under the name Entropy Engine, is a plug-and-play computer card that fits most network servers and creates truly random numbers at a rate of up to 200 million bits each second and can deliver them on-demand over a network to existing encryption applications and devices performing cryptographic operations across datacenters, cloud computing systems, mobile phones, and the IoT. Entropy Engine is more than 10 times higher performing than other quantum devices currently on the market and is one of the world's most cost-effective, quantum-powered random number generators.

The second alliance, between Los Alamos and Ernst and Young, commercialized PathScan, a network-anomaly detection tool that searches for deviations in normal communication patterns that might indicate a cyber intruder. Unlike traditional security tools that look for malware or network signatures, PathScan searches for deviations from normal patterns of communication that are indicative of an intruder's presence.

PathScan's three-step approach builds statistical models to characterize the normal flows of traffic between each pair of communicating computers; actively enumerates multi-hop paths of communication; and passively monitors each path and tests whether the flows observed are expected in the context of the statistical models or whether they are unlikely and, therefore, show indicators of a possible adversary moving through the network. PathScan was also designed to work with an organization's legacy information security framework and does not require significant infrastructure development or vast stores of data to operate. Its network collection is passive, with limited impact to operations.[14]

10.6 National Renewable Energy Laboratory

National Renewable Energy Laboratory (NREL) focuses on energy challenges ranging from breakthroughs in fundamental science to new clean technologies to integrated energy systems that are critical to power the nation and the economy. This includes advances in the science and engineering of energy efficiency, sustainable transportation, and renewable power technologies and the knowledge to integrate and optimize energy systems. Through partnerships and licensing of its intellectual property rights, NREL seeks to reduce private sector risk in early stage technologies, enable investment in the adoption of renewable energy and energy efficiency technologies, reduce U.S. reliance on foreign energy sources, reduce carbon emissions, and increase U.S. industrial competitiveness.[15]

As part of the U.S. Department of Energy's Grid Modernization Initiative and Grid Modernization Laboratory Consortium, NREL collaborates with industry, academia, and other research organizations to find solutions to improve the ability of the grid to identify, anticipate, detect, protect against, and respond to threats and hazards. Securing the grid from cyberattacks is complex and since objective voices are hard to come by NREL established the CPSSEC and Resilience R&D Center.

NREL researchers and leading cybersecurity vendors designed and built the Test Bed for Secure Distributed Management which comprises hardware or software systems that mimic the communications, power systems, and cybersecurity layers for a utility's distribution system. The test bed incorporates a nine-layer security architecture (seven-layer OSI model + two upper layers of GridWise Architecture Council Stack). It is applicable to any multisite information system in any industry that has real-time transactions between different actors (end users and/or systems), including online energy devices, electric vehicles, wind turbines, home energy networks, thermostats, and demand response systems.

NREL offers a cybersecurity assessment service designed to help companies maximize their cybersecurity efforts and dollars. Using a tool that draws on two of the best known and most respected security guidance documents in the electric sector, NREL's assessment gives immediate visibility to the maturity of a company's cybersecurity operations relative to industry standards. A customized road map is then created that identifies actionable items and prioritizes them so the company knows where to focus first.[16]

10.7 Oak Ridge National Laboratory

The Cyber and Information Security Research (CISR) Group at Oak Ridge National Laboratory (ORNL) conducts research in cyber warfare, situational understanding, visual analytics, and information dominance to defend the nation's critical infrastructures against attacks from known and future adversaries, understand the threat to provide real-time actionable intelligence from diverse data, secure the supply chain and critical infrastructure, and continuing operational capabilities, and defeat known and future adversaries. The objective is rapid research development and delivery of innovative end-to-end integrated solutions to cyber and information security problems.[17] Research projects at the CISR cover a wide range of areas including

- Beholder: exploiting timing information to detect remote intrusion and zero-day attacks
- Choreographer: modifies DNS mappings to detect malicious content and connections, and to break the intruder kill chain
- Concordia: executable fragment forensics, clustering of software executable, similarity measures for malware, correlation and fusion of cyber information
- SCREAM: scalable real-time enterprise asset mapping/monitoring
- SFP: secure file protection
- STASH: ultra secure two-factor authentication using quantum technology
- SAPPY: end-to-end unbreakable encryption over traditional channels based on quantum technology
- USB-ARM: automated prevention of inadvertent and malicious injection of virus and malware
- VUD: automated vulnerability detection for compiled smart grid software
- NV (Nessus Vulnerability Visualization): web-based visualization tool for analyzing system vulnerabilities
- Pico: national malware repository for automated security analysis and exploitation
- Situational understanding and discovery of cyberattacks (SiTU): timely discovery and understanding of novel and sophisticated cyberattacks from vast quantities of cyber data
- Situation and Threat Understanding by Correlating Contextual Observations (STUCCO): leveraging endogenous and exogenous data sources to provide context to cybersecurity events
- Hyperion: automated sleeper code detection, vulnerability detection for defense or offense, zero-day malware detection and mitigation
- Miru: nondestructive automated hardware functionality analysis for supply chain security
- Perseus: detecting counterfeit hardware
- Programmable Logic Controllers (PLC) Logic Audit Control (PLAC): auditing system to verify contents of PLC are free of tampering
- Thor: software tamper resistance (e.g., digital rights management), hardware tamper resistance, key management, number generation
- Marco Polo: real-time geophysical location of internet users for prosecution of online criminals; and pinpoint potential adversaries
- SCREAM Plus: monitors potential adversary networks; locate vulnerabilities[18]

A central concern in modeling and simulating electric grids and the information infrastructure that monitors and controls them is hybrid modeling and simulation. ORNL has an extensible framework for integrating continuous and hybrid system models into discrete-event simulations. It includes a set of numerical integration schemes for solving ordinary differential equations and can be easily extended by end users who require specialized or especially robust continuous system simulation algorithms. This is useful for

- Simulating network-centric systems with continuous and discrete event subcomponents
- Building comprehensive, integrated modeling of networked controllers and plants
- Easy extension by end users who require specific continuous system simulation algorithms

This capability is further augmented with a software-in-the-loop simulation system that may be used to embed live control software into a simulated physical infrastructure. The focus of this simulation technology is on understanding cyber-physical impacts of existing control software and a framework for designing next generation controllers.

Cyber threats to EDS are real and increasingly innovative, complex, and sophisticated. Flaws in system components, communication methods, and common operating systems make modern EDS vulnerable to cyber infiltration and sabotage, and dependence on GPS timing for grid phase synchronization makes GPS spoofing or jamming attacks a serious concern. ORNL is developing a reference architecture for distributed enterprise-level cyber-physical intelligence (DELPHI) enabling secure, resilient operation of all aspects of EDS. DELPHI will provide persistent enterprise-level situational awareness of the grid, detecting and identifying attacks as they occur, autonomously implementing response/recovery protocols to ensure resilient operation. This research encompasses both cyber and physical-layer based detection and identification of real-world threat scenarios including network infiltration, malware insertion, and wireless/GPS spoofing. Detection of cyber-based attacks is being accomplished by learning signatures associated with anomalous behavior in the ICS monitoring and control traffic, and signatures associated with anomalous behavior in individual ICS nodes. Detection of physical-layer attacks is done by generating Radio Frequency Distinct Native Attribute (RF-DNA) based fingerprints for electrical equipment, authorized wired and wireless devices in the ICS network, authorized firmware loads and GPS transmission and then comparing consequent activity/transmission with these fingerprints detecting GPS spoofing attacks, authenticating valid firmware loads and identifying and denying access to unauthorized or rogue devices. DELPHI leverages ORNL's unique capabilities in advanced behavior-based network intrusion detection technologies, intelligent energy motoring and delivery systems, ICS security and learning-from-signals and will be demonstrated on ORNL's state-of-the-art energy delivery infrastructure and smart metering test facilities.

ORNL maintains the capability to test power grid components' behavior under cyber threat and place the results within a virtual interconnection scale simulation platform to examine threats and consequences. The Extreme Cyber Test Bed (ECTB) represents a unique national capability providing the ability to address such catastrophic consequences as failure of transmission gear, failure of distribution-scale circuit systems, loss of the capacity to adapt to rapidly accelerating experimental tempo, and isolation from the power grid. ECTB extends pilot-scale cyber threat research, development, and testing to the extreme end of the consequence spectrum, allowing detailed analysis of threats for new hardware, software, and procedures. This testbed is being jointly developed with the Nevada National Security Site, University of Tennessee, University of Nevada Las Vegas, Mississippi State University, and Louisiana Tech University.

ORNL has recently applied its quantum information expertise to the challenge of securing the electric grid. Multiple projects are aimed at identifying the best application space for quantum information, and for reducing the cost of quantum key distribution (QKD). In the first of these projects, the capabilities of commercially available QKD systems are evaluated for their suitability in various grid applications. The goal is to help guide future development by finding the best match between capabilities and needs. The cost of QKD is being reduced through collaboration with General Electric (GE) and ID Quantique. The three-year project was to develop a technology that makes a quantum channel accessible to multiple clients, rather than just the usual endpoints. By spreading the cost of the QKD system over multiple parties, the cost per user is reduced dramatically. Finally, the unique capabilities of QKD are being used to deliver quantum-verifiable timing signals to components on the grid. The project combines the high precision of optical timing signals with the quantum security of single photons.

The Next Generation Secure Scalable Communication Network for Smart Grid research project addresses the significant gap between commercially available communications systems and those needed to satisfy the demanding requirements associated with the electric utility industry. The key objectives for the project are (1) security in lower layers: next generation spread spectrum techniques to develop secure PHY (physical) and MAC (multiple access) layer specific for smart grid applications. The three security aspects of the communication technology are confidentiality, integrity, and availability, (2) scalability and self-configuring: advanced multiuser techniques and interference mitigation techniques are needed for seamless scalability of devices, (3) end-use applications—the next generation radios have to secure-by-design with end-use application, deployment requirements, and interoperability considerations incorporated at the design phase, and finally (4) robust control—future smart grid demands a communication platform to facilitate robust close-loop control systems. Future smart grid control systems operated over multi-scale (wide-area, time, and criticality) requires supporting communication systems with deterministic QoS guarantees. ORNL developed secure communication techniques using novel hybrid spread spectrum techniques and code division multiple access to enable seamless, secure, scalable communication platform for future smart grids.

Detection of embedded vulnerabilities prior to deployment is being addressed by ORNL's Hyperion system that has been developed in partnership with EnerNex and Sensus for direct static analysis of compiled control software embedded in devices. The Hyperion system generates a new artifact, the behavior from the compiled software. This behavior catalog presents a set of conditions and the software behavior under each of these conditions, and can be coupled with other analysis techniques to reveal the specific conditions for an event of interest such as disconnecting power or computing usage in order to assure that a system will perform correctly and be free of exploitable vulnerabilities when delivered to the field.

ORNL is developing, in partnership with GE Research, technology that exploits fine-grained timing data collected from remote SCADA and network devices to reveal the presence of software and network intrusions. The Beholder technology is focused first on detecting timing patterns that are indicative of anti-detection methods, and second on detecting significant deviations from a device baseline. For the latter detection, ORNL has been investigating phase-space dissimilarity measures. Initial experiments have confirmed the general feasibility of this approach; ORNL is now working to develop a system for testing and detection in the field under realistic conditions, and to measure any potential impact of running the Beholder system on availability and reliability.[19]

10.8 Pacific Northwest National Laboratory

PNNL's cybersecurity capability is focused on protecting the cyber-based systems that monitor and control critical infrastructure. Through the application of state-of-the-art technologies, clients with both traditional development and operational issues related to cybersecurity are supported. One initiative covers Intrinsically Secure Computing (ISC) which involves software and systems that will inherently respond to and defend themselves against internal and external threats. ISC contains trusted engineering so implicit trust is replaced with explicit trust. Once communications can be trusted, it is easier to defend against a security breach and respond to events. While designed in security is the ultimate goal, the need to protect other systems remains important. PNNL's cybersecurity capability incorporates the corrective and forensic security measures needed to support and maintain legacy and modern systems such as SCADA systems.

Control systems were built with reliable operations in mind, not security. Couple that with the life cycle of control system equipment which may be 20 to 30 years old. The goal is to develop and migrate technology from the IT world to the control system world without adversely impacting reliable operations. This requires collaboration with national and international standards bodies, vendors, and universities to arrive at better solutions.

The PNNL Electricity Infrastructure Operations Center (EIOC) and SCADA laboratory can measure the impact of vendor security products on control systems communication. The EIOC provides a test environment where it can examine the impacts of vendor projects using live data. One result of these impact assessments is suggestions for enhancing and improving vendor products.[17] Below is a summary of Atlanta Regional Commission (ARC) Initiative projects:

- Module integration interface for Resilient Cyber System (MiiRCS). In order to support integration of the ARC research tools, provides a framework needed that will help define the technical integration points of the various modules, create a sample set of integrations for reference, and function effectively on the ARC testbed. PNNL is designing and implementing technologies in the capacities of Discovery, Reasoning, Decider, and Actuator (a variation of the Observe-Orient-Decide-Act [OODA] loop) within a common platform to enable resilient operation of enterprise cyber systems. The technical approach to achieving the objectives consists of three broad tasks: categorization of technologies, design and implementation, and evaluation and optimization.
- Directly supporting the development of methodologies and capabilities to evaluate, test, probe, and own cyber enterprise networks calls for leveraging the state of practice TTP to build upon existing efforts in penetration testing and vulnerability assessments. Testing will be conducted within the CyberNET testbed, a unique capability that provides the ability to emulate enterprise network environments to enable controlled experimentation that would not be possible in operational environments. CyberNET offers a sterile and dynamic playground that is easily configurable and customizable where researchers can build, test, evaluate, or otherwise conduct their research in an enterprise-like environment. CyberNET accelerates the research of scientists and engineers while reducing cost, time, and redundancies across the cybersecurity domain. Enhanced modeling and simulation, supported by real world datasets, will increase realism in models, leading to more relevant research.
- Different states and behaviors of dynamic cyber networks can be identified using methods from topological data analysis, coupled with novel forms of graph statistics, applied to cyber graph data. To complement traditional data analysis methods, topological methods are effective in identifying the shapes or structures of a data set, as distinct from the details. Topological measures may thus be especially effective in distinguishing states of a cyber-network within its resiliency cycle. PNNL is complementing these topological methods with novel graph statistical methods and investigates the correlation between these statistical metrics and the appearances of topological features. Given the relative importance of graph data in the real-world and computational challenges surrounding it, the high-risk/high-reward approaches

to analyzing graph data problems will provide researchers a new avenue for understanding their data.

- Implementing cutting edge concepts in automation, algorithms, and infrastructure can severely increase the complexity for the human managing all of it, negating the increase in cost for the adversary, unless we start early and evaluate the role of cyber defenders in a new paradigm of resilient infrastructure. Researchers are identifying the defender's role in resilient cybersecurity, how to best convey needed information to them for situational awareness, and how to provide the ability to investigate malicious activity. Studies are being conducted across many organizations to (1) identify key awareness challenges presented by resilient technologies, (2) study various approaches for conveying network awareness while the underlying infrastructure is dynamic, and (3) find why certain data attributes are required to potentially answer the question in a different manner. Studies will be compiled and assessed for insight on how to proceed forward with enabling defenders in the future; prototypes will then be developed, incorporating concepts from resiliency applications, and validated with the defender community.

- Rendezvous: optimization and *stochastic* algorithms for asymmetric resilient infrastructure is a broadly accepted idea in cyber defense is that a cyber system cannot be successfully defended on a continual basis against malicious attacks. While the economic constraints restrict the amount of resources available to defenders of a system, the attackers operate at a relatively low cost leading to the well understood asymmetry in cyber defense. Researchers are developing a mathematical framework to understand and enable defenders with a limited budget to gain the asymmetrical advantage over the attackers. Specifically, based on fundamental concepts such as multi-objective optimization, stochasticity, and attacker–defender multistage Stackelberg games, are being developed for efficient proactive strategies for defenders to disrupt the cyber kill chain in order to increase the cost for attackers while minimizing the costs to defend while satisfying the constraints with available resources.

- A fundamental assumption of the ARC Initiative is that significant improvements in sustaining the functionality of cyber systems in the face of ongoing attacks requires thinking strategically about the problem and conducting research that is defensible, repeatable, and has enduring impact. The initiative has engaged scientists from other research domains to develop science practices that are relevant to cybersecurity research with the intent of enhancing the quality and impact of the research results.

- CyberFit lays the groundwork for cyber operations, cyber research, and cyber engineering to team up and create a culture of cyber fitness, for better standing up against adversaries. While there has long been a positive attitude between cyber operations, researchers, and software engineers, the culture gap and lack of interaction between these groups has been problematic. The

CyberFit approach to removing this culture gap is to lay a foundation of teamwork and technology. CyberFit Trench Talks provide the communication, feedback, and engagement foundation of teamwork, while the CyberFit Data Warehouse is the technology that provides data, novel technology, and finally solutions to problems. Together the Data Warehouse and the Trench Talks provide the teamwork and technology foundation for a blended culture of CyberFitness.

■ Kritikos is a (near) real-time enterprise introspection method for discovering cyber assets, identifying the functional relationships and dependencies between assets, and assessing the importance of the assets in terms of the business processes that they serve.

■ Multi-scale, multidimensional graph analytics tools for cybersecurity developed graph-theoretic models to characterize a complex cyber system at multiple scales. The models will be used to provide continuous metrics-based updates to drive an asymmetric resilient infrastructure. The algorithms in the software framework include multi-scale graph modeling, spectral analysis, role mining, shortest-path, and analysis of graph models.

■ Chimera aims to understand how the network properties of redundancy, diversity, and independence effect resiliency; particularly availability of system elements. These properties must be measured in a scientific manner and the second-order effects of these properties must be understood. For example, the diversity of a network topology may be improved by installing components from different vendors. However, one component may be measurably superior to another. Therefore, diversity may introduce additional vulnerabilities that actually decrease the resilience of the network.[20]

10.9 Sandia National Laboratories

Sandia National Laboratories performs work for industry responding to certain types of federal government solicitations. A strong science, technology, and engineering foundation enables Sandia's mission through a research staff working at the forefront of innovation, collaborative research with universities and companies, and discretionary research projects with significant potential impact. This is in keeping with Sandia's vision to be a premier science and engineering laboratory for national security and technology innovation.[21] Fundamental research helps Sandia's efforts in cybersecurity and are focused on three broad areas: trusted hardware, software, and systems; networks and systems architectures and analysis; and effective cyber defense systems.

The Cyber Engineering Research Institute (CERI) is a virtual organization spanning Sandia's two main sites. New Mexico's CERI facility (the Cyber Engineering Research Laboratory) is located in the Sandia Science and Technology Park. The California CERI facility (the Cybersecurity Technologies Research Laboratory) is located in the Livermore Valley Open Campus. CERI focuses on exploratory research in cybersecurity and facilitates partnerships with academia and industry.[22]

The Human Performance Laboratory uses a variety of cognitive neuroscience methods, including electroencephalography (EEG), eye tracking, and behavioral measures, to study human cognition. The research conducted in the laboratory focuses on investigating techniques for improving cognitive performance. The findings from this research can be applied in cyber and other domains, such as improving training techniques, assessing learning and memory, and helping people to avoid errors.

The IDEA laboratory enables Cyber Engineering Research Laboratory (CERL) researchers, visitors, and customers to sit elbow-to-elbow and interactively explore large, complex data sets. This laboratory facilitates collaborative research for methods to visualize, analyze, and make decisions with large, complex data.

Research and Engineering for Cyber Operations and Intelligence Laboratory (RECOIL) is a controlled environment for performing cyber exercises that can be used for human-centered cybersecurity research and training. RECOIL expands upon the successful Tracer Fire cybersecurity training, a live exercise program that Sandia developed for the DOE. RECOIL exercises are regularly performed with students and cybersecurity professionals from academia, industry, and government agencies. RECOIL facilitates partnerships between CERI researchers and academia.[23]

As part of ongoing research to help prevent and mitigate disruptions to computer networks on the Internet, researchers at Sandia National Laboratories in California have turned their attention to smartphones and other handheld computing devices. Sandia cyber researchers linked together 300,000 virtual handheld computing devices running the Android operating system so they can study large networks of smartphones and find ways to make them more reliable and secure. Android dominates the smartphone industry and runs on a range of computing gadgets.

The work is expected to result in a software tool that will allow others in the cyber research community to model similar environments and study the behaviors of smartphone networks. Ultimately, the tool will enable the computing industry to better protect handheld devices from malicious intent. The project builds on the success of earlier work in which Sandia focused on virtual Linux and Windows desktop systems. The Android project, dubbed MegaDroid, is expected to help researchers at Sandia and elsewhere who struggle to understand large-scale networks. Soon, Sandia expects to complete a sophisticated demonstration of the MegaDroid project that could be presented to potential industry or government collaborators.

A key element of the Android project is a spoof GPS. The researchers simulated GPS data of a smartphone user in an urban environment, an important experiment since smartphones and such key features as Bluetooth and Wi-Fi capabilities are highly location dependent and thus could easily be controlled and manipulated by rogue actors. The researchers then fed that data into the GPS input of an Android VM. Software on the VM treats the location data as indistinguishable from real GPS data, which offers researchers a much richer and more accurate emulation environment from which to analyze and study what hackers can do to smartphone networks. The main challenge in studying Android-based machines is the sheer complexity of the software. Google, which developed the Android operating system, wrote some 14 million lines of code into the software, and the system runs on top of a Linux kernel, which more than doubles the amount of code.

This latest development by Sandia cyber researchers represents a significant steppingstone for those hoping to understand and limit the damage from network disruptions due to glitches in software or protocols, natural disasters, acts of terrorism, or other causes. These disruptions can cause significant economic and other losses for individual consumers, companies, and governments. The research builds upon the Megatux project that started in 2009, in which Sandia scientists ran a million virtual Linux machines, and on a later project that focused on the Windows operating system, called MegaWin. Sandia researchers created those virtual networks at large scale using real Linux and Windows instances in VMs.[24]

Control system cybersecurity, including grid control, has operated as a niche for some time. That status is ending, however, as the electric grid now operates in a world where grid vulnerabilities can be easily discovered through open Internet research. Electric power systems and power-system operators are more reliant on telemetry, automated controls, and communications than ever before in an effort to improve energy reliability, safety, and cost effectiveness. More specifically, emerging advancements in phasor measurement units (PMUs), distributed energy resources (DER), smart-grid technologies, cloud computing services, and grid cyber vulnerability and assessments represent significant cybersecurity threats to the continuity of delivered power. To mitigate the additional risk, deploying cybersecurity controls must be commensurate with the deployment of these enabling technologies. Cybersecurity across the national electric grid is made difficult by a highly constrained solution space. Constraints on addressing grid cybersecurity include

- Strong and growing levels of technical ability in adversaries
- 20-year technology refresh cycle
- Limited avenues for utilities to fund security
- System owner reluctance to adding hardware or software that could potentially impact warranties
- A focus on availability over integrity or confidentiality of data[24]

The National SCADA Test Bed is a DOE Office of Electricity Delivery and Energy Reliability (OE) sponsored resource to help energy control systems. It combines state-of-the-art operational system testing facilities with research, development, and training to discover and address critical security vulnerabilities and threats to the energy sector. Sandia research efforts range from autonomous agent systems applied to SCADA, cryptographic security, system assessment, and red-team activities. Sandia is able to complement its communication and control capabilities with actual generation and load facilities for DER.[25]

10.10 Summary

The Energy Department's National Labs address large scale, complex R&D challenges with a multidisciplinary approach that places an emphasis on translating basic science to innovation. A key mission of the DOE Office of Electricity Delivery and Energy Reliability (OE) is to enhance the reliability and resiliency of the energy infrastructure. This chapter provides background on DOE FFRDCs.

- FFRDCs are government-funded entities that have long-term relationships with one or more federal agencies to perform R&D and related tasks. FFRDCs are typically entirely federally funded, or nearly so, but they are operated by contractors or other nongovernmental organizations.
- The DOE launched the Grid Modernization Laboratory Consortium, a strategic partnership between DOE headquarters and the DOE National Laboratories to bring together leading experts and resources to collaborate on the goal of modernizing the electric grid.
- The DOE supported national laboratories are approaching cybersecurity research from a number of perspectives and capitalizing on their unique disciplines and abilities to research new technologies to secure the cyber infrastructure.
- The ASCR Program, which is part of the Office of Science, sponsors research to support DOE's leadership in scientific computation. Security of networks and middleware is a critical element in the ASCR Next Generation Networking research program.
- The CEDS Program operates with the goal that, by 2020, resilient EDS will be designed, installed, operated, and maintained to survive cyber-incidents while sustaining critical functions.
- One of the many undertakings of the Grid Modernization Laboratory Consortium is to develop a multiyear program plan for grid modernization. The plan will outline an integrated systems approach to transforming the nation's grid by incorporating numerous program activities within DOE as well as activities undertaken by national stakeholders.

10.11 Seminar Discussion Topics

Discussion topics for graduate or professional-level seminars are

- Which national laboratory do seminar participants feel are doing the most interesting cybersecurity research?

- What experience have seminar participants had working with any of the DOE national laboratories?
- What areas of cybersecurity research being conducted by the national laboratories do seminar participants think are the most important? Why?

Key Terms

cyber-physical systems (CPS): combine the cyber and physical worlds with technologies that can respond in real time to their environments including the IoT, industrial Internet, and co-engineered interacting networks of physical and computational components

steganographic channels: steganography means covered writing or covered, concealed messages, or messages in image, or video within another file, message, image, or video. A steganographic channel in a communications network is when the channel is hidden in another channel or made difficult to detect in some manner

stochastic: is an event or system is one that is unpredictable because of a random variable

References

1. DOE. *Office of Electricity Delivery & Energy Reliability. Mission.* Retrieved December 1, 2016, http://www.energy.gov/oe/mission
2. DOE. *Cybersecurity and Emerging Threats Research and Development (CET R&D).* Retrieved December 1, 2016, http://www.energy.gov/oe/mission/cybersecurity-and-emerging-threats-research-and-development-cet-rd
3. DOE. *Launch of the Grid Modernization Laboratory Consortium.* November 17, 2014. Retrieved December 1, 2016, http://energy.gov/articles/launch-grid-modernization-laboratory-consortium
4. DOE. *Grid Modernization Update Electricity Advisory Committee.* March 26, 2015. Retrieved December 1, 2016, http://energy.gov/sites/prod/files/2015/04/f21/01-Mar2015EAC-NatlLabConsortium.pdf
5. Argonne National Laboratory. *Cyber Operations, Analysis, and Research (COAR).* November 8, 2016. Retrieved December 2, 2016, https://coar.risc.anl.gov/category/cyber-research/
6. INL. *Securing the Electrical Grid from Cyber and Physical Threats.* Retrieved December 2, 2016, https://www.inl.gov/research-programs/grid-resilience/
7. INL. *Improving Wireless Communication Reliability and Security.* Retrieved December 2, 2016, https://www.inl.gov/research-programs/wireless-research/
8. LBNL. *Cybersecurity for Energy Delivery Systems Research and Development.* Retrieved December 2, 2016, https://crd.lbl.gov/departments/data-science-and-technology/idf/research/cybersecurity-energy-systems/
9. LBNL. *Livermore, Berkeley National Labs Leading Project to Increase Power Grid Cybersecurity.* Retrieved December 2, 2016, https://crd.lbl.gov/news-and-publications/news/2016/livermore-berkeley-national-labs-leading-project-to-increase-power-grid-cybersecurity/

10. Los Alamos National Laboratory. *Our History.* Retrieved December 3, 2016, http://www.lanl.gov/about/history-innovation/index.php
11. Los Alamos National Laboratory. *Cyber Security Science.* Retrieved December 3, 2016, http://csr.lanl.gov/projects/
12. Los Alamos National Laboratory. *For Cybersecurity, in Quantum Encryption We Trust.*
13. Los Alamos National Laboratory. *Lab Hosts Multi-Lab Cyber Security Games.*
14. Los Alamos National Laboratory. *Addressing Cybersecurity.* Retrieved December 3, 2016, http://www.lanl.gov/projects/feynman-center/about/news/2016-03-17-addressing-cybersecurity.php
15. NREL. *About NREL.* Retrieved December 3, 2016, http://www.nrel.gov/about/
16. NREL. *Security and Resilience.* Retrieved December 3, 2016, http://www.nrel.gov/grid/security-resilience.html
17. PNNL. *Cyber Security Protecting Our Nation's Critical Infrastructure.* Retrieved December 3, 2016, http://eioc.pnnl.gov/research/cybersecurity.stm
18. ORNL. *Cyber and Information Security Research.* Retrieved December 3, 2016, http://www.ioc.ornl.gov/about/
19. ORNL. *Energy Security Projects.* Retrieved December 3, 2016, http://web.ornl.gov/sci/electricity/research/security/projects/
20. PNNL. *Asymmetric Resilient Cybersecurity.* Retrieved December 3, 2016, http://cybersecurity.pnnl.gov/projects.stm
21. Sandia National Laboratories. *About.* Retrieved December 4, 2016, http://www.sandia.gov/about/index.html
22. Sandia National Laboratories. *Cybersecurity.* Retrieved December 4, 2016, http://www.sandia.gov/missions/defense_systems/cybersecurity.html
23. Sandia National Laboratories. *Cyber Engineering Research Laboratory (CERL).* Retrieved December 4, 2016, http://www.cs.sandia.gov/CERI/cerl.html
24. Sandia National Laboratories. *Cyber and Physical Security.* Retrieved December 4, 2016, http://energy.sandia.gov/energy/ssrei/gridmod/cyber-security-for-electric-infrastructure/
25. Sandia National Laboratories. *National Supervisory Control and Data Acquisition (SCADA).* Retrieved December 4, 2016, http://energy.sandia.gov/energy/ssrei/gridmod/cyber-security-for-electric-infrastructure/scada-systems/

Chapter 11

Cybersecurity Research for Critical Industry Sectors

Since the events of September 11, 2001, many governments have supported the implementation of stronger security measures in their own country as well as in the countries of their treaty or trading partners. In the United States, the DHS has provided a leadership role in promoting threat analysis and security efforts. DHS and The Office of the President have identified 16 critical infrastructure sectors whose assets, systems, and networks are important to sustaining national interest including economic stability and sustainability.[1] This chapter reviews these critical sectors and the NIST cybersecurity framework being used to address cybersecurity issues in many of them.

11.1 U.S. Critical Industry Sectors

PPD-21 lists the critical industry sectors and assigns responsibility for monitoring threats and fostering the growth of improved security to specific federal agencies or departments.[2] The sectors and corresponding federal agencies are shown in Figure 11.1.

There are 16 critical infrastructure sectors whose assets, systems, and networks, whether physical or virtual, are considered so vital to the United States that their incapacitation or destruction would have a debilitating effect on security, national economic security, national public health or safety, or any combination thereof. The 16 critical infrastructure sectors are elaborated on below.

Critical Industry Sector[5]	Sector-Specific Agency
Chemical	Department of Homeland Security (DHS)
Commercial facilities	DHS
Communications	DHS
Critical manufacturing	DHS
Dams	DHS
Defense industrial base	Department of Defense (DOD)
Emergency services	DHS
Energy	Department of Energy (DOE)
Financial services	Department of the Treasury
Food and agriculture	Department of Agriculture (USDA) and Department of Health and Human Services (DHHS)
Government facilities	DHS and General Services Administration (GSA)
Healthcare and public health	DHHS
Information technology	DHS
Nuclear reactors, materials, and waste	DHS
Transportation systems	DHS and Department of Transportation (DOT)
Water and wastewater systems	Environmental Protection Agency (EPA)

Figure 11.1   Critical industry sectors and federal agencies charged with security leadership.

The chemical sector is an integral component of the economy, relying on and supporting a wide range of other critical infrastructure sectors. The sector can be divided into five main segments, based on the end product produced and each of these segments has distinct characteristics, growth dynamics, markets, new developments, and issues:

- Basic chemicals
- Specialty chemicals
- Agricultural chemicals
- Pharmaceuticals
- Consumer products

The majority of chemical sector facilities are privately owned, requiring DHS to work closely with the private sector and its industry associations to: set goals and objectives; identify assets; assess risks; prioritize needs; and implement protective programs. DHS has also issued regulatory Chemical Facility Anti-Terrorism

Standards (CFATS) for any facility that manufactures, uses, stores, or distributes certain chemicals at or above specified quantities or concentrations.[3]

The commercial facilities sector includes a diverse range of sites that draw large crowds of people for shopping, business, entertainment, or lodging. Facilities within the sector operate on the principle of open public access, meaning that the general public can move freely without the deterrent of highly visible security barriers. The majority of these facilities are privately owned and operated, with minimal interaction with the federal government and other regulatory entities. DHS is designated as the sector-specific agency (SSA) for the commercial facilities sector. The commercial facilities sector consists of eight subsectors:

- Entertainment and media (e.g., motion picture studios, broadcast media)
- Gaming (e.g., casinos)
- Lodging (e.g., hotels, motels, conference centers)
- Outdoor events (e.g., theme and amusement parks, fairs, campgrounds, parades)
- Public assembly (e.g., arenas, stadiums, aquariums, zoos, museums, convention centers)
- Real estate (e.g., office and apartment buildings, condominiums, mixed use facilities, self-storage)
- Retail (e.g., retail centers and districts, shopping malls)
- Sports leagues (e.g., professional sports leagues and federations)[4]

The communications sector is an integral component of the economy, underlying the operations of all businesses, public safety organizations, and government. PPD-21 identifies the communications sector as critical because it provides an enabling function across all critical infrastructure sectors. Over the last 25 years, the sector has evolved from predominantly a provider of voice services into a diverse, competitive, and interconnected industry using terrestrial, satellite, and wireless transmission systems. The transmission of these services has become interconnected; satellite, wireless, and wireline providers depend on each other to carry and terminate their traffic and companies routinely share facilities and technology to ensure interoperability. DHS is designated as the SSA for the communications sector.

The private sector, as owners and operators of the majority of communications infrastructure, is the primary entity responsible for protecting sector infrastructure and assets. Working with the federal government, the private sector is able to predict, anticipate, and respond to sector outages and understand how they might affect the ability of the national leadership to communicate during times of crisis, impact the operations of other sectors, and affect response and recovery efforts. The communications sector is closely linked to other sectors, including

- The energy sector, which provides power to run cellular towers, central offices, and other critical communications facilities and also relies on communications to aid in monitoring and controlling the delivery of electricity.

■ The IT sector, which provides critical control systems and services, physical architecture, and Internet infrastructure, and also relies on communications to deliver and distribute applications and services.

■ The financial services sector, which relies on communications for the transmission of transactions and operations of financial markets.

■ The emergency services sector (ESS), which depends on communications for directing resources, coordinating response, operating public alert and warning systems, and receiving emergency 9-1-1 calls.

■ The transportation systems sector, which provides the diesel fuel needed to power backup generators and relies on communications to monitor and control the flow of ground, sea, and air traffic.[5]

The critical manufacturing sector is crucial to the economic prosperity and continuity of the United States. A direct attack on or disruption of certain elements of the manufacturing industry could disrupt essential functions at the national level and across multiple critical infrastructure sectors. DHS is designated as the SSA for the critical manufacturing sector. The critical manufacturing sector identified several industries to serve as the core of the sector:

■ Primary metals manufacturing including iron and steel mills and ferro alloy manufacturing, alumina and aluminum production and processing, and nonferrous metal production and processing.

■ Machinery manufacturing including engine and turbine manufacturing, power transmission equipment manufacturing, and earth moving, mining, agricultural, and construction equipment manufacturing.

■ Electrical equipment, appliance, and component manufacturing including electric motor manufacturing, transformer manufacturing, and generator manufacturing.

■ Transportation equipment manufacturing including vehicles and commercial ships manufacturing, aerospace products and parts manufacturing, and locomotives, railroad and transit cars, and rail track equipment manufacturing.[6]

The dams sector delivers critical water retention and control services including hydroelectric power generation, municipal and industrial water supplies, agricultural irrigation, sediment and flood control, river navigation for inland bulk shipping, industrial waste management, and recreation. Its key services support multiple critical infrastructure sectors and industries. Dams sector assets irrigate at least 10% of U.S. cropland, help protect more than 43% of the U.S. population from flooding, and generate about 60% of electricity in the Pacific Northwest. There are more than 87,000 dams in the United States and approximately 65% are privately owned and approximately 77% are regulated by state dam safety offices. The dams sector has interdependencies with a wide range of other sectors, including communications, energy, food and agriculture, transportation systems, and water. DHS is designated as the SSA for the dams sector.[7]

The defense industrial base sector is the worldwide industrial complex that enables R&D, as well as design, production, delivery, and maintenance of military weapons systems, subsystems, and components or parts, to meet U.S. military requirements. The defense industrial base partnership consists of DoD components, more than 100,000 defense industrial base companies and their subcontractors who perform under contract to the DoD, companies providing incidental materials and services to the DoD, and government-owned/contractor-operated and government-owned/government-operated facilities. Defense industrial base companies include domestic and foreign entities, with production assets located in many countries. The sector provides products and services that are essential to mobilize, deploy, and sustain military operations. The DoD is designated as the SSA for the defense industrial base sector. The defense industrial base sector does not include the commercial infrastructure of providers of services such as power, communications, transportation, or utilities that the DoD uses to meet military operational requirements. These commercial infrastructure assets are addressed by other SSAs.[8]

The ESS is a community of millions of highly skilled, trained personnel, along with the physical and cyber resources, that provide a wide range of prevention, preparedness, response, and recovery services during both day-to-day operations and incident response. The ESS includes geographically distributed facilities and equipment in both paid and volunteer capacities organized primarily at the federal, state, local, tribal, and territorial levels of government, such as city police departments and fire stations, county sheriff's offices, DoD police and fire departments, and town public works departments. The ESS also includes private sector resources, such as industrial fire departments, private security organizations, and private emergency medical services providers. The mission of the ESS is to save lives, protect property and the environment, assist communities impacted by disasters, and aid recovery during emergencies. DHS is designated as the SSA for the ESS.

Five distinct disciplines compose the ESS, encompassing a wide range of emergency response functions and roles: law enforcement, fire and emergency services, emergency medical services, emergency management, and public works. The ESS also provides specialized emergency services through individual personnel and teams. These specialized capabilities may be found in one or more various disciplines, depending on the jurisdiction: tactical teams (i.e., SWAT), hazardous devices team/public safety bomb disposal, public safety dive teams/maritime units; canine units, aviation units (i.e., police and medical evacuation helicopters), hazardous materials (i.e., HAZMAT), search and rescue teams, public safety answering points (i.e., 9-1-1 call centers), fusion centers, private security guard forces, and National Guard civil support.[9]

The energy infrastructure fuels the economy of the twenty-first century. Without a stable energy supply, health and welfare are threatened, and the economy cannot function. More than 80% of the country's energy infrastructure is owned by the private sector, supplying fuels to the transportation industry, electricity to households and businesses, and other sources of energy that are integral to growth and production across the nation.

The energy infrastructure is divided into three interrelated segments: electricity, oil, and natural gas. The electricity segment contains more than 6,413 power plants (this includes 3,273 traditional electric utilities and 1,738 nonutility power producers) with approximately 1,075 gigawatts of installed generation. Approximately 48% of electricity is produced by combusting coal (primarily transported by rail), 20% in nuclear power plants, and 22% by combusting natural gas. The remaining generation is provided by hydroelectric plants (6%), oil (1%), and renewable sources (solar, wind, and geothermal) (3%). The heavy reliance on pipelines to distribute products across the nation highlights the interdependencies between the energy and transportation systems sector.

The energy sector is well aware of its vulnerabilities and is leading a significant voluntary effort to increase its planning and preparedness. Cooperation through industry groups has resulted in substantial information sharing of best practices across the sector. Many sector owners and operators have extensive experience abroad with infrastructure protection and have more recently focused their attention on cybersecurity. The DOE is designated as the SSA for the energy sector.[10]

The financial services sector represents a vital component of the national critical infrastructure. Large-scale power outages, recent natural disasters, and an increase in the number and sophistication of cyberattacks demonstrate the wide range of potential risks facing the sector. The financial services sector includes thousands of depository institutions, providers of investment products, insurance companies, other credit and financing organizations, and the providers of the critical financial utilities and services that support these functions. Financial institutions vary widely in size and presence, ranging from some of the world's largest global companies with thousands of employees and many billions of dollars in assets, to community banks and credit unions with a small number of employees serving individual communities. The Department of Treasury is designated as the SSA for the financial services sector. Whether an individual savings account, financial derivatives, credit extended to a large organization, or investments made to a foreign country, these products allow customers to

- Deposit funds and make payments to other parties
- Provide credit and liquidity to customers
- Invest funds for both long and short periods
- Transfer financial risks between customers[11]

The food and agriculture sector is almost entirely under private ownership and is composed of an estimated 2.1 million farms, 935,000 restaurants, and more than 200,000 registered food manufacturing, processing, and storage facilities.

This sector accounts for roughly one-fifth of U.S. economic activity. The food and agriculture sector has critical dependencies with many sectors, but particularly with the following:

- Water and wastewater systems, for clean irrigation and processed water
- Transportation systems, for movement of products and livestock
- Energy, to power the equipment needed for agriculture production and food processing
- Chemical, for fertilizers and pesticides used in the production of crops[12]

The government facilities sector includes a wide variety of buildings, located in the United States and overseas, that are owned or leased by federal, state, local, and tribal governments. Many government facilities are open to the public for business activities, commercial transactions, or recreational activities while others that are not open to the public contain highly sensitive information, materials, processes, and equipment. These facilities include general-use office buildings and special-use military installations, embassies, courthouses, national laboratories, and structures that may house critical equipment, systems, networks, and functions. In addition to physical structures, the sector includes cyber elements that contribute to the protection of sector assets (e.g., access control systems and closed-circuit television systems) as well as individuals who perform essential functions or possess tactical, operational, or strategic knowledge. The government facilities sector-specific plan details how the National Infrastructure Protection Plan (NIPP) risk management framework (RMF) is implemented within the context of the unique characteristics and risk landscape of the sector. The national monuments and icons sector was consolidated within the government facilities sector in 2013 under PPD-21. DHS and the General Services Administration (GSA) are designated as the co-SSAs for the government facilities sector.[13]

The healthcare and public health sector protects all sectors of the economy from hazards such as terrorism, infectious disease outbreaks, and natural disasters. Because the vast majority of the sector's assets are privately owned and operated, collaboration and information sharing between the public and private sectors is essential to increasing resilience of the healthcare and public health critical infrastructure. Operating in all U.S. states, territories, and tribal areas, the sector plays a significant role in response and recovery across all other sectors in the event of a natural or man-made disaster. While healthcare tends to be delivered and managed locally, the public health component of the sector, focused primarily on population health, is managed across all levels of government: national, state, regional, local, tribal, and territorial.

The healthcare and public health sector is highly dependent on fellow sectors for continuity of operations and service delivery, including communications, emergency services, energy, food and agriculture, IT, transportation systems, and water and wastewater systems. The Healthcare and Public Health Sector-Specific Plan details how the NIPP RMF is implemented within the context of the unique characteristics and risk landscape of the sector. The Department of Health and Human Services (DHHS) is designated as the SSA for the healthcare and public health sector.[14]

The IT sector is central to the nation's security, economy, and public health and safety as businesses, governments, academia, and private citizens are increasingly dependent upon IT sector functions. These virtual and distributed functions produce and provide hardware, software, and IT systems and services, and in collaboration with the communications sector, the Internet. The sector's complex and dynamic environment makes identifying threats and assessing vulnerabilities difficult and requires that these tasks be addressed in a collaborative and creative fashion. IT sector functions are operated by a combination of entities which are often owners and operators and their respective associations that maintain and reconstitute the network, including the Internet. Although IT infrastructure has a certain level of inherent resilience, its interdependent and interconnected structure presents challenges as well as opportunities for coordinating public and private sector preparedness and protection activities. DHS is designated as the SSA for the IT sector.[15]

The nuclear reactors, materials, and waste sector accounts for approximately 20% of the U.S. electrical generation which is provided by 99 commercial nuclear plants. The Sector-Specific Plan details how the NIPP RMF is implemented within the context of the unique characteristics and risk landscape of the sector. DHS is designated as the SSA for the nuclear reactors, materials, and waste sector.[16]

DHS and the United States Department of Transportation (USDOT) are designated as the co-SSAs for the transportation systems sector. The transportation system quickly, safely, and securely moves people and goods through the country and overseas. The transportation systems sector consists of seven key subsectors, or modes:

- Aviation includes aircraft, air traffic control systems, and about 19,700 airports, heliports, and landing strips. Approximately 500 provide commercial aviation services at civil and joint-use military airports, heliports, and sea plane bases. In addition, the aviation mode includes commercial and recreational aircraft (manned and unmanned) and a wide variety of support services, such as aircraft repair stations, fueling facilities, navigation aids, and flight schools.
- Highway and motor carrier encompasses more than 4 million miles of roadway, more than 600,000 bridges, and more than 350 tunnels. Vehicles include trucks, including those carrying hazardous materials; other commercial vehicles, including commercial motor coaches and school buses; vehicle and driver licensing systems; traffic management systems; and cyber systems used for operational management.
- Maritime transportation system consists of about 95,000 miles of coastline, 361 ports, more than 25,000 miles of waterways, and intermodal landside

connections that allow the various modes of transportation to move people and goods to, from, and on the water.

■ Mass transit and passenger rail includes terminals, operational systems, and supporting infrastructure for passenger services by transit buses, trolleybuses, monorail, heavy rail also known as subways or metros, light rail, passenger rail, and vanpool/rideshare. Public transportation and passenger rail operations provided an estimated 10.8 billion passenger trips in 2014.

■ Pipeline systems consist of more than 2.5 million miles of pipelines spanning the country and carrying nearly all of the nation's natural gas and about 65% of hazardous liquids, as well as various chemicals. Above-ground assets, such as compressor stations and pumping stations, are also included.

■ Freight rail consists of seven major carriers, hundreds of smaller railroads, over 138,000 miles of active railroad, over 1.33 million freight cars, and approximately 20,000 locomotives. An estimated 12,000 trains operate daily. The DoD has designated 30,000 miles of track and structure as critical to mobilization and resupply of U.S. military forces.

■ Postal and shipping moves about 720 million letters and packages each day and includes large integrated carriers, regional and local courier services, mail services, mail management firms, and chartered and delivery services.[17]

In the water and wastewater systems sector, there are approximately 153,000 public drinking water systems and more than 16,000 publicly owned wastewater treatment systems in the United States. More than 80% of the U.S. population receives their potable water from these drinking water systems, and about 75% of the U.S. population has its sanitary sewerage treated by these wastewater systems.

The water and wastewater systems sector is vulnerable to a variety of attacks, including contamination with deadly agents; physical attacks, such as the release of toxic gaseous chemicals; and cyberattacks. The result of any variety of attack could be large numbers of illnesses or casualties and/or a DoS that would also impact public health and economic vitality. The sector is also vulnerable to natural disasters. Critical services, such as firefighting and healthcare (hospitals), and other dependent and interdependent sectors, such as energy, food, and agriculture, and transportation systems, would suffer negative impacts from a DoS in the water and wastewater systems sector. The Environmental Protection Agency (EPA) is designated as the SSA for the water and wastewater systems sector. PPD-21 changed the name of the water sector to the water and wastewater systems sector in 2013.[18]

The DHS Office of Cybersecurity and Communications (CS&C), within the NPPD, is responsible for enhancing the security, resilience, and reliability of the cyber and communications infrastructure. CS&C works to prevent or minimize disruptions to critical information infrastructure in order to protect the public, the economy, and government services. CS&C leads efforts to protect the federal.gov domain of civilian government networks and to collaborate with the private sector to increase the security of critical networks in the.com domain. In addition, the

NCCIC serves as a 24/7 cyber monitoring, incident response, and management center and as a national point of cyber and communications incident integration.[19]

Formerly, the Infrastructure Analysis and Strategy Division (IASD) within the Office of Infrastructure Protection (IP), Office of Cyber and Infrastructure Analysis (OCIA) was established as an office of the NPPD in 2014. OCIA has an important role in DHS's efforts to implement PPD-21, which calls for integrated analysis of critical infrastructure, and EO 13636, identifying critical infrastructure where cyber incidents could have catastrophic impacts to public health and safety, the economy, and national security. OCIA builds on the recent accomplishments of the Department's Homeland Infrastructure Threat and Risk Analysis Center (HITRAC) and manages the National Infrastructure Simulation and Analysis Center (NISAC) to advance understanding of emerging risks crossing the cyber-physical domain. OCIA represents an integration and enhancement of DHS's analytic capabilities, supporting stakeholders and interagency partners.[20]

11.2 EO for Improving Critical Infrastructure Cybersecurity

On February 12, 2013, President Barack Obama signed an EO designed to move the federal government rapidly forward on the mission to improving critical infrastructure cybersecurity. The premise behind the order was that repeated cyber intrusions into critical infrastructure demonstrate the need for improved cybersecurity. The national and economic security of the United States depends on the reliable functioning of the critical infrastructure in the face of such threats.

Cybersecurity information sharing was to be expanded based on the advice of subject matter experts regarding the content, structure, and types of information most useful to critical infrastructure owners and operators in reducing and mitigating cyber risks.

The NIST was to lead the research on and the development of a framework to reduce cyber risks to critical infrastructure (the Cybersecurity Framework). The Cybersecurity Framework was to include a set of standards, methodologies, procedures, and processes that align policy, business, and technological approaches to address cyber risks and incorporate voluntary consensus standards and industry best practices to the fullest extent possible. In addition, the Cybersecurity Framework was to provide a prioritized, flexible, repeatable, performance-based, and cost-effective approach, including information security measures and controls, to help owners and operators of critical infrastructure identify, assess, and manage cyber risk with a focus on identifying cross-sector security standards and guidelines applicable to critical infrastructure.

The SSAs and other interested agencies were to coordinate with the Sector Coordinating Councils to review the Cybersecurity Framework and, if necessary, develop implementation guidance or supplemental materials to address sector-specific risks and operating environments. A risk-based approach was called for to identify critical infrastructure where a cybersecurity incident could reasonably result in catastrophic regional or national effects on public health or safety, economic security, or national security.[21]

11.3 The NIST Framework for Improving Critical Infrastructure Cybersecurity

The Cybersecurity Framework focuses on using business drivers to guide cybersecurity activities and considers cybersecurity risks as part of the organization's risk management processes. The Framework consists of three parts: the *Framework Core*, the *Framework Profile*, and the *Framework Implementation Tiers*. The Framework Core is a set of cybersecurity activities, outcomes, and informative references that are common across critical infrastructure sectors, providing the detailed guidance for developing individual organizational Profiles. Through use of the Profiles, the Framework will help an organization align its cybersecurity activities with its business requirements, risk tolerances, and resources. The Tiers provide a mechanism for organizations to view and understand the characteristics of their approach to managing cybersecurity risk.

The Framework is not a one-size-fits-all approach to managing cybersecurity risk for critical infrastructure. Organizations will continue to have unique risks and face different threats, have different vulnerabilities, and have different risk tolerances and thus how they implement the practices in the Framework will vary. Organizations can determine activities that are important to critical service delivery and can prioritize investments to maximize the impact of each dollar spent. Ultimately, the Framework is aimed at reducing and better managing cybersecurity risks. Use of this voluntary Framework is the next step to improve the cybersecurity of the critical infrastructure.

The Framework is a living document and will continue to be updated and improved as industry provides feedback on implementation. As the Framework is put into practice, lessons learned will be integrated into future versions. This will ensure it is meeting the needs of critical infrastructure owners and operators in a dynamic and challenging environment of new threats, risks, and solutions. The Framework provides a common taxonomy and mechanism for organizations to

- Describe their current cybersecurity posture
- Describe their target state for cybersecurity
- Identify and prioritize opportunities for improvement within the context of a continuous and repeatable process
- Assess progress toward the target state
- Communicate among internal and external stakeholders about cybersecurity risk

The Framework Core is a set of cybersecurity activities, desired outcomes, and applicable references that are common across critical infrastructure sectors. The Core presents industry standards, guidelines, and practices in a manner that allows for communication of cybersecurity activities and outcomes across the organization from the executive level to the implementation/operations level. The Framework Core consists of five concurrent and continuous functions: identify, protect, detect, respond, and recover. When considered together, these functions provide a high-level, strategic view of the lifecycle of an organization's management of cybersecurity risk. The Framework Core then identifies underlying key categories and subcategories for each function, and matches them with example informative references such as existing standards, guidelines, and practices for each subcategory.

The Framework Implementation Tiers provide context on how an organization views cybersecurity risk and the processes in place to manage that risk. The Tiers describe the degree to which an organization's cybersecurity risk management practices exhibit the characteristics defined in the Framework (e.g., risk and threat aware, repeatable, and adaptive). The Tiers characterize an organization's practices over a range, from partial (Tier 1) to adaptive (Tier 4). These Tiers reflect a progression from informal, reactive responses to approaches that are agile and risk-informed. During the Tier selection process, an organization should consider its current risk management practices, threat environment, legal and regulatory requirements, business/mission objectives, and organizational constraints.

A Framework Profile represents the outcomes based on business needs that an organization has selected from the Framework categories and subcategories. The Profile can be characterized as the alignment of standards, guidelines, and practices to the Framework Core in a particular implementation scenario. Profiles can be used to identify opportunities for improving cybersecurity posture by comparing a Current Profile with a Target Profile. To develop a Profile, an organization can review all of the categories and subcategories and, based on business drivers and a risk assessment, determine which are most important; they can add categories and subcategories as needed to address the organization's risks. The Current Profile can then be used to support prioritization and measurement of progress toward the Target Profile, while factoring in other business needs including cost-effectiveness and innovation. Profiles can be used to conduct self-assessments and communicate within an organization or between organizations. The Framework Core elements work together as follows.

Functions organize basic cybersecurity activities at their highest level. These functions are identify, protect, detect, respond, and recover. They aid an organization in expressing its management of cybersecurity risk by organizing information, enabling risk management decisions, addressing threats, and improving by learning from previous activities. The functions also align with existing methodologies for incident management and help show the impact of investments in cybersecurity. For example, investments in planning and exercises support timely response and recovery actions, resulting in reduced impact to the delivery of services.

Categories are the subdivisions of a function into groups of cybersecurity outcomes closely tied to programmatic needs and particular activities. Examples of categories include asset management, access control, and detection processes.

Subcategories further divide a *category* into specific outcomes of technical and/ or management activities. They provide a set of results that, while not exhaustive, help support achievement of the outcomes in each category. Examples of subcategories include external information systems are catalogued, data-at-rest is protected, and notifications from detection systems are investigated.

Informative references are specific sections of standards, guidelines, and practices common among *critical infrastructure* sectors that illustrate a method to achieve the outcomes associated with each subcategory. The informative references presented in the Framework Core are illustrative and not exhaustive. They are based upon cross-sector research and guidance most frequently referenced during the Framework development process.

The five Framework Core Functions are defined below. These functions are not intended to form a serial path, or lead to a static desired end state. Rather, the functions can be performed concurrently and continuously to form an operational culture that addresses dynamic cybersecurity risk.

Identify: develop the organizational understanding to manage cybersecurity risk to systems, assets, data, and capabilities. The activities in the identify function are foundational for effective use of the Framework. Understanding the business context, the resources that support critical functions, and the related cybersecurity risks enables an organization to focus and prioritize its efforts, consistent with its risk management strategy and business needs. Examples of outcome categories within this function include: asset management; business environment; governance; risk assessment; and risk management strategy.

Protect: develop and implement the appropriate safeguards to ensure delivery of critical infrastructure services. The protect function supports the ability to limit or contain the impact of a potential *cybersecurity event*. Examples of outcome categories within this function include: access control; awareness and training; data security; information protection processes and procedures; maintenance; and protective technology.

Detect: develop and implement the appropriate activities to identify the occurrence of a cybersecurity event. The detect function enables timely discovery of cybersecurity events. Examples of outcome categories within this function include: anomalies and events; security continuous monitoring; and detection processes.

Respond: develop and implement the appropriate activities to take action regarding a detected cybersecurity event. NIST developed a Compendium of informative references gathered from the RFI input, Cybersecurity Framework workshops, and stakeholder engagement during the Framework development process. The Compendium includes standards, guidelines, and practices to assist with implementation. The Compendium is not intended to be an exhaustive list, but rather a starting point based on initial stakeholder input. The Compendium and other supporting material can be found at http://www.nist.gov/cyberframework/

The respond function supports the ability to contain the impact of a potential cybersecurity event. Examples of outcome categories within this function include: response planning; communications; analysis; mitigation; and improvements.

Recover: develop and implement the appropriate activities to maintain plans for resilience and to restore any capabilities or services that were impaired due to a cybersecurity event. The recover function supports timely recovery to normal operations to reduce the impact from a cybersecurity event. Examples of outcome categories within this function include: recovery planning; improvements; and communications.

The Framework Profile is the alignment of the functions, categories, and sub-categories with the business requirements, risk tolerance, and resources of the organization. A Profile enables organizations to establish a roadmap for reducing cybersecurity risk that is well aligned with organizational and sector goals, considers legal/regulatory requirements and industry best practices, and reflects risk management priorities. Given the complexity of many organizations, they may choose to have multiple profiles, aligned with particular components and recognizing their individual needs.

Framework Profiles can be used to describe the current state or the desired target state of specific cybersecurity activities. The Current Profile indicates the cybersecurity outcomes that are currently being achieved. The Target Profile indicates the outcomes needed to achieve the desired cybersecurity risk management goals. Profiles support business/mission requirements and aid in the communication of risk within and between organizations. This Framework document does not prescribe Profile templates, allowing for flexibility in implementation.

An organization can use the Cybersecurity Framework as a key part of its systematic process for identifying, assessing, and managing cybersecurity risk. The Framework is not designed to replace existing processes; an organization can use its current process and overlay it onto the Framework to determine gaps in its current cybersecurity risk approach and develop a roadmap to improvement. Utilizing the Framework as a cybersecurity risk management tool, an organization can determine activities that are most important to critical service delivery and prioritize expenditures to maximize the impact of the investment.

The Framework is designed to complement existing business and cybersecurity operations. It can serve as the foundation for a new cybersecurity program or a mechanism for improving an existing program. The Framework provides a means of expressing cybersecurity requirements to business partners and customers and can help identify gaps in an organization's cybersecurity practices. It also provides a general set of considerations and processes for considering privacy and civil liberties implications in the context of a cybersecurity program.[22]

The content of the Cybersecurity Framework document and supporting material is very comprehensive and detailed. This section just provides a brief overview of the basic concepts and processes. Complete documentation can be found at: https://www.nist.gov/cyberframework

11.4 SSAs Cybersecurity Progress

The U.S. GAO conducted a study in 2015 to determine the extent to which SSAs have

- Identified the significance of cyber risks to their respective sectors' networks and ICSs
- Taken actions to mitigate cyber risks within their respective sectors
- Collaborated across sectors to improve cybersecurity
- Established performance metrics to monitor improvements in their respective sectors

To conduct the review, GAO analyzed policy, plans, and other documentation and interviewed public and private sector officials for eight of nine SSAs with responsibility for 15 of 16 sectors.

SSAs determined the significance of cyber risk to networks and ICSs for all 15 of the sectors in the scope of GAO's review. Specifically, they determined that cyber risk was significant for 11 of 15 sectors. Although the SSAs for the remaining four sectors had not determined cyber risks to be significant during their 2010 sector-specific planning process, they subsequently reconsidered the significance of cyber risks to the sector. For example, commercial facilities SSA officials stated that they recognized cyber risk as a high-priority concern for the sector as part of the updated sector planning process. SSAs and their sector partners are to include an overview of current and emerging cyber risks in their updated sector-specific plans.

SSAs generally took actions to mitigate cyber risks and vulnerabilities for their respective sectors and developed, implemented, or supported efforts to enhance cybersecurity and mitigate cyber risk with activities that aligned with a majority of actions called for by the NIPP. SSAs for 12 of the 15 sectors had not identified incentives to promote cybersecurity in their sectors as proposed in the NIPP; however, the SSAs are participating in a working group to identify appropriate incentives. In addition, SSAs for 3 of 15 sectors had not yet made significant progress in advancing cyber-based R&D within their sectors because it had not been an area of focus for their sector. DHS guidance for updating the sector-specific plans directs the SSAs to incorporate the NIPP's actions to guide their cyber risk mitigation activities, including cybersecurity-related actions to identify incentives and promote R&D.

All SSAs that GAO reviewed used multiple public–private and cross-sector collaboration mechanisms to facilitate the sharing of cybersecurity-related information. For example, the SSAs used councils of federal and nonfederal stakeholders, including coordinating councils and cybersecurity and ICS working groups, to coordinate with each other. In addition, SSAs participated in the NCCIC, a national center at DHS to receive and disseminate cyber-related information for public and private sector partners.

The DoD, DoE, and DHHS established performance metrics for their three sectors. However, the SSAs for the other 12 sectors had not developed metrics to measure and report on the effectiveness of all of their cyber risk mitigation activities or their sectors' cybersecurity posture. This was because, among other reasons, the SSAs rely on their private sector partners to voluntarily share information needed to measure efforts. The NIPP directs SSAs and their sector partners to identify high-level outcomes to facilitate progress toward national goals and priorities. Until SSAs develop performance metrics and collect data to report on the progress of their efforts to enhance the sectors' cybersecurity posture, they may be unable to adequately monitor the effectiveness of their cyber risk mitigation activities and document the resulting sector-wide cybersecurity progress.

GAO recommended that certain SSAs collaborate with sector partners to develop performance metrics and determine how to overcome challenges to reporting the results of their cyber risk mitigation activities. Four of these agencies concurred with GAO's recommendations, while two agencies did not comment on the recommendations. The GAO report provides great detail on what each SSAs had accomplished and the report is a profile of where each SSA was at in the process of working with their respective sectors.[23] A full copy of the report is available at: http://www.gao.gov/products/GAO-16-79

11.5 Summary

In the United States, DHS has provided a leadership role in promoting threat analysis and security efforts. DHS and The Office of the President have identified 16 critical infrastructure sectors whose assets, systems, and networks, are important to sustaining national interest including economic stability and sustainability.[1] NIST has conducted research and lead development efforts on the cybersecurity framework which SSAs have encouraged organizations in their respective sectors to use when developing or improving cybersecurity plans. Key points covered in this chapter include

- There are 16 critical infrastructure sectors whose assets, systems, and networks, whether physical or virtual, are considered so vital to the United States that their incapacitation or destruction would have a debilitating effect on security, national economic security, national public health or safety, or any combination thereof.
- The DHS Office of CS&C, within the NPPD, is responsible for enhancing the security, resilience, and reliability of the cyber and communications infrastructure.
- A risk-based approach was called for to identify critical infrastructure where a cybersecurity incident could reasonably result in catastrophic regional or national effects on public health or safety, economic security, or national security.

- The Cybersecurity Framework is not a one-size-fits-all approach to managing cybersecurity risk for critical infrastructure.
- An organization can use the Cybersecurity Framework as a key part of its systematic process for identifying, assessing, and managing cybersecurity risk.
- SSAs determined the significance of cyber risk to networks and ICSs for all 15 of the sectors in the scope of GAO's review. Specifically, they determined that cyber risk was significant for 11 of 15 sectors.

11.6 Seminar Discussion Topics

Discussion topics for graduate or professional-level seminars are

- What experience have seminar participants had working with the Cybersecurity Framework?
- What areas of the Cybersecurity Framework do seminar participants think are the most important? Why?
- Are seminar participants knowledgeable of alternatives to the Cybersecurity Framework that help organizations in determining the status of their cybersecurity efforts? If yes, what are those alternatives?

Key Terms

category: the subdivision of a function into groups of cybersecurity outcomes, closely tied to programmatic needs and particular activities. Examples of categories include asset management, access control, and detection processes

critical infrastructure: systems and assets, whether physical or virtual, so vital to the United States that the incapacity or destruction of such systems and assets would have a debilitating impact on cybersecurity, national economic security, national public health or safety, or any combination of those matters

cybersecurity event: a cybersecurity change that may have an impact on organizational operations (including mission, capabilities, or reputation)

framework core: a set of cybersecurity activities and references that are common across critical infrastructure sectors and are organized around particular outcomes. The Framework Core comprises four types of elements: functions, categories, subcategories, and informative references

framework implementation tiers: a lens through which to view the characteristics of an organization's approach to risk or how an organization views cybersecurity risk and the processes in place to manage that risk

framework profile: a representation of the outcomes that a particular system or organization has selected from the framework categories and subcategories

References

1. U.S. Department of Homeland Security Critical Infrastructure Sectors. October 2015. Retrieved December 8, 2016, https://www.dhs.gov/critical-infrastructure-sectors
2. The White House. *Presidential Policy Directive–Critical Infrastructure Security and Resilience (PRESIDENTIAL POLICY DIRECTIVE/PPD-21).* February 2013. Retrieved December 8, 2016, https://www.whitehouse.gov/the-press-office/2013/02/12/presidential-policy-directive-critical-infrastructure-security-and-resil
3. DHS. *Chemical Sector.* Retrieved December 8, 2016, https://www.dhs.gov/chemical-sector
4. DHS. *Commercial Facilities Sector.* Retrieved December 8, 2016, https://www.dhs.gov/commercial-facilities-sector
5. DHS. *Communications Sector.* Retrieved December 8, 2016, https://www.dhs.gov/communications-sector
6. DHS. *Critical Manufacturing Sector.* Retrieved December 8, 2016, https://www.dhs.gov/critical-manufacturing-sector
7. DHS. *Dams Sector.* Retrieved December 8, 2016, https://www.dhs.gov/dams-sector
8. DHS. *Defense Industrial Base Sector.* Retrieved December 8, 2016, https://www.dhs.gov/defense-industrial-base-sector
9. DHS. *Emergency Services Sector.* Retrieved December 8, 2016, https://www.dhs.gov/emergency-services-sector
10. DHS. *Energy Sector.* Retrieved December 8, 2016, https://www.dhs.gov/energy-sector
11. DHS. *Financial Services Sector.* Retrieved December 8, 2016, https://www.dhs.gov/financial-services-sector
12. DHS. *Food and Agriculture Sector.* Retrieved December 8, 2016, https://www.dhs.gov/food-and-agriculture-sector
13. DHS. *Government Facilities Sector.* Retrieved December 8, 2016, https://www.dhs.gov/government-facilities-sector
14. DHS. *Healthcare and Public Health Sector.* Retrieved December 8, 2016, https://www.dhs.gov/healthcare-public-health-sector
15. DHS. *Information Technology Sector.* Retrieved December 8, 2016, https://www.dhs.gov/information-technology-sector
16. DHS. *Nuclear Reactors, Materials, and Waste Sector.* Retrieved December 8, 2016, https://www.dhs.gov/nuclear-reactors-materials-and-waste-sector
17. DHS. *Transportation Systems Sector.* Retrieved December 8, 2016, https://www.dhs.gov/transportation-systems-sector
18. DHS. *Water and Wastewater Systems Sector.* Retrieved December 8, 2016, https://www.dhs.gov/water-and-wastewater-systems-sector
19. DHS. *Office of Cybersecurity and Communications.* Retrieved December 8, 2016, https://www.dhs.gov/office-cybersecurity-and-communications
20. DHS. *Office of Cyber and Infrastructure Analysis (OCIA).* Retrieved December 8, 2016, https://www.dhs.gov/office-cyber-infrastructure-analysis
21. The White House Office of the Press Secretary. *Executive Order Improving Critical Infrastructure Cybersecurity.* February 12, 2013. Retrieved December 8, 2016, https://www.whitehouse.gov/the-press-office/2013/02/12/executive-order-improving-critical-infrastructure-cybersecurity

22. NIST. *Framework for Improving Critical Infrastructure Cybersecurity Version 1.0*. February 12, 2014. Retrieved December 9, 2016, https://www.nist.gov/cyberframework

23. GAO. *Critical Infrastructure Protection: Sector-Specific Agencies Need to Better Measure Cybersecurity Progress*. GAO-16-79: November 19, 2015. Retrieved December 9, 2016, http://www.gao.gov/products/GAO-16-79

Chapter 12

Cybersecurity Research for Consumer Protection

A considerable amount of cybersecurity research is directed at protecting the national infrastructure and the military capability of the United States. However, there are several research initiatives that are definitely focused on protecting consumers. Agencies like the Food and Drug Administration (FDA), the National Highway Transportation Safety Administration (NHTSA), and the Federal Aviation Administration (FAA) have specific responsibilities to protect the general public. This chapter examines some of the cybersecurity research efforts that are directed at protecting consumers.

12.1 Automotive Cybersecurity and Automated Vehicle Research

Cybersecurity, within the context of road vehicles, is the protection of automotive electronic systems, communication networks, control algorithms, software, users, and underlying data from malicious attacks, damage, unauthorized access, or manipulation. A top USDOT priority is enhancing vehicle cybersecurity to mitigate cyber threats that could present unreasonable safety risks to the public or compromise sensitive information such as consumers' personal data. On behalf of USDOT, the NHTSA is actively engaged in vehicle cybersecurity research and employs a proactive and collaborative approach to protect vehicle owners from safety-related cybersecurity risks. NHTSA has been actively engaging stakeholders and working to broadly enhance cybersecurity capabilities.

NHTSA believes that it important for the automotive industry to make vehicle cybersecurity an organizational priority. This includes proactively adopting and using well-researched available guidance and existing standards and best practices. Prioritizing vehicle cybersecurity also means establishing other internal processes and strategies to ensure that systems will be reasonably safe under expected real-world conditions, including those that may arise due to potential vehicle cybersecurity vulnerabilities.

NHTSA cybersecurity research focuses on solutions to harden the vehicle's electronic architecture against potential attacks and to ensure that vehicle systems take appropriate and safe actions, even when an attack is successful. A layered approach to vehicle cybersecurity reduces the probability of an attack's success and mitigates the ramifications of potential unauthorized access. The following fundamental vehicle cybersecurity protections serve as a small subset of potential actions which can move the motor vehicle industry toward a more cyber-aware posture:

■ Limit developer/debugging access in production devices
■ Control keys
■ Control vehicle maintenance diagnostic access
■ Control access to firmware
■ Limit ability to modify firmware
■ Control proliferation of network ports, protocols, and services
■ Use segmentation and isolation techniques in vehicle architecture design
■ Control internal vehicle communications
■ Log events
■ Control communication to back-end servers
■ Control wireless interfaces

NHTSA cybersecurity research has also shown that the automotive industry should consider that consumers may bring aftermarket devices (e.g., insurance dongles) and personal equipment (e.g., cell phones) onto cars and connect them with vehicle systems through the interfaces that manufacturers provide (Bluetooth, USB, OBD-II port, etc.). The automotive industry should consider the incremental risks that could be presented by these devices and provide reasonable protections.

In addition, aftermarket device manufacturers should consider that their devices are interfaced with CPS and could impact safety-of-life. Even though the primary purpose of the system may not be safety related (e.g., telematics device collecting fleet operational data), if not properly protected, they could be used as proxy to influence the safety-critical system behavior on vehicles. Aftermarket devices could be also brought on to all ages and types of vehicles with varying levels of cybersecurity protections on the vehicle side of the interface. Therefore, these devices should include strong cybersecurity protections on the units since they could impact the safety of vehicles regardless of their intended primary function. NHTSA urges that the NIST RMF Security Life Cycle and NIST standards be used in the process.

In addition, NHTSA cybersecurity research has also shown that the automotive industry should also consider the serviceability of vehicle components and systems by individuals and third parties. The automotive industry should provide strong vehicle cybersecurity protections that do not unduly restrict access by authorized alternative third-party repair services.[1]

Automated Vehicle Research is another area where the USDOT's Intelligent Transportation System Joint Program Office (ITS JPO) has established a program within the overall ITS program. As a first step, the program has developed a 2015–2019 Multimodal Program Plan for Vehicle Automation, a key component of the ITS JPO's ITS Strategic Plan 2015–2019. The program plan establishes the vision, role, and goals, as well as a broad research roadmap for automation research. USDOT cybersecurity research aims to enable and accelerate the development and deployment of automated vehicles; ensure safe and efficient operations of emerging technologies and systems; and maximize public benefits by leveraging connected vehicle technologies, infrastructure-based solutions, and other approaches.

There are critical research questions regarding driver transitions between automated and manual driving modes, such as how drivers perform over time when using these systems. An initial study, funded by the NHTSA and the ITS JPO, addressed human factors research questions focused on drivers transitioning into and out of *automated driving*. The results support development of initial human factors driver-vehicle interface principles. Project partners include the Virginia Tech Transportation Institute, Battelle, Bishop Consulting, General Motors, Google, and the Southwest Research Institute.[2] Additional current research includes

- Introduction of cooperative vehicle-highway systems to improve speed harmonization
- Simulation for research on automated longitudinal vehicle control
- High-performance vehicle streams simulation
- Partial automation for *truck platooning* (Port Authority Trans-Hudson Corporation/Caltrans)
- Development of a platform technology for automated vehicle research
- Vehicle automation program management and planning
- Human factors evaluation of level 2 and level 3 automated driving concepts
- Cooperative adaptive cruise control investigation of key human factors issues
- Development of functional descriptions and test methods for emerging automated vehicle applications
- Transportation system benefit study of highly automated vehicles
- Lane changing/merge foundational research[3]

12.2 Cybersecurity Research for eEnabled Aircraft

The FAA has been focusing some of its cybersecurity research efforts on the rapidly changing design of commercial aircraft. Just over a decade ago, the potential for cybersecurity issues in new commercial aircraft and in the systems that communicate wirelessly between aircraft, airport ground equipment, and flight control systems began to emerge. Aircraft Original Equipment Manufacturers (OEMs) are developing *eEnabled* technologies that they are increasingly deploying into aircraft. The definition of eEnabled is any device, system, or combination of devices/components and systems that communicate with technologies other than point-to-point including interfaces between aircraft components and interfaces between aircraft and off-aircraft entities. Examples of eEnabled technologies include electronic flight bags (EFBs), WANs, cellular, Wi-Fi—802.11b/g, and Ethernet.

Legacy aircraft (e.g., B737, A320) have limited connections with external networks such as EFBs, Gatelink, and wireless Local Area Networks (LANs). However, eEnabled aircraft (e.g., B787, B747-8, A380, Bombardier C-Series) have many new and integrated external network connections (e.g., software data loading, broadband 802.11 connections, etc.) with airlines, airports, aircraft manufacturers, air navigation service providers, and repair organizations. The introduction of eEnabled technologies into new commercial aircraft is leading to unprecedented global connectivity that creates a new environment for the aviation sector. Aircraft navigation and communication functions are transitioning from operating as isolated and independent systems, to being integrated into a networked system that is dependent on exchanging digital information between the eEnabled aircraft and external networks located on the ground and on other eEnabled aircraft.

Due to the proliferation of these new connective technologies, it became necessary to reexamine security and safety of the aircraft to protect it against unwanted cyber intrusion. It would be essential to include cybersecurity within the certification criteria and processes. In addition, the FAA recommends that the cybersecurity approach of the new eEnabled aircraft should be coordinated with the move toward the Next Generation Air Traffic Control (NextGen) system, NextGen. In that major initiative, the FAA will be addressing cybersecurity throughout the aviation and air transportation sectors.[4]

NextGen will evolve from a ground-based system of air traffic control to a satellite-based system of air traffic management which includes enhanced use of GPS and weather systems, as well as enhanced data networking and the use of digital communications. Security architectures and information sharing will be a vital element of this highly connected system, ensuring all system elements maintain appropriate levels of trust. This highly connected NextGen environment parallels the move toward connected vehicle systems and applications where automobiles and infrastructure will be connected.

In 2007, the FAA engaged the Volpe Center to research the requirements for airborne network security to ensure aircraft safety. The study required robust involvement from other government agencies including DHS and DoD, aircraft OEMs, suppliers, and academia. Because the cybersecurity of aircraft should be an international effort, the government of the United Kingdom was also involved.

Also in 2007, the FAA helped lead the establishment of a standards development group in the Radio Technical Commission for Aeronautics (RTCA). This group (SC-216) developed the Security Assurance and Assessment Processes for Safety-related Aircraft Systems (DO-326). Published in December 2010, this process document is intended to augment current guidance for aircraft certification to handle the information security threat. It addresses only aircraft type certification but is intended as the first of a series of documents on aeronautical systems security that together will address information security for the overall Aeronautical Information System Security (AISS) of airborne systems with related ground systems and environment.

The FAA has also staffed an internal national cybersecurity team to research and work on developing a standardized approach to address the cybersecurity vulnerabilities of aircraft equipment being installed during type certification, amended type certification, supplemental type certification (STC), and field approval projects throughout the Aircraft Certification Service and Flight Standards Service. Future work activities by the RTCA SC-216 group include examination and update of the FAA Instructions for Continued Airworthiness Order to address operational cybersecurity guidance for airline and maintenance repair organizations for eEnabled aircraft.

In order to gain hands-on understanding and experience regarding how the various eEnabled components were integrated and what cybersecurity vulnerabilities may be present, the FAA engaged the Volpe Center and Wichita State University (WSU) to develop the airborne network security simulator (ANSS). The goals for ANSS are to

- Identify potential information security threats in a synthetic environment by simulating next generation aircraft communications systems
- Share knowledge, tools, and methodologies with academia and other interested stakeholders to extend research value
- Act as a coordinating authority for cybersecurity risk mitigation within the international aerospace and aviation community
- Recommend appropriate technical and procedural standards for security risks to aid in the development of regulatory guidelines and policies
- Influence industry bodies on cybersecurity best practice with respect to specifications, procedures, and recommendations used by the industry

One of the key issues in the cybersecurity challenge for the FAA is that, at this time, aircraft are not fully integrated with all of the eEnabled technologies and systems. This creates a difficult type certification (TC) and STC problem with respect to cybersecurity.

A different set of challenges may emerge as many of the legacy aircraft may be retrofitted with newer avionics as required to operate in a NextGen (U.S.) or Single European Sky ATM Research, SESAR (Europe) operational environment. Even older legacy aircraft will need to consider the importance of cybersecurity. Many scheduled for retrofit with the newer technology are subject to the same cybersecurity threats. This also increases complexity to the STC process by requiring a new security baseline for each aircraft model and subtype configuration.

The challenge will be how to properly mitigate and manage the installation and use of newer IP-enabled external networks onto a legacy aircraft that was not originally designed to provide such capabilities. While the existing backplane has fewer capabilities for an external access to any part of the aircraft, previously isolated systems were never designed to protect or manage themselves while operating with some of the newer external access methods.[5]

In 2010, the FAA and Volpe Center conducted a survey of aircraft OEMs, supply chain vendors, type certification inspection (DERs), and government/military organizations. The goal of the study was to gather information to be used to aid in future FAA planning related to regulations, directives, standards, guidance, training, and research regarding aircraft network security.

The survey results showed that the vast majority of respondents had aggressive plans for developing and adding eEnabled technologies into airframes: 63% of organizations planned to include eEnabled technologies and within three to five years and that number would grow to 83%. The inclusion of these technologies is a logical business decision for aircraft manufacturers and airlines.

STC involving the incorporation of eEnabled technologies on legacy aircraft as well as the need to type certify new aircraft that are eEnabled will be a major workload for the FAA in the next few years. In addition, the survey findings show the need for eEnabled certification will expand by 63% to 83% over the next five years. This will influence the FAA in the following areas:

- FAA workload increases and workforce cybersecurity training increases
- OEM workload increases and workforce cybersecurity training increases
- Airline workload increases and workforce cybersecurity training increases
- Need for additional policy and rulemaking
- Supply chain issues—the need to ensure cybersecurity requirements are communicated and met by sub-tier vendors[6]

12.3 Cybersecurity Research for Medical Devices and Hospital Networks

The U.S. FDA has for several years been aware of cybersecurity vulnerabilities and incidents that could directly impact medical devices or hospital network operations. Many medical devices contain *configurable embedded computer systems* that can be vulnerable to cybersecurity breaches. In addition, as medical devices are increasingly interconnected, via the Internet, hospital networks, other medical devices, and smartphones, there is an increased risk of cybersecurity breaches, which could affect how a medical device operates.

The FDA is researching cybersecurity issues in medical devices and recommends that manufacturers and health care facilities take steps to assure that appropriate safeguards are in place to reduce the risk of failure due to cyberattack, which could be initiated by the introduction of malware into medical equipment or unauthorized access to configuration settings in medical devices and hospital networks.

The FDA has also recommended that hospitals and health care facilities take steps to evaluate network security and protect hospital systems. In evaluating network security, hospitals and health care facilities should consider

- Restricting unauthorized access to the network and networked medical devices
- Making certain appropriate antivirus software and firewalls are up to date
- Monitoring network activity for unauthorized use
- Protecting individual network components through routine and periodic evaluation, including updating security patches and disabling all unnecessary ports and services
- Developing and evaluating strategies to maintain critical functionality during adverse conditions[7]

The FDA cybersecurity research findings have evolved into a guidance document entitled Content of Premarket Submissions for Management of Cybersecurity in Medical Devices, which recommends that manufacturers consider cybersecurity risks as part of the design and development of a medical device. Then also submit documentation to the FDA about the risks identified and controls in place to mitigate those risks. The guidance also recommends that manufacturers submit their plans for providing patches and updates to operating systems and medical software.

As medical devices become more interconnected and interoperable, they can improve the care patients receive and create efficiencies in the healthcare system. Some medical devices, like computer systems, can be vulnerable to security breaches, potentially impacting the safety and effectiveness of the device. By carefully considering possible cybersecurity risks while designing medical devices, and having a plan to manage system or software updates, manufacturers can reduce the vulnerability in their medical devices.

The FDA's concerns about cybersecurity vulnerabilities include malware infections on network-connected medical devices or computers, smartphones, and tablets used to access patient data; unsecured or uncontrolled distribution of passwords; failure to provide timely security software updates and patches to medical devices and networks; and security vulnerabilities in off-the-shelf software designed to prevent unauthorized access to the device or network. The FDA has been working closely with other federal agencies and the medical device industry to identify and communicate with stakeholders about vulnerabilities.[8]

12.4 Cybersecurity Research for Protecting Personal Technologies

The NSF has funded several research projects designed to protect consumers that use *personal mobile technologies*. Those research projects are covered in more depth in Chapter 8. A brief summary of each project included in Chapter 8 is as follows:

- Pocket Security Smartphone Cybercrime in the Wild studies how, when, and where people use smartphones and the relationship between these usage patterns and the likelihood of being a victim of cybercrime. This research is the first step to a better scientific understanding how the physical world surrounding smartphones use enables cybercrime.[9]
- Technological Con-Artistry: An Analysis of Social Engineering is a study of one of the most serious threats in the world today to the security of cyberspace. Social engineering is a process by which people with access to critical information regarding information systems security are tricked or manipulated into surrendering such information to unauthorized persons, thereby allowing access to otherwise secure systems. This research will examine who social engineers are, why they engage in social engineering, the processes they use to conceive of and implement social engineering projects, and how they view information privacy and security and justify their behavior.[10]
- A Socio-Technical Approach to Privacy in a Camera-Rich World project is designed to a gain a deeper understanding of the privacy implications of camera technologies from both a social and technical perspective. Cameras are now pervasive on consumer devices, including smartphones, laptops, tablets, and new wearable devices like Google Glass and the Narrative Clip lifelogging camera.[11]
- Security and Privacy for Wearable and Continuous Sensing Platforms research project studies security and privacy for wearable devices. These devices offer many benefits to end users in terms of real-time access to information and the augmentation of human memory, but they are also likely to introduce new and complex privacy and security problems.[12]

In October 2014, the NIST established the NCCoE's with the goal of accelerating the adoption of secure technologies to address the most pressing cybersecurity challenges.[13] NCCoE's cybersecurity research on personal mobile technologies are covered in more depth in Chapter 9 and include

- Derived PIV Credentials will help businesses authenticate individuals who use mobile devices and need access to controlled facilities, information systems, and applications. The goal of the building block effort is to demonstrate a feasible security platform based on federal PIV standards.[14]
- MDS poses a unique set of challenges to individuals and enterprises. A set of security controls and countermeasures that address mobile threats in a holistic manner must be identified, necessitating a broader view of the entire mobile security ecosystem. This view must go beyond devices to include, as an example, the cellular networks and cloud infrastructure used to support mobile applications and native mobile services.[15]

As part of ongoing research to help prevent and mitigate disruptions to computer networks on the Internet, researchers at Sandia National Laboratories in California have turned their attention to smartphones and other handheld computing devices. Sandia cyber researchers linked together 300,000 virtual handheld computing devices running the Android operating system so they can study large networks of smartphones and find ways to make them more reliable and secure. Ultimately, the tool will enable the computing industry to better protect handheld devices from malicious intent. The Android project, dubbed MegaDroid, is expected to help researchers at Sandia and elsewhere who struggle to understand large-scale networks. The main challenge in studying Android-based machines is the sheer complexity of the software. Google, which developed the Android operating system, wrote some 14 million lines of code into the software, and the system runs on top of a Linux kernel, which more than doubles the amount of code.[16] More detail on this project is provided in Chapter 10.

12.5 The U.S. Federal Trade Commission Focus on Consumer Protection

The U.S. Federal Trade Commission (FTC) is the nation's consumer protection agency. The FTC works to prevent fraudulent, deceptive, and unfair business practices in the marketplace and to protect the security and privacy of consumers. The FTC is the only federal agency with both consumer protection and competition jurisdiction in broad sectors of the economy. The FTC pursues vigorous and effective law enforcement; advances consumers' interests by sharing its expertise with federal and state legislatures and U.S. and international government agencies; develops policy and research tools through hearings, workshops, and conferences; and creates practical and plain-language educational programs for consumers and businesses in a global marketplace with constantly changing technologies. The FTC's work is performed by the Bureaus of Consumer Protection, Competition and Economics.[17]

The IoT has the potential to offer enormous benefits to consumers. Innovative companies are already selling connected devices, apps, sensors, services, etc., unlike anything that has been done before. As with any online activity, it is important to protect consumers' sensitive data from thieves. The IoT, however, adds new security dimensions to consider. For example, an insecure connection could give a hacker access not just to the confidential information transmitted by the device, but to everything else on a user's network. And in the IoT, the risk is not just to data. If a home automation system is not secure, a criminal could override the settings to unlock the doors. And just think of the consequences if a hacker were able to remotely recalibrate a medical device.

Businesses and law enforcers have a shared interest in ensuring that consumers' expectations about the security of these new products are met. Like any other industry in its infancy, the IoT must prove itself worthy of consumer confidence. When it comes to security, technology is ever-changing, but certain time-tested tenets have emerged. Based on input from industry, consumers, academics, and others, the FTC has researched the challenges to creating a secure IoT and developed a series of principles that companies should consider when designing and marketing products that will be connected to the IoT:

- Encourage a culture of security at your company. Designate a senior executive who will be responsible for product security.
- Train staff to recognize vulnerabilities and reward them when they speak up. If you work with service providers, clearly articulate in contracts the high standards demanded from them.
- Implement security by design rather than grafting security on as an afterthought and build it into products or services at the outset of the planning process.
- Implement a defense-in-depth approach that incorporates security measures at several levels.
- Walk through how consumers will use the product or service in a day-to-day setting to identify potential risks and possible security soft spots.
- Carefully consider the risks presented by the collection and retention of consumer information.
- Default passwords quickly become widely known. Do not use them unless you require consumers to change the default during set-up.
- Standard encryption techniques are available for data the device transmits and for what it stores. Select stronger encryption methods over weaker ones (e.g., you can do better than Wired Equivalent Privacy [WEP]).
- Add random data to hashed data to make it harder for attackers to compromise.
- Consider using rate limiting, a system for controlling the traffic sent or received by a network to reduce the risk of automated attacks.

- Consider investing additional resources in the design, implementation, and testing of authentication. If the risks are substantial, is it appropriate to put two-factor authentication in place, for example, requiring the use of a password and a secure token.
- Consider how to limit permissions.
- Take advantage of readily available security tools.
- Test the security measures before launching the product.
- Select the secure choice as the default setting.
- Use initial communications with customers to educate them about the safest use of the product.
- Establish an effective approach for updating security procedures.
- Keep your ear to the ground. Some recent law enforcement actions have cited companies' failure to follow up when credible sources warned them about security vulnerabilities in their products. It is wise to take advantage of the wealth of expertise that is already out there and listen to what people are saying about the products and the technologies used.
- Use a set-up wizard to walk consumers through the process of implementing security features.
- Build in a dashboard or profile management portal to make it easier for consumers to find the security settings for the device, configure them, and change them later.
- Use icons, lights, or other methods to signal when an update is available or when the device is connected to the Internet.[18]

12.6 The IoT Learns to Fly with Unmanned Aircraft Systems

Talk about complicated! An unmanned aircraft system (UAS) is an unmanned aircraft (UA) with associated support equipment, control station, data links, telemetry, communications, and navigation equipment necessary to operate it. A UA is considered an aircraft under both 49 U.S.C. § 40102 and 14 C.F.R. § 1.1. Currently, the federal government has established regulations for UAS operation using U.S. codes and federal regulations on the federal level and by statute on the state level. Currently, the FAA has focused primarily on safety. While the FAA has a major roles in providing guidance and regulation for UAS operations and management, it is important to note that other users also play important roles. As such, airports, law enforcement, pilots, and the UAS operators also have important responsibilities in the safe and appropriate operation of UAS within the National Airspace System (NAS).[19]

The FAA is responsible for the safe and efficient movement of aircraft in the air and on the ground. Per the FAA Modernization and Reform Act of 2012, the FAA is amending its regulations to adopt specific rules for the operation of UAS into the

NAS. Regardless of the type of UAS operation, FAA regulations and Federal Codes prohibit any conduct that endangers individuals and property within the NAS. Specifically these guidelines:

- Require the FAA to regulate aircraft and UAS operations in the NAS (49 U.S.C. § 40103)
- Authorize government public safety agencies to operate UAS under certain restrictions (FAA: A.C.001.1-A)
- Ban all UA and remote control aircraft operations within three miles and up to 3,000 feet in altitude from all major sporting events as detailed in the Notice to Airmen (NOTAM) 4/3621

Twenty-three leading research institutions and one hundred leading industry and government partners comprise the Alliance for System Safety of UAS through Research Excellence, or ASSURE. They provide the expertise and infrastructure that the FAA Center of Excellence for Unmanned Aircraft Systems demands.[20]

The present U.S. air traffic control system is not well equipped to handle UAS traffic, underscoring the importance of the Next Generation Air Transportation System (NextGen), which will allow UAS to be operated safely and efficiently inside domestic airspace. FAA aircraft certification rules must also keep up with the demand for UAS design, production, and operation in the United States. Listed below are the different project categories for research conducted by ASSURE members and partners:

- Air traffic integration. The overall level of safety in the National Aerospace System is preserved through NAS integration, which requires adherence to rigorous airworthiness standards and airspace regulations. While they apply equally to manned aircraft, they also recognize the distinguishing characteristics of UAS. This research encompasses those UAS that operate like fixed wing manned aircraft that require use of ramps, taxiways, and runways to complete ground operations.
- Collaborative decision making (CDM) is a joint government/industry initiative aimed at improving air traffic flow management (ATFM) through increased information exchange among aviation community stakeholders. These stakeholders work together to create technological and procedural solutions to the ATFM challenges faced by the NAS. New entrants into the NAS such as UAS are not being considered.
- Airworthiness. Advances in technology have greatly increased the affordability and accessibility of UAS to potential commercial operators and the general public. Accordingly, when the FAA develops and issues regulations that enable the commercial and private operation of UAS in the NAS below 400 feet, we can expect a significant increase in the number of aircraft operating in this space. In addition to the significant number of new aircraft operating in this space, these UAS will be operating in airspace that puts them in closer

proximity to people than conventional aircraft now operate (currently it is rare for aircraft to operate in this arena).

■ Control and communication (C²) research is the development of an appropriate C² link between the UA and the control station to support the required performance of the UA in the NAS and to ensure that the pilot always maintains a threshold level of control of the aircraft. Efforts will focus on completing development of C² link assurance and mitigation technologies and methods for incorporating them into the development of standards for the certification of the UAS.

■ Detect and avoid (DAA). This research area focuses on issues related to the detection of potential threats to remain well clear and avoid collisions. It explores sensors, the data produced from sensors, the management and use of that data, and the operational outcome that is considered safe and acceptable.

■ Human factors. When the pilot controls the aircraft from a remote control station, several human factors issues emerge with respect to the pilot, the air traffic controller, and their interactions to safely operate UAS in the NAS. Human factors issues in manned aviation are well known, but further analyses regarding integration of UAS into the NAS is required.

■ Low altitude operations safety. The substantial increase in air traffic below 400 feet that is expected with the integration of small UA systems in the NAS also significantly raises the exposure of the general population to the potential effects of a UAS mishap.

■ Training. The FAA's role in training is to establish policy, guidance, and standards. Airmen training standards are under development and need to be synchronized with regulatory guidance. This research centers on UAS pilot training and pilot certification and the differences and similarities between manned and unmanned pilot training and certification.[21]

UAS holds the potential to provide significant benefits to both industry and consumers in myriad ways. These include using UAS to inspect cell phone towers without risking human lives, monitor crop growth, and take aerial photos of real estate. The best practices agreed to by privacy and consumer advocates, industry, news organizations, and trade associations represent an important step in building consumer trust, giving users the tools to innovate in this space in a manner that respects privacy, and providing accountability and transparency. The voluntary best practices are consistent with safe harbor principles and encourage UAS users to

■ Inform affected persons of UAS use and the collection of data
■ Take care in the collection and storage of information that identifies a particular person
■ Limit the use and sharing of such data
■ Secure data
■ Monitor and comply with the law as it evolves[22]

Aircraft systems information security protection (ASISP) is a major concern and there are many sources of information processing security standards and guidance that might be able to be used in the ASISP context including the FTC, Federal Information Processing Standards (FIPS), NIST Cybersecurity Framework, and the International Standards Organization (ISO) 7001 standard for information security management.[23]

12.7 Summary

Agencies like the FDA, the NHTSA, and the FAA have specific responsibilities to protect the general public. This chapter examined cybersecurity research efforts that are directed at protecting the consumer. Key points covered include

- Cybersecurity, within the context of road vehicles, is the protection of automotive electronic systems, communication networks, control algorithms, software, users, and underlying data from malicious attacks, damage, unauthorized access, or manipulation.
- A layered approach to vehicle cybersecurity reduces the probability of an attack's success and mitigates the ramifications of potential unauthorized access.
- Just over a decade ago, the potential for cybersecurity issues in new commercial aircraft and in the systems that communicate wirelessly between aircraft, airport ground equipment, and flight control systems began to emerge.
- In order to gain hands-on understanding and experience regarding how the various eEnabled components were integrated and what cybersecurity vulnerabilities may be present, FAA engaged the Volpe Center and WSU to develop the ANSS.
- The FDA has been aware of cybersecurity vulnerabilities and incidents that could directly impact medical devices or hospital network operations for several years.
- The FDA cybersecurity research findings have evolved into a guidance document entitled Content of Premarket Submissions for Management of Cybersecurity in Medical Devices.
- The NSF has funded several research projects designed to protect consumers that use personal mobile technologies.
- Sandia cyber researchers linked together 300,000 virtual handheld computing devices running on the Android operating system so they can study large networks of smartphones and find ways to make them more reliable and secure.
- The FTC is the only federal agency with both consumer protection and competition jurisdiction in broad sectors of the economy.
- The IoT has the potential to offer enormous benefits to consumers. Innovative companies are already selling connected devices, apps, sensors, services, etc.,

unlike anything that has been done before. Twenty-three leading research institutions and one hundred leading industry, government partners comprise the Alliance for System Safety of UAS through Research Excellence, or ASSURE.

12.8 Seminar Discussion Topics

Discussion topics for graduate or professional-level seminars are

- Which areas of cybersecurity research to protect consumers do seminar participants feel are the most interesting? Why?
- What experience have seminar participants had working in any of the areas of cybersecurity research designed to protect consumers?
- What experience have seminar participants had with government agencies, private corporations, or academic institutions that have worked with any of the research initiatives designed to protect consumers?

Key Terms

automated driving: operating a vehicle that performs one or more driving functions through the use of vehicle automation systems

configurable embedded computer systems: a computer system that is embedded in another device which can be configured prior to embedding as well as after installation

eEnabled: is any device, system, or combination of devices/components and systems that communicate with technologies other than point-to-point including interfaces between aircraft components and interfaces between aircraft and off-aircraft entities

personal mobile technologies: include individually owned devices such as cell phones, tablets, laptops, and digital media

truck platooning: is an extension of cooperative adaptive cruise control and forward collision avoidance technology that provides automated lateral and longitudinal vehicle control to maintain a tight formation of vehicles with short following distances

References

1. USDOT. *National Highway Traffic Safety Administration. Cybersecurity Best Practices for Modern Vehicles.* (Report No. DOT HS 812 333). October, 2016. Retrieved December 7, 2016, http://www.nhtsa.gov/staticfiles/nvs/pdf/812333_ CybersecurityForModernVehicles.pdf

2. USDOT. *Intelligent Transportation System Joint Program Office. Automated Vehicle Research*. Retrieved December 7, 2016, http://www.its.dot.gov/automated_vehicle/avr_plan.htm

3. USDOT. *National Highway Traffic Safety Administration. A Summary of Cybersecurity Best Practices*. October 2014. Retrieved December 7, 2016, http://ntl.bts.gov/lib/52000/52800/52889/812075_CybersecurityBestPractices.pdf

4. FAA. *2016 National Aviation Research Plan (NARP)*. Retrieved December 7, 2016, https://www.faa.gov/about/office_org/headquarters_offices/ang/offices/tc/about/campus/faa_host/rdm/media/pdf/2016narp.pdf

5. FAA. *Handbook for Networked Local Area Networks in Aircraft*. Retrieved December 7, 2016, https://www.faa.gov/aircraft/air_cert/design_approvals/air_software/media/ar-08-35.pdf

6. USDOT. *National Transportation Systems Center. About*. Retrieved December 7, 2016, https://www.volpe.dot.gov/about-us

7. FDA. *Cybersecurity for Medical Devices and Hospital Networks: FDA Safety Communication*. June 17, 2013. Retrieved December 7, 2016, http://www.fda.gov/Safety/MedWatch/SafetyInformation/SafetyAlertsforHumanMedicalProducts/ucm357090.htm

8. FDA. *The FDA Takes Steps to Strengthen Cybersecurity of Medical Devices*.

9. NSF. *Pocket Security—Smartphone Cybercrime in the Wild. Award Abstract # 1619084*. September 12, 2016. Retrieved November 29, 2016, https://www.nsf.gov/awardsearch/showAward?AWD_ID=1619084&HistoricalAwards=false

10. NSF Technological Con-Artistry: An Analysis of Social Engineering. *Award Abstract #1616804*. September 6, 2016. Retrieved November 29, 2016, https://www.nsf.gov/awardsearch/showAward?AWD_ID=1616804&HistoricalAwards=false

11. NSF. *A Socio-Technical Approach to Privacy in a Camera-Rich World. Award Abstract #1408730*. August 26, 2014. Retrieved November 30, 2016, https://www.nsf.gov/awardsearch/showAward?AWD_ID=1408730&HistoricalAwards=false/

12. NSF. *Security and Privacy for Wearable and Continuous Sensing Platforms. Award Abstract #1513584*. January 25, 2016. Retrieved November 30, 2016, https://www.nsf.gov/awardsearch/showAward?AWD_ID=1513584&HistoricalAwards=false

13. NIST. *About the National Cybersecurity Center of Excellence*. Retrieved December 4, 2016, https://nccoe.nist.gov/sites/default/files/library/fact-sheets/nccoe-fact-sheet.pdf

14. NCCoE. *Derived PIV Credentials*. Retrieved December 4, 2016, http://nccoe.nist.gov/projects/building_blocks/piv_credentials

15. NCCoE. *Mobile Device Security*. Retrieved December 4, 2016, http://nccoe.nist.gov/projects/building_blocks/mobile_device_security

16. Sandia National Laboratories. *Cyber and Physical Security*. Retrieved December 4, 2016, http://energy.sandia.gov/energy/ssrei/gridmod/cyber-security-for-electric-infrastructure/

17. FTC. *About the FTC*. Retrieved December 7, 2016, https://www.ftc.gov/about-ftc

18. FTC. *Careful Connections: Building Security in the Internet of Things*. Retrieved December 7, 2016, https://www.ftc.gov/tips-advice/business-center/guidance/careful-connections-building-security-internet-things

19. Florida Department of Transportation. *Unmanned Aircraft Systems (UAS)*. Retrieved December 8, 2016, http://www.fdot.gov/aviation/uas.shtm

20. FAA Center of Excellence for Unmanned Aircraft Systems. *ASSURE*. Retrieved December 8, 2016, http://www.assureuas.org/index.php

21. FAA Center of Excellence for Unmanned Aircraft Systems. *Research Focus Areas.* Retrieved December 8, 2016, http://www.assureuas.org/projects/

22. U.S. Department of Commerce. *Finding Common Ground on Unmanned Aircraft Systems (UAS).* May 19, 2016. Retrieved December 8, 2016, https://www.commerce.gov/news/blog/2016/05/finding-common-ground-unmanned-aircraft-systems-uas

23. FAA. UAS Integration Office. *FAA Unmanned Aircraft Systems (UAS) Cyber Security Initiatives.* February 11, 2015. Retrieved December 8, 2016, http://csrc.nist.gov/groups/SMA/ispab/documents/minutes/2015-02/2015-feb_george-ispab.pdf

Chapter 13

Cybersecurity Usability Obstacles and Research

Usability has only recently become an important concern in the cybersecurity field. The cybersecurity field is relatively young and but there is a growing recognition of the fact that users themselves are a key component in organizational security programs. If users find a cybersecurity measure too difficult, they will try to circumvent it which of course harms organizational and personal security. Therefore, it is in every organization's interest to design cybersecurity measures in such a way that they take into account the perceptions, characteristics, needs, abilities, and behaviors of users themselves.[1] This chapter covers the usability research and how that is being applied to cybersecurity as well as some of the many obstacles to usability.

13.1 The NIST Usability of Cybersecurity Team

The NIST Usability of Cybersecurity Team is part of the CNCI Research and Development effort. The multidisciplinary team includes experts in computer science, cognitive psychology, cybersecurity, and HCI. As a relatively young field, cybersecurity usability has little empirical data from which to develop usability best practices.

Usability is very context specific and influenced by a number of factors, such as the nature of the user population, organizational culture, and the specifications of the organization's systems and cybersecurity measures themselves. The goal of the team is to provide guidance for policymakers, system engineers, and security professionals so that they can make better decisions that enhance the usability of cybersecurity in their organizations. Ideally, these decisions should

■ Have a basis in real empirical data
■ Create solutions that are secure in practice, not just in theory
■ Take user needs and behavior into account

The NIST Usability of Cybersecurity Team conducts research into specific areas of cybersecurity usability in order to gather empirical data and discover best practices. This includes research on passwords, password policies, and password typing studies that explore the relationship between password length, complexity of the password rules, and human memory. In addition, the team studies multi-factor authentication and users' perception of security and privacy in order to determine users' mental models and develop personas, training, educational requirements, and integrating the usability, security, and software engineering life cycles.[2]

Other NIST usability research is being conducted in collaboration with the Office of the National Coordinator (ONC) for Health Information Technology (HIT) and the Agency for Healthcare Research and Quality (AHRQ). The project is a multiyear research program aimed at building a principled framework for measuring the usability of healthcare IT systems. The ultimate goal is to discover principles for how systems can be built to prevent critical errors and promote safe, effective, and efficient use by all end users (doctors, nurses, administrators, patients, and others). The research program is proceeding on two tracks:

■ The human factors tasks, users, and systems track examines key scenarios of use, describes user populations and their characteristics, and identifies the key design features of healthcare IT systems that lead to usability successes and failures.
■ The organizational usability processes track focuses on existing usability engineering practices in HIT organizations. The practices will be compared to industry standards and best practices. The collaboration also will research existing methodologies for formal usability evaluation to inform our efforts to develop usability assessment procedures.[3]

HIT holds significant potential to provide tools, electronic health records (EHR) in particular, that enables the healthcare system to better respond to the healthcare needs of American diversity and avoids disparities from occurring. To ensure that EHRs can live up to that potential, NIST and Johns Hopkins are partnering in a research program aimed at developing human factors guidelines for preventing disparities related to EHR adoption. The objectives of the research are to ensure

■ Clinical personnel EHR use is not associated with unintended consequences that lead to the creation or exacerbation of healthcare disparities
■ EHR design and development workers have the needed resources and guidance to support the most usable and accessible EHR system development

NIST will employ the research findings to develop technical guidance that provides the basis for HIT design decisions (based on universal design principles) that will decrease or eliminate potential health-care disparities among end users. Implementing identified best practices and comprehensive technical guidelines will help support safe, effective, error-free EHR use among an increasingly diverse population of potential users.

Accessibility barriers to HIT devices for the one in five Americans with disabilities are a closely related area of concern that electronic health record systems (EHRs) have the potential to address. By providing guidance for HIT design, NIST has an opportunity to achieve a nationwide impact that is truly welcoming to all people, regardless of ability. Even though Section 508 applies only to the federal sector, NIST believes it is important to promote the use of accessibility standards on a voluntary basis. For that reason, NIST supports HIT standards for accessibility of electronic and IT promulgated by the U.S. Access Board. It also is working to develop test methods to validate HIT accessibility conformance. The positive impact of accessible HIT includes not only improved health, but also improvements in the employment and education of people with disabilities.[4]

NIST participates on the ISO/IEC JTC 1/SC 7 and ISO/TC 159/SC 4 as the WG28 Joint Working Group, U.S. delegation co-convener, to develop standards for usability documentation. This family of documents provides a definition of the type and scope of formats and the high-level structure to be used for documenting required usability information and the results of usability evaluation. These standards define the content of the context of use, user needs, user requirements, user interaction specification, UI specification, user report format, and field data report.[5]

13.2 The Basics of Usability Research

Cybersecurity usability is a new field but usability research and testing are rather well-established disciplines. The research and analysis of *user experience (UX)* focuses on gaining a deep understanding of users, what they need, what they value, their abilities, and also their limitations.[6] *Usability testing* refers to evaluating a product or service by testing it with representative users. During a test, participants will try to complete typical tasks while observers watch, listen, and take notes. The goal is to identify any usability problems, collect qualitative and quantitative data, and determine the participant's satisfaction with the product.[6]

Usability testing lets the design and development teams identify problems before they are built into a product. The earlier the issues are identified and fixed, the less expensive the fixes will be in terms of both staff time and possible impact to the product development schedule and time to market. During a usability test, researchers

- Learn if participants are able to complete specified tasks successfully
- Identify how long it takes to complete specified tasks

- Find out how satisfied participants are with a website or other product
- Identify changes required to improve user performance and satisfaction
- Analyze the performance to see if it meets usability objectives

Effective usability testing does not require a formal usability lab for testing. It can be done in a fixed laboratory having two or three connected rooms outfitted with audiovisual equipment or in any space as long as someone is observing the user and taking notes. Testing costs depend on the type of testing performed, size of testing team, and the number of participants for testing.[7]

The *System Usability Scale (SUS)* provides a quick and dirty reliable tool for measuring usability. It consists of a 10-item questionnaire with five response options for respondents; from strongly agree to strongly disagree. It allows developers and testers to evaluate a wide variety of products and services, including hardware, software, mobile devices, websites, and applications. SUS has become an industry standard, with references in over 1,300 articles and publications. The noted benefits of using SUS include that it

- Is a very easy scale to administer to participants
- Can be used on small sample sizes with reliable results
- Is valid and it can effectively differentiate between usable and unusable systems

When a SUS is used, participants are asked to score the following 10 items with one of five responses that range from strongly agree to strongly disagree:

1. I think that I would like to use this system frequently
2. I found the system unnecessarily complex
3. I thought the system was easy to use
4. I think that I would need the support of a technical person to be able to use this system
5. I found the various functions in this system were well integrated
6. I thought there was too much inconsistency in this system
7. I would imagine that most people would learn to use this system very quickly
8. I found the system very cumbersome to use
9. I felt very confident using the system.
10. I needed to learn a lot of things before I could get going with this system

Interpreting scoring can be complex. The participant's scores for each question are converted to a new number, added together, and then multiplied by 2.5 to convert the original scores of 0–40 to 0–100. Though the scores are 0–100, these are not percentages and should be considered only in terms of their percentile ranking.

Based on research, a SUS score above 68 would be considered above average and anything below 68 is below average, however, the best way to interpret results involves normalizing the scores to produce a percentile ranking.[8]

The DigitalGov User Experience Program focuses exclusively on improving federal digital products such as websites, mobile sites, and APIs. The program believes that a little user research can make government a lot better and wants to help make digital products better. It teaches federal employees how to make products and services more user-friendly, save money via user research, and create successful UXs. The DigitalGov User Experience Program offers services as follows to federal agencies at no charge:

■ Usability training for federal employees: the free workshops and webinars help participants to conduct UX activities including audience research, task analysis, and usability tests and evaluations.
■ The UX community supports monthly calls, live events, and the UX listserve.
■ Usability test support through occasional educational tests to demonstrate why usability tests are so important.
■ The DigitalGov team will present to stakeholders how usability can improve government services.
■ Usability case studies that are filled with before and after screenshots of government products improved by user research.
■ Usability starter kit that has templates and samples.[9]

13.3 Usability Research Activities

A search of the NSF awards conducted in December 2016 of awards related to cybersecurity showed just over 800 awards that were addressing cybersecurity in some manner. These included awards that were related to educational programs as well as research projects. The purpose of the search was to determine if the topic of usability was being addressed in the awards. A further filtering of the awards yielded about 100 research or development projects with usability as a significant factor in the project. Examples of the types of projects with usability as a significant factor include

■ Electronic health record (EHR) systems
■ The use of communication and storage technologies by journalists
■ Increasing scientists' ability to make visualization animations and video narratives for storytelling
■ Identifying potentially problematic ballots before deploying them on Election Day
■ The development of assistive robots for healthcare
■ How people will interact with new computer systems in dual-task settings such as operating on board navigation systems while driving
■ Research on lightweight, energy-efficient, and usable security mechanisms in mobile networks for IoT applications

- Enhancing the functionality and usability of the next-generation Internet
- Research on a completely new approach to communications security in the IoT to be deployed in a greater number of security-sensitive applications
- Eye tracking technology for HCI studies, usability testing, medical research, and experiments in psychology
- Mobile UIs that are more accessible to diverse user communities
- Improving usability of two-factor authentication
- Development of compact data representations and usability driven functionalities that are privacy-preserving
- Incorporation of usable privacy technology into the social network fabric

Integration of human factors concerns into homeland security technologies is of interest to DHS. The goals are to improve utility and operator safety and assessments of public acceptance of homeland security technologies. DHS is also interested the use of technology to discern critical aspects of human behavior. Homeland Security Science, Technology, Engineering, and Math (HS-STEM) disciplines that DHS are necessary to support research associated with this area include computer science, engineering, health sciences, psychology, and social sciences.[10]

The 2002 Help America Vote Act has given NIST a key role in helping to realize nationwide improvements in voting systems. To assist the Election Assistance Commission (EAC) with the development of voluntary voting system guidelines, Help America Vote Act of 2002 (HAVA) established the Technical Guidelines Development Committee (TGDC) and directs NIST to chair the TGDC. NIST usability research activities include

- Security of computers, computer networks, and computer data storage used in voting systems
- Methods to detect and prevent fraud
- Protection of voter privacy
- The role of human factors (usability) in the design and application of voting systems, including assistive technologies for individuals with disabilities (including blindness) and varying levels of literacy[11]

The EAC's Accessible Voting Technology Initiative (AVTI) supports accessibility research on transformative technologies and approaches. Through the AVTI, the EAC has produced over 45 solutions for assisting voters with disabilities. The initiatives include the EAC's Military Heroes grant to provide assistance needed for recently injured military personnel to participate in elections. As mandated by the Help America Vote Act, the EAC Language Accessibility Program studies and promotes accessibility (usability) in voting, registration, polling places, and voting equipment. The materials they issue are the product of collaboration among working groups comprising election officials, advocacy groups, and research and public policy organizations.[12]

13.4 MDS Usability

The FTC is the only federal agency with both consumer protection and competition jurisdiction in broad sectors of the economy. The FTC pursues vigorous and effective law enforcement; advances consumers' interests by sharing its expertise with federal and state legislatures and U.S. and international government agencies; develops policy and research tools through hearings, workshops, and conferences; and creates practical and plain-language educational programs for consumers and businesses in a global marketplace with constantly changing technologies. The FTC's work is performed by the Bureaus of Consumer Protection, Competition and Economics. That work is aided by the Office of General Counsel and seven regional offices.[13]

In June 2013, the FTC hosted a public forum to examine the state of mobile security. Mobile technologies, such as smartphones and tablets provide consumers with an always-connected and convenient means of engaging in their daily activities, including email, shopping, banking, and surfing the web. While consumers reap many benefits through these technologies, they may not be aware of, or appreciate, the potential risks. Since the ordinary use of mobile devices involves the collection, transmission, and storage of consumers' sensitive personal information, mobile threats such as lost or stolen devices, or malicious or privacy-infringing applications can place consumers at serious risk of identity theft or financial harm. In light of these issues, the forum convened four panels consisting of security researchers, academics, and industry representatives to engage in a wide-ranging conversation on the mobile threat landscape, industry efforts to secure the mobile ecosystem, and consumers' mobile security expectations.

The first panel, composed of experts in mobile threat analysis, examined the most common threat vectors in the mobile environment, the likelihood that U.S. consumers will encounter these threats, and the potential evolution of these threats. Panelists agreed that due to ease-of-distribution and other factors malicious applications are the most common threat vector. Although malware infections have been relatively low in the United States, panelists warned that malicious applications are likely to become more sophisticated as their developers use advanced techniques to circumvent the defenses developed by mobile platforms.

Building on this discussion, the second panel consisted of representatives from mobile platform providers, which play a critical role in mobile security. The panel debated various approaches to mitigating mobile threats and securing the end-UX, discussing the benefits and limitations of features such as sandboxing, trusted UIs, and application review processes. Although the platforms have taken different approaches in some of these areas, the panelists all agreed that it is important to provide application developers with the resources and incentives to create secure applications.

The third panel considered the role that other members of the mobile ecosystem, such as telecommunication carriers and third-party developers, should play in ensuring end-user security. Given that the current system is complex, dynamic, and includes many players, the panelists agreed that there are unique security challenges the ecosystem faces such as inefficiencies when rolling out patches and updates, but that security should be a focal point for every player in the mobile ecosystem.

Finally, the fourth panel explored consumer behaviors with respect to mobile security. Panelists noted that even though device loss and theft are the most common problems faced by consumers, many consumers do not take advantage of existing options, such as password authentication, to protect mobile devices. The panel discussed potential solutions, such as biometrics, that may be more consumer-friendly and help drive the adoption of better security practices.[14]

After the panels, Nithan Sannappa, an attorney in the Division of Privacy and Identity Protection analyzed the content of the panels in a series of blog posts exploring several important issues regarding user privacy and security in mobile computing which are cited in this section. Key observations made by Nithan Sannappa in the posts included

- Consumers typically have a one-to-one relationship with their smartphone or other mobile device. That is, they generally do not share their smartphone with other users. In the early days of personal computing, however, multiple people often shared a single computer in places such as the office, the classroom, or the public library.
- Given these environmental conditions, desktop operating systems were primarily concerned with protecting a user's files from the potentially prying eyes of other users. Operating systems included security features such as multiple login accounts to address this threat, but typically assumed that applications installed by the user could be trusted with global access to device resources, including the user's personal information.
- With the rapid evolution of the Internet and the spread of malware, it soon became clear that not all applications could be trusted. In designing the next generation of computing devices, modern operating system architects included advanced security features, such as sandboxing to address the threats posed by untrusted applications.[15]
- There are two approaches to implementing permission-based access controls predominating in mobile operating systems: run-time and install-time. *Run-time permissions* rely on system dialogs that prompt the user when an application attempts to access a particular resource. Users can then decide, on a case-by-case basis, whether to give an application access to that resource. *Install-time permissions* require the developer to identify all of the protected resources that an application can access, and to declare these permissions at the time of installation.
- Based on the permissions displayed, the user can choose whether or not to install the application. If the user chooses to install the application, the operating system grants the application access to all of the resources specified by

the developer. As with any user-facing security feature, the usability of permissions has been widely debated in the security community.

■ Operating system architects began experimenting with permission-based access controls in the desktop era. In an effort to thwart malware, User Access Control (UAC) prompted the user with a run-time system dialog when an application attempted to perform a sensitive task. Subsequent studies, however, demonstrated that users did not necessarily understand or act appropriately when presented with the UAC run-time dialogs.

■ Moreover, researchers have noted, a decade of usability research has shown that users may become habituated to run-time warnings making them ineffective. Developers have observed that run-time dialogs in mobile operating systems can be similarly problematic since an application usually barrages users with a stack of dialogs on its first launch which can lead to the user carelessly dismissing all of them without reading them. Thus, effective usability is compromised.

■ Recent studies, however, have demonstrated that users also often ignore or do not fully understand install-time permissions. Based on experiences and the available research, there appear to be important usability concerns with both run-time and install-time permissions. In both cases, users may not fully understand the implications of granting access, or may be so habituated to the prompts that they do not pay attention when making access decisions. In light of these usability concerns, one may question whether permission-based access controls provide any value as a privacy or security-enhancing mechanism. First, researchers have demonstrated that permissions can have a positive impact in limiting application access to privacy and security-sensitive APIs. Second, researchers have noted that permissions may allow advanced users to raise concerns with developers and flag questionable application behavior for other users. Indeed, anecdotal evidence suggests that developers often respond to user concerns regarding permissions.

■ Despite a history of usability concerns, permissions appear to be a useful tool in increasing transparency and encouraging developers to adhere to the principle of least privilege. The FTC has long supported the idea of layered disclosures presented in a context that is useful for consumers. From this perspective, permissions in mobile operating systems are clearly an improvement over the opacity of traditional operating systems, which often led to disclosures buried in lengthy legal documents.

■ Nonetheless, increasing the usability and efficacy of permissions remain important challenges to address. Participants at the 2013 workshop noted that providing users with greater context regarding information flows is an important part of addressing these challenges. Researchers have applied the concept of contextual integrity to permissions suggesting that in order to minimize habituation and increase user comprehension; mobile operating systems should only ask users to make security decisions when information flows defy user expectations.

■ By providing incentives and opportunities for developers to adhere to the principle of least privilege, mobile operating systems can help minimize the situations in which users must confront such information flows. In addition, by providing greater context for access requests, mobile operating systems can help users make informed decisions about such information flows.[16]

■ With applications often using data for multiple purposes, it is unsurprising that users may question whether a defined purpose is the only use for that data. For example, an application that collects location data to support a navigation feature may also include a third-party advertising library that collects the same information to provide geo-targeted ads. With studies finding that the purpose for which an app requests a certain permission has a major impact on people's willingness to grant that permission, consumers must be able to trust developers to disclose all material purposes for an application's access to a resource. Researchers have suggested that application markets could play a role in this disclosure process.[17]

The FTC has also researched mobile apps for kids and findings raise several alarms about cybersecurity usability at disclosure on what data is being collected from their children, how it is being shared, or who will have access to it. The FTC also found that many of the apps surveyed included interactive features, such as connecting to social media, and sent information from the mobile device to ad networks, analytics companies, or other third parties, without disclosing these practices to parents.

FTC staff examined hundreds of apps for children and looked at disclosures and links on each app's promotion page in the app store, on the app developer's website, and within the app. According to the report, most apps failed to provide any information about the data collected through the app, let alone the type of data collected, the purpose of the collection, and who would obtain access to the data. Even more troubling, the results showed that many of the apps shared certain information with third parties such as device ID, geolocation, or phone number without disclosing that fact to parents so they could decide which apps to grant what permissions. In this case, cybersecurity usability was thwarted by app developers. Further, a number of apps contained interactive features such as advertising, the ability to make in-app purchases, and links to social media without disclosing these features to parents prior to download. The survey found that

■ Parents were not being provided with information about what data an app collects, who will have access to that data, and how it will be used. Only 20% of the apps staff reviewed disclosed any information about the app's privacy practices.

■ Many apps (nearly 60% of the apps surveyed) were transmitting information from a user's device back to the app developer or, more commonly, to an advertising network, analytics company, or other third party.

- A relatively small number of third parties received information from a large number of apps which means the third parties that receive information from multiple apps could potentially develop detailed profiles of the children based on their behavior in different apps.
- 58% of the apps reviewed contained advertising within the app, while only 15% disclosed the presence of advertising prior to download.
- 22% of the apps contained links to social networking services, while only 9% disclosed that fact.
- 17% of the apps reviewed allow kids to make purchases for virtual goods within the app, with prices ranging from 99 cents to $29.99. Although both app stores provided certain indicators when an app contained in-app purchasing capabilities, these indicators were not always prominent and, even if noticed, could be difficult for many parents to understand.[18]

In a follow-up study, the FTC reviewed 364 kids' apps in Google Play or the Apple App Store. It was found that164 of them (45%) had privacy policies that could be viewed from a direct link on the app store page. Of the apps surveyed, an additional 38 include privacy policies in harder-to-find places, for example, within the app or on the app developer's webpage. However, information that is difficult for parents to locate is not likely to be of much benefit to them. Of all the apps, 48 included short form disclosures in their app descriptions about the sharing of personal information with third parties, the use of persistent identifiers, in-app purchases, social network integration, or the presence of advertising. The conclusion was that a significant portion of kids' apps still leave parents in the dark about the data collected about their children.[19]

13.5 Growth in the Use of Handheld Computers for Internet Access

Cybersecurity usability is rapidly becoming more critical every year especially since there is tremendous growth in the use of handheld computing devices for Internet access. Although many American households still have desktop computers with wired Internet connections, many others also have laptops, smartphones, tablets, and other devices that connect people to the Internet via wireless modems and fixed wireless Internet networks, often with mobile broadband data plans.

There is evidence that certain groups rely on handheld computers more than others. In some cases, the pattern is similar to that of overall computer ownership, with young households reporting higher rates of having only handheld computers than older householders. In other instances, however, the pattern for using only handheld devices is directly opposite that of overall computer ownership. Black and Hispanic households, for example, were more likely than both White and Asian households to report owning only a handheld device. The same pattern appears by income, with low-income households reporting handheld ownership alone at much higher rates than more affluent households.

In 2013, 83.8% of U.S. households reported computer ownership, with 78.5% of all households having a desktop or laptop computer, and 63.6% having a handheld computer such as a smartphone or other handheld wireless computer. In 2013, 74.4% of all households reported Internet use, with 73.4% reporting a high-speed connection. The most common household connection type was via a cable modem (42.8%), followed by mobile broadband (33.1%).

The Census Bureau has asked questions in the Current Population Survey (CPS) about computer use since 1984. As part of the 2008 Broadband Data Improvement Act, the U.S. Census Bureau began asking about computer and Internet use in the 2013 American Community Survey (ACS). Federal agencies use these statistics to measure and monitor the nationwide development of broadband networks and to allocate resources intended to increase access to broadband technologies, particularly among groups with traditionally low levels of access. State and local governments can use these statistics for similar purposes. Understanding how people in specific cities and towns use computers and the Internet will also help businesses and nonprofits better serve their communities.[20]

13.6 Literacy in the United States

Literacy levels are very important when it comes to dealing with cybersecurity usability. As discussed in previous sections, in this chapter using security settings and permissions is challenging for a great many people and when they do not understand what their handheld computing device is try to tell them they often skip right through the process not knowing the potential consequences. In addition, instructions for privacy and security settings in some applications and on social media platforms can be confusing to read and take considerable time to go through and those frustrations can lead to people not selecting appropriate security settings.

The National Assessment of Adult Literacy is a nationally representative assessment of English literacy among American adults age 16 and older. Sponsored by the National Center for Education Statistics (NCES), NAAL is the nation's most comprehensive measure of adult literacy since the 1992 National Adult Literacy Survey (NALS). NAAL not only provides information on adults' literacy performance but also on related background characteristics that are of interest to researchers, practitioners, policymakers, and the general public. The ratings for different levels of literacy are defined as follows:

- Below basic: no more than the most simple and concrete literacy skills
- Basic: can perform simple and everyday literacy activities
- Intermediate: can perform moderately challenging literacy activities
- Proficient: can perform complex and challenging literacy activities

In prose literacy, or the knowledge and skills needed to understand and use information from texts including editorials, news stories, poems, and fiction there was not much change in the percentage of the U.S. population scoring in the four different levels of literacy between 1992 and 2003 (1992: below basic 14% basic 28% intermediate 43% proficient 15%) (2003: below basic 14% basic 29% intermediate 44% proficient 13%).

In document literacy or the knowledge and skills required to locate and use information contained in various formats, including job applications, payroll forms, transportation schedules, maps, tables, and graphics there was an increase in the percentage of the population that scored at the intermediate level in 2003 (1992: below basic 14% basic 22% intermediate 49% proficient 15%) (2003: below basic 12% basic 22% intermediate 53% proficient 13%).

In quantitative literacy or the knowledge and skills required to apply arithmetic operations, either alone or sequentially, to numbers embedded in printed materials, such as balancing a checkbook, calculating a tip, completing an order form, or determining the amount of interest on a loan from an advertisement there was an improvement from 1992 to 2003 (1992: below basic 26% basic 32% intermediate 30% proficient 13%) (2003: below basic 22% basic 33% intermediate 33% proficient 13%).[21]

The Program for the International Assessment of Adult Competencies (PIAAC) is a cyclical, large-scale study that was developed under the auspices of the Organization for Economic Cooperation and Development (OECD). Adults were surveyed in 24 participating countries in 2012 and 9 additional countries in 2014.

The goal of PIAAC is to assess and compare the basic skills and the broad range of competencies of adults around the world. The assessment focuses on cognitive and workplace skills needed for successful participation in twenty-first century society and the global economy. Specifically, PIAAC measures relationships between individuals' educational background, workplace experiences and skills, occupational attainment, use of information and communications technology, and cognitive skills in the areas of literacy, numeracy, and problem solving.

PIAAC is a complex assessment: the data collection has been conducted in multiple languages, in numerous countries with diverse populations, cultures, education, and life experiences. In the United States, the PIAAC assessment is conducted in English only; however, the PIAAC survey background questions are administered either in English or Spanish. All participating countries follow the quality assurance guidelines set by the OECD consortium, and closely follow all the agreed-upon standards set for survey design, implementation of the assessment, and the reporting of results.

PIAAC builds on knowledge and experiences gained from previous international adult assessments, the International Adult Literacy Survey (IALS) and the Adult Literacy and Lifeskills Survey (ALL). PIAAC enhances and expands on these previous assessments' frameworks and, at the same time, improves upon their design and methodologies. IALS measured literacy proficiency for each domain on a scale of 0–500 points. Literacy ability in each domain was expressed by a score, defined as the point at which a person has an 80% chance of successful performance from among the set of tasks of varying difficulty included in the assessment. The five levels of literacy that correspond to measured ranges of scores achieved are

- Level 1 indicates persons with very low skills, where the individual may, for example, be unable to determine the correct amount of medicine to give a child from information printed on the package.
- Level 2 respondents can deal only with material that is simple, clearly laid out, and in which the tasks involved are not too complex. It denotes a weak level of skill, but more than at level 1. It identifies people who can read, but test poorly. They may have developed coping skills to manage everyday literacy demands, but their low level of proficiency makes it difficult for them to face novel demands, such as learning new job skills.
- Level 3 is considered a suitable minimum for coping with the demands of everyday life and work in a complex, advanced society. It denotes roughly the skill level required for successful secondary school completion and college entry. Like higher levels, it requires the ability to integrate several sources of information and solve more complex problems.
- Levels 4 and 5 describe respondents who demonstrate command of higher-level information processing skills.[22]

Problem solving in technology-rich environments (PS-TRE) is an innovative addition to adult literacy and large-scale assessments. In the PIAAC PS-TRE framework, PS-TRE is defined as: using digital technology, communication tools, and networks to acquire and evaluate information, communicate with others, and perform practical tasks.

PS-TRE measures skills and abilities that are required for solving problems while operating in a technology-rich environment. Specifically, it assesses the cognitive processes of problem solving: goal setting, planning, selecting, evaluating, organizing, and communicating results. The environment in which PS-TRE assesses these processes is meant to reflect the reality that digital technology has revolutionized access to information and communication capabilities over the past decades.

In particular, the Internet has immensely increased instantaneous access to large amounts of information in multiple formats and has expanded capabilities of instant voice, text, visual, and graphic communications across the globe. In order to effectively operate in this environment, it is necessary to have mastery of foundational computer (Information and Communications Technology [ICT]) skills, including (a) skills associated with manipulating input and output devices (e.g., the mouse, keyboard, and digital displays), (b) awareness of concepts and knowledge of how the environment is structured (e.g., files, folders, scrollbars, hyperlinks, and different types of menus or buttons), and (c) the ability to interact effectively with digital information (e.g., how to use commands such as save, delete, open, close, move, highlight, submit, and send). Such interaction involves familiarity with electronic texts, images, graphics, and numerical data, as well as the ability to locate, evaluate, and critically judge the validity, accuracy, and appropriateness of accessed information. These skills constitute the core aspects of the PIAAC PS-TRE assessment.

PS-TRE items present tasks of varying difficulty to be performed in simulated software applications using commands and functions commonly found in the technology environments of email, web pages, and spreadsheets. These tasks range from purchasing particular goods or services online and finding interactive health information to managing personal information and business finances.

PIAAC recognizes the diversity of digital technologies and the fact that they are evolving at a rapid pace, but due to implementation constraints the first round of PIAAC will be limited to using computers and computer networks. The PS-TRE assessments are only computer administered. The percentage of U.S. adults age 16 to 74 at each level of proficiency on the PIAAC PS-TRE scale in 2012 are as follows[23]:

- Below level 1 24%
- Level 1 41%
- Level 2 30%
- Level 3 5%

The PIAAC literacy framework expands the definition of literacy used in IALS and ALL1 and provides a broad definition of literacy: literacy is understanding, evaluating, using, and engaging with written text to participate in society, to achieve one's goals, and to develop one's knowledge and potential.

This definition (a) highlights the ranges of cognitive processes involved in literacy, (b) focuses on a more active role of individuals in society (participating), and (c) includes a range of text types, such as narrative and interactive texts, in both print and electronic formats.

While this is a broader definition than IALS and ALL, selected items from those assessments are used to provide a link to IALS and ALL. PIAAC items include continuous texts (e.g., sentences and paragraphs), noncontinuous texts (e.g., schedules, graphs, maps), and electronic texts (including hypertext, or text in interactive environments, such as forms and blogs). Task activities are presented in home, work, and community contexts, addressing various purposes adults pursue in their lives.

Based on the PIAAC framework, literacy tasks include items (in both modes) that cover a range of difficulties (low, middle, and high) to present a comprehensive picture of the range of skills of adults in each country.[24] The percentage of U.S. adults age 16 to 74 at each level of proficiency on the PIAAC literacy scales in 2012 are as follows:

- Below level 1 20%
- Level 1 34%
- Level 2 28%
- Level 3 10%

The primary goal of PIAAC's numeracy assessment is to evaluate basic mathematical and computational skills that are considered fundamental for functioning in everyday work and social life. In the PIAAC numeracy framework, numeracy is defined as: the ability to access, use, interpret, and communicate mathematical information and ideas, to engage in and manage mathematical demands of a range of situations in adult life.

PIAAC numeracy assessment items (a) cover as many aspects as are defined in the framework, (b) are, as much as possible, authentic and culturally appropriate, (c) cover different levels of ability, and (d) are nationally adapted to use the standard measuring systems of the participating country. New items in paper-and-pencil and computer formats have been developed, and items from ALL and IALS are used as well.[25] The percentage of U.S. adults age 16 to 74 at each level of proficiency on the PIAAC numeracy scales in 2012 are as follows:

- Below level 1 9%
- Level 1 20%
- Level 2 34%
- Level 3 28%
- Levels 4 and 5 10%

Based on studies prior to PIAAC, it was found that in the United States over seven million adults had very low literacy skills. Many other countries participating in PIAAC also had large numbers of adults with low literacy skills. The primary goal of the PIAAC reading components framework is to provide information about the literacy skills of adults at the lower end of the literacy spectrum specifically, whether they have the foundational skills to develop the higher literacy and numeracy abilities necessary for functioning in society.

The reading components assessment focuses on elements of reading that are comparable across the range of languages in the participating countries: reading vocabulary, sentence comprehension, and basic passage comprehension.

The reading vocabulary section asks participants to identify the best word to label different graphic illustrations. This task measures whether participants can identify common, concrete print words used in everyday adult interactions in the community, home, and workplace. It is not meant to determine the vocabulary knowledge (breadth or depth) of the participants.

The sentence comprehension section asks participants to identify whether sentences of varying grammatical/syntactic complexity make sense. This task measures whether participants can understand and correctly judge the accuracy of the content of sentences.

The basic passage comprehension section asks participants to make a choice between a correct and an incorrect word to complete a sentence within a passage. This task measures whether respondents comprehend text in context and can appropriately use words in ways that characterize fluency.

The reading component portion of the assessment is optional for countries participating in PIAAC. In countries that chose to adopt the reading components tasks, participants who do not take the computer-based assessment and those who fail to pass the computer-administered ICT and literacy/numeracy core items are directed to these tasks.[26]

In the 2003 study, adults household income was divided into eight categories: less than $10,000, $10,000–$14,999, $15,000–$19,999, $20,000–$29,999, $30,000-$39,999, $40,000–$59,999, $60,000–$99,999, and $100,000 or greater. It was found that average prose, document, and quantitative literacy were higher for adults in each increasing level of household income, with two exceptions. On the prose and quantitative scales, the differences in average literacy between adults who lived in households with incomes of $10,000–$14,999 and adults who lived in households with incomes of $15,000–$19,999 were not statistically significant. On the document scale, the difference in average literacy between adults who lived in households with incomes below $10,000 and adults who lived in households with incomes between $10,000 and $14,999 was not statistically significant.

With each higher level of prose, document, and quantitative literacy (from below basic through proficient), the percentage of adults with household incomes below $10,000 decreased. For example, 26% of adults with below basic prose literacy lived in households with incomes below $10,000 compared with 14% of adults with basic prose literacy, 5% of adults with intermediate prose literacy, and 2% of adults with proficient prose literacy.

At the top of the income scale, the percentage of adults living in households with incomes above $100,000 was higher at each higher level of literacy. For example, 2% of adults with below basic prose literacy lived in households with incomes of $100,000 or more, while 6% of adults with basic prose literacy, 16% of adults with intermediate prose literacy, and 30% of adults with proficient prose literacy lived in households with incomes of $100,000 or more.[27]

13.7 Summary

Usability has recently become an important concern in the cybersecurity field but usability research is a rather well-established discipline. There are numerous obstacles to achieve cybersecurity usability but there are also proven methods to perform appropriate usability testing for cybersecurity applications. If users find a cybersecurity measure too difficult, they will try to circumvent it and compromise security. Key points covered in this chapter include

- NIST has established a Usability of Cybersecurity Team is part of the CNCI Research and Development effort.
- Electronic Health Record systems (EHRs) are also facing usability challenges and NIST is working to provide guidance to EHRs developers on usability.

- The NSF has made several grant awards to address cybersecurity usability and related issues.
- The 2002 Help America Vote Act has given NIST a key role in helping to realize nationwide improvements in the usability and security of voting systems and to assist the EAC with the development of voluntary voting system guidelines.
- Since the ordinary use of mobile devices involves the collection, transmission, and storage of consumers' sensitive personal information, mobile threats such as lost or stolen devices, or malicious or privacy-infringing applications can place consumers at serious risk of identity theft or financial harm.
- There are two approaches to implementing permission-based access controls that predominate in mobile operating systems: run-time and install-time.
- Based on experiences and the available research, there appear to be important usability concerns with both run-time and install-time permissions.
- There appear to be important usability concerns with both run-time and install-time permissions. In both cases, users may not fully understand the implications of granting access, or may be so habituated to the prompts that they do not pay attention when making access decisions.
- The FTC has also researched mobile apps for kids and findings raise several alarms about cybersecurity usability at disclosure on what data is being collected from children, how it is being shared, or who will have access to it.
- Cybersecurity usability is rapidly becoming more critical every year especially since there is tremendous growth in the use of handheld computing devices for Internet access.
- Low-income households are reporting handheld computing device ownership alone at much higher rates than more affluent household groups and rely on handheld computers more than others.
- The PS-TRE assessments of U.S. adults age 16 to 74 show that about half of the population are challenged when tested on solving problems using computing technology.
- In the 2003 literacy study, it was found that average prose, document, and quantitative literacy was higher for adults in each increasing level of household income, and lower for lower income households.
- The lower income population is facing cybersecurity risks because of their tendency to rely on handheld computing devices for Internet use and because they also have lower literacy scores which makes using technology more challenging.

13.8 Seminar Discussion Topics

Discussion topics for graduate or professional-level seminars are

- What experience have seminar participants had with usability testing?

- How much usability testing do seminar participants think should be done on a cybersecurity application for mobile computing devices before the application is made publically available?
- What do seminar participants think is the best way to teach mobile computing device users with low literacy skills how to manage cybersecurity? Why?
- What do seminar participants think is the best way to teach children how to manage cybersecurity for their mobile computing device? Why?

Key Terms

install-time permissions: require the developer to identify all of the protected resources that an application can access, and to declare these permissions at the time of installation. Based on the permissions displayed, the user can choose whether or not to install the application

run-time permissions: are the permissions that users give to a computing device when a system dialog box prompts the user when an application attempts to access a particular resource. Users can then decide, on a case-by-case basis, whether to give an application access to that resource

system usability scale (SUS): is widely used reliable tool for measuring usability of a wide variety of products and services, including hardware, software, mobile devices, websites, and applications

usability testing: is the evaluation of a product or service by testing it with representative users and during a test, participants will try to complete typical tasks while observers watch, listen, and take notes

user experience (UX): is what happens during HCI from the human perspective

References

1. NIST Security. *Usability of Security*. Retrieved December 10, 2016, http://csrc.nist.gov/security-usability/HTML/about.html
2. NIST. *About Us*. Retrieved December 10, 2016, http://csrc.nist.gov/security-usability/HTML/about.html
3. NIST Health Information Technology (IT). *Safety-Related Usability Framework*. Retrieved December 10, 2016, https://www.nist.gov/healthcare/health-it-usability/safety-related-usability-framework
4. NIST Health Information Technology (IT). *Human Factor Guidelines and Accessibility*. Retrieved December 10, 2016, https://www.nist.gov/healthcare/health-it-usability/human-factor-guidelines-and-accessibility
5. NIST Information Technology Laboratory. *Information Access. Industry Usability Reporting*. Retrieved December 10, 2016, https://www.nist.gov/itl/iad/industry-usability-reporting

6. Usability.gov. *User Experience Basics.* Retrieved December 10, 2016, https://www.usability.gov/what-and-why/user-experience.html
7. Usability.gov. *Usability Testing.* Retrieved December 10, 2016, https://www.usability.gov/how-to-and-tools/methods/usability-testing.html
8. Usability.gov. *System Usability Scale (SUS).* Retrieved December 10, 2016, https://www.usability.gov/how-to-and-tools/methods/system-usability-scale.html
9. DigitalGov. *DigitalGov User Experience Program.* Retrieved December 10, 2016, https://www.usability.gov/how-to-and-tools/guidance/gsa-first-fridays-program.html
10. DHS. *DHS Education Programs.* Retrieved December 11, 2016, http://www.orau.gov/dhseducation/about/researchAreas.html#HF
11. NIST. *NIST and the Help America Vote Act (HAVA).* Retrieved December 11, 2016, https://www.nist.gov/itl/voting
12. EAC. *Voting Accessibility.* Retrieved December 11, 2016, https://www.eac.gov/voter_resources/voting_accessibility.aspx
13. FTC. *About.* Retrieved December 11, 2016, https://www.ftc.gov/about-ftc/
14. FTC. *Mobile Security: Potential Threats and Solutions.* June 4, 2013. Retrieved December 11, 2016, https://www.ftc.gov/news-events/events-calendar/2013/06/mobile-security-potential-threats-solutions
15. Nithan Sannappa. FTC. *Secure APIs and the Principle of Least Privilege.* May 7, 2015. Retrieved December 11, 2016, https://www.ftc.gov/news-events/blogs/techftc/2015/05/secure-apis-principle-least-privilege
16. Nithan Sannappa. FTC. *Usability and Transparency Considerations of Permission-Based Access Controls.* May 14, 2015. Retrieved December 11, 2016, https://www.ftc.gov/news-events/blogs/techftc/2015/05/usability-transparency-considerations-permission-based-access
17. Nithan Sannappa. FTC. *Enhancing Permissions through Contextual Integrity.* May 21, 2015. Retrieved December 11, 2016, https://www.ftc.gov/news-events/blogs/techftc/2015/05/enhancing-permissions-through-contextual-integrity
18. FTC. *FTC's Second Kids' App Report Finds Little Progress in Addressing Privacy Concerns Surrounding Mobile Applications for Children.* December 10, 2012. Retrieved December 11, 2016, https://www.ftc.gov/news-events/press-releases/2012/12/ftcs-second-kids-app-report-finds-little-progress-addressing
19. FTC. *Kids' Apps Disclosures Revisited.* September 3, 2015. Retrieved December 11, 2016, https://www.ftc.gov/news-events/blogs/business-blog/2015/09/kids-apps-disclosures-revisited
20. U.S. Census Bureau. *Computer and Internet Use in the United States: 2013.* November 2014. Retrieved December 11, 2016, www.census.gov/history/pdf/2013computeruse.pdf
21. National Center for Education Statistics. *National Assessment of Adult Literacy (NAAL).* Retrieved December 11, 2016, https://nces.ed.gov/naal/
22. National Center for Education Statistics. *The Program for the International Assessment of Adult Competencies (PIAAC).* Retrieved December 12, 2016, http://nces.ed.gov/surveys/piaac/
23. National Center for Education Statistics. *Problem Solving in Technology-Rich Environments Domain.* Retrieved December 12, 2016, http://nces.ed.gov/surveys/piaac/problem-solving.asp
24. National Center for Education Statistics. *Literacy Domain.* Retrieved December 12, 2016, http://nces.ed.gov/surveys/piaac/literacy.asp

25. National Center for Education Statistics. *Numeracy Domain*. Retrieved December 12, 2016, http://nces.ed.gov/surveys/piaac/numeracy.asp

26. National Center for Education Statistics. *Reading Components Domain*. Retrieved December 12, 2016, http://nces.ed.gov/surveys/piaac/reading-components.asp

27. National Center for Education Statistics. *Literacy in Everyday Life Results from the 2003 National Assessment of Adult Literacy*. April 2007. Retrieved December 12, 2016, http://nces.ed.gov/Pubs2007/2007480.pdf

Chapter 14

Conclusions

The cybersecurity efforts of the U.S. government are slowly maturing and starting to show more solid progress including the coordination and prioritization of cybersecurity research activities. Major legislation passed by the U.S. Congress and the executive actions of President Obama have prompted greater progress in these efforts. They have created the CNCI,[1] the Federal Information Security Modernization Act of 2014,[2] and the Cybersecurity Act of 2015 and The CNAP.[3]

The desperately needed cybersecurity research efforts are spread across numerous agencies that provide technical expertise in their areas of responsibility. The agencies are clearly focused on cybersecurity research to meet the needs of the realms and industry sectors for which they have responsibility. Thus, the goal of reducing overlap has been achieved as has the goal of assuring that there is appropriately focused research to support the diverse and critical needs of the U.S. economy.

It is likely that the Congressional actions will stay in place but it is also likely that the executive actions will be modified by incoming presidents and cabinets. The research goals and objectives will likely stay in place but the organization of oversight and priority setting will be modified by new cabinets. The changes will mostly be propaganda focused with new administrations criticizing past administrations and self-glorifying their changes and laying claim to their new, but not likely improved, management approaches.

14.1 Threat Level Red

Cyber incidents reported by U.S. federal government agencies continues to increase[4] and high-profile hacking and attack incidents have become commonplace with hacks or data thefts reported by Yahoo, Sony, the U.S. Office of Personnel Management, Target stores, and numerous others including the Democratic National Committee. To address these trends, a portion of government cybersecurity research has been focused on leap ahead technology, strategies, and programs. The goal is to develop technologies that provide increases in cybersecurity by orders of magnitude above current systems and which can be deployed within five to ten years. In addition, the federal government, through efforts such as the NICE, plans to enhance cybersecurity education and training nationwide and hire more cybersecurity experts to secure federal agencies.[4]

It is widely accepted that cyberspace has moved well beyond websites and social media applications. We are now in the age of the IoT. Through the integration of computers, sensors, and networking in physical devices, the IoT fuses the physical and digital worlds to develop new capabilities and services, which in turn create new opportunities.[5]

14.2 A Stronger and Better Organized DHS

The DHS has a leading role in protecting the United States from calamity and catastrophe. DHS was conceived and recommended by the U.S. Commission on National Security in the late 1990s out of a conviction that the entire range of U.S. national security policies and processes required reexamination in the light of new circumstances. Those circumstances encompassed not only the changed geopolitical reality after the Cold War, but also the significant technological, social, and intellectual changes that were occurring. Prominent among such changes was the information revolution and the accelerating discontinuities in a range of scientific and technological areas. Another was the increased integration of global finance and commerce, or globalization.[6]

Formed in the twenty-first century in 2002 from the combination of 22 departments and agencies, DHS work includes customs, border, and immigration enforcement; emergency response to natural and manmade disasters; antiterrorism work; and cybersecurity. DHS pursues cybersecurity research to improve security for its numerous activities as well as the government and critical industry sectors. This includes cybersecurity support for the National Strategy for Global Supply Chain Security and the Customs-Trade Partnership Against Terrorism.[7] Of particular interest to DHS are technologies that can be developed and transitioned to commercial products or used in federal, state, and local government systems. It is not likely that the missions of DHS will change greatly in the future. There is always the-better-than-the-past-administration rhetoric that new administrations bring with them but DHS has survived both Republican and Democratic administrations and the U.S. Congress will likely have the final word on any significant changes to DHS.

14.3 Over a Century of Service from NIST

The NIST has a leading role in the cutting-edge research and standard setting that is necessary to address cyber threats from around the globe. Founded in 1901, NIST is one of the oldest physical science laboratories in the United States. Congress established the agency to remove a major challenge to U.S. industrial competitiveness at the time when the country's second-rate measurement infrastructure that lagged behind the capabilities of the United Kingdom, Germany, and other economic rivals. NIST's cybersecurity program supports the promotion of innovation and industrial competitiveness of the United States by advancing measurement science, standards, and related technology through several important R&D programs. NIST performs several critical R&D functions in support of the U.S. government and participates in the standard setting process with its counterparts in countries around the world. The cybersecurity framework, developed by NIST in collaboration with numerous organizations, has become a widely used tool to evaluate cybersecurity activities in critical industry sector organizations and aid those organizations in planning their improvements in cybersecurity.[8]

14.4 Game Changing Capabilities from DARPA, IARPA, and In-Q-Tel

While NIST works with existing and emerging technologies, the DARPA is the principal agency within the DoD for high-risk, high-payoff research, development, and demonstration of new technologies and systems. This includes transforming revolutionary concepts and even seeming impossibilities into practical game changing capabilities. The ultimate results have included precision weapons and stealth technology, the Internet, automated voice recognition and language translation, and GPS receivers small enough to embed in myriad consumer devices.

DARPA's scientific investigations run the gamut from laboratory efforts to the creation of full-scale technology demonstrations in the fields of biology, medicine, computer science, chemistry, physics, engineering, mathematics, material sciences, social sciences, neurosciences, and more. Since 2010, DARPA has had success in transitioning new technologies from the research environment to military users, including DoD acquisition programs and warfighters. DARPA maintains a portfolio-level database that identifies these outcomes by program.

DARPA's technological approach focuses on radical innovation that addresses future warfighting needs, rather than developing technologies that address current warfighting needs. This approach shapes how the agency defines, pursues, and tracks technology transition. DARPA considers a successful transition to be one where its program, or a portion of its program, influences or introduces new knowledge. This knowledge is often passed through program performers, which DARPA relies on to execute technology development in its programs. Typical performers include commercial enterprises; other DoD entities, such as military service laboratories and research agencies; and academic institutions. Further, DARPA generally does not develop technologies to full maturity. Instead, the agency focuses on demonstrating the feasibility of new technologies, which includes verifying that the concepts behind the technologies have potential for real-life applications. As a result, most DARPA technologies require additional development before they are ready for operational or commercial use. However, the agency's process for tracking technology transition outcomes is not designed to capture transitions that occur after a program completes and does not provide DARPA with an effective means for updating its database.[9]

In a similar fashion as DARPA, the IARPA invests in high-risk, high-payoff research programs to tackle some of the most difficult challenges of the agencies and disciplines in the IC. IARPA collaborates across the IC to ensure that research addresses relevant future needs. This cross-community focus ensures the ability to: address cross-agency challenges; leverage both operational and R&D expertise from across the IC; and coordinate transition strategies with agency partners.

Modeled after the DARPA, IARPA was established in 2006 with the mandate to: conduct *cross-community research*; target new opportunities and innovations; and generate revolutionary capabilities. IARPA was tasked to accomplish these objectives by drawing upon the technical and operational expertise that resides within the intelligence agencies.[10]

It is likely that the evolution of IARPA will follow a similar path to the evolution of DARPA. However, the IARPA customer base, although diverse in its missions and operational styles, is not as diverse as the DARPA customer base. There will be a continued long-term evolution of research areas for both organizations which will likely be impacted by new technologies and new missions and theaters of operation. The mega thrust of both agencies will be impacted by the expanded utilization and commercialization of space. The new frontier will require resilient and secure networks for space operations, vehicles, and stations. They may very well have their own Internet which will facilitate commerce and industry in space as well as help in U.S. defense efforts that are space based.

The advances in science and technology provide a unique opportunity to transform intelligence applying expanded analytic, collection, and processing capabilities, and to improve cross-component collaboration through the IC system for information sharing. Innovative programs such as In-Q-Tel provide CIA and the IC with effective reach into the cutting-edge creativity of the U.S. private sector.[11]

Small or newer companies often do not to target the U.S. federal government market because it can be difficult to target or slow to access. Because those companies often need to penetrate their markets quickly to generate cash flow, government customers can miss the chance to influence product development. Moreover, private venture capital firms sometimes discourage small companies they invest in from doing business with the government because of the complexity of the procurement process and long lead time on procurement decisions. This means that agencies are often two to three years behind the commercial market for technology, especially in areas like IT where there is rapid innovation.[12] In-Q-Tel is seeking business plans from companies that are developing cutting-edge technology and more information about submitting ideas is available on the website.

14.5 The Cross-Community Innovation Ecosystem of DoD

The U.S. military has several diverse challenges in cybersecurity R&D of cyber capabilities. First is the strategic research needs to develop leap ahead transforming technology to maintain cyber superiority which is largely handled by DARPA and other military research laboratories. Second is the combined strategic and applied research, development, and deployment of the technology required to protect the DoD at the enterprise level. Third is the applied research, development, and deployment of the technology required to enable and protect missions of the diversity of capabilities provided by the air force, army, navy, and marines. Fourth is the applied research, development, and deployment of the technology required to enable and protect the specific units and missions within the four branches of services. Finally is the tactical and action research required to enable and protect all military forces and missions that are in progress as they face emerging and possibly previously unknown cyber threats.

DoD cybersecurity research is conducted in Cross-Community Innovation Ecosystem. The military centric research is handled by the OSD, the AFRL, the ONR, the ARL, and the respective R&D units within the research structure of DoD and military branches and in each of their research ecosystems. Research focus areas are split up among the laboratories based on their expertise as follows:

- The OSD programs emphasize game-changing research over incremental approaches, and enhance the organizational ties and *experimental infrastructure* needed to accelerate transition of new technologies into practice.
- The AFRL efforts in cybersecurity aim to create a firm, trustable foundation in cyberspace, and then to build assured mission capabilities upon it. New technologies are needed to be aware of missions and threats, compute optimal assurance solutions, and implement protection as needed via mission agility or infrastructure reinforcement.
- The ARL contributes to a number of the Strategic Plan's objectives with a particular focus on Moving Target technologies within its Cyber Maneuver Initiative. The Cyber Maneuver Initiative aims to improve defense against APTs.
- The ONR focuses on long- and medium-term scientific and technology areas that have the potential for delivering significant improvements in the robustness, resiliency, security, and operational effectiveness of cyber environments.[13]

The DoD complex is seemingly endless with coordinating committees, special units, specific directives, and roadmaps. In July 2016, the OSD issued a memo on Cybersecurity Operational Test and Evaluation Priorities and Improvements that identified areas where the DoD operational test and evaluation community should accelerate development of the tools and techniques necessary to conduct cybersecurity assessments which emulate the full range of potential threats in a consistent and rigorous way.[14] Various DoD research centers often use Sources Sought Notices, OT Agreements for Prototype Projects, and Broad Area Announcements to collect information about potential contractor capabilities and interest in advanced R&D projects.

14.6 The SoS at NSA

The NSA has a leading role in conducting the research necessary to develop standards and technology required to protect the critical communications and computer systems necessary to keep the United States both operational and thriving. The nature of NSA is such that most things will happen in secret. However, NSA does do considerable unclassified cybersecurity research, which is applied in the development of advisories, guidance, and standards. NSA has several research efforts exploring the Tailored Trustworthy Spaces theme, including exploration of risk through behavioral analytics and large-scale data analysis, a novel means to detect modifications to computing systems and network analytics, and efforts to customize system controls. Other areas of NSA activity include

- Exploring Moving Target technologies by conducting a full-scope analysis of the Moving Target problem and solution space. NSA plans to develop movement prototypes and evaluate several critical enabling functions.
- NSA sponsors the SoS Initiative for the promotion of a foundational cybersecurity science that is needed to mature the cybersecurity discipline and to underpin advances in cyber defense. The SoS initiative works to: engage the academic community for foundational research; promote rigorous scientific principles; and grow the SoS community.[15]
- The IA programs at the NSA deliver mission enhancing IA technologies, products, and services including capability packages which provide product-neutral information for a given operational requirement, which helps customers successfully implement their own solutions. A *capability package* identifies critical architectural components, while also describing the role each component plays in protecting data.[16]
- The NSA TTP transfers NSA-developed technology to industry, academia, and other research organizations, benefitting the economy and the agency mission. The program has an extensive portfolio of patented technologies across multiple technology areas.[17]

■ The NSA and the DHS jointly sponsor the National CAE-CD program. The goal of the program is to reduce vulnerability in national information infrastructure by promoting higher education and research in cyber defense and producing professionals with cyber defense expertise.[18]

14.7 The Progress of Science from NSF

A very significant source of funding for research, including cybersecurity research is the NSF. It is an independent federal agency created by Congress in 1950 to promote the progress of science; to advance national health, prosperity, and welfare; and to secure national defense. With an annual budget of $7.5 billion (FY 2016), NSF is the funding source for approximately 24% of all federally supported basic research conducted by U.S. colleges and universities. In many fields such as mathematics, computer science, and the social sciences, NSF is the major source of federal backing. There are about 12,000 new awards per year, with an average duration of three years. Most of these awards go to individuals or small groups of investigators. Others provide funding for research centers, instruments, and facilities that allow scientists, engineers, and students to work at the outermost frontiers of knowledge. NSF-funded researchers have won some 223 Nobel Prizes as well as other honors too numerous to list. NSF also funds equipment that is needed by scientists and engineers but is often too expensive for any one group or researcher to afford.[19]

NSF has long supported cybersecurity research to protect the frontiers of cyberspace through investments in basic research that have resulted in innovative ways to secure information and ensure privacy on the Internet with the development of algorithms that form the basis for electronic commerce, software security bug detection, and spam filtering.[20] NSF funds research and education in most fields of science and engineering. It does this through grants, and cooperative agreements to more than 2,000 colleges, universities, K-12 school systems, businesses, informal science organizations, and other research organizations throughout the United States. The foundation accounts for about one-fourth of federal support to academic institutions for basic research.[21]

14.8 The National Laboratories are National Treasures

FFRDCs that are funded and overseen by the DOE and DoD conduct several research projects related to cybersecurity. DOE projects focus largely on the management and sustainability of the electric power grid. R&D laboratories fill voids where in-house and private sector R&D centers are unable to meet agency core area needs. Specific objectives for these FFRDCs are to

■ Maintain over the long term a competency in technology areas where the government cannot rely on in-house or private sector capabilities

■ Develop and transfer important new technology to the private sector so the government can benefit from a wider, broader base of expertise[22]

Several FFRDCs claim that they have cybersecurity capabilities but do not explain or elaborate on their activities related to cybersecurity research. This may just be a transparency issue or it is also possible they are doing very little to pursue cybersecurity research. This gap in information leaves doubts about their activities even they report having capabilities. The GAO and the DoD Inspector General's Office and others have raised concerns that FFRDC mission statements are too broad and do not clearly identify the specialized tasks that FFRDCs should perform. Congress and others have repeatedly raised questions about the adequacy of DoD policy guidance and oversight as well as concerns regarding whether DoD policy guidance ensures that sponsors adequately justify awarding noncompetitive contracts for the operation of the FFRDCs.[23]

A key mission of the DOE Office of Electricity Delivery and Energy Reliability (OE) is to enhance the reliability and resiliency of the energy infrastructure. Within DOE OE's CEDS Program, cybersecurity R&D is tailored to the unique performance requirements, designs, and operational environments of EDS. The Strategic Plan research themes, particularly Designed-In Security and Tailored Trustworthy Spaces are strongly supported by the strategies and milestones outlined in the CEDS Program. Other elements of DOE also perform related cybersecurity research. The ASCR Program, which is part of the Office of Science, sponsors research to support DOE's leadership in scientific computation. Security of networks and middleware is a critical element in the ASCR Next Generation Networking research program. The NNSA within DOE also sponsors cybersecurity research to support its unique mission requirements.[24]

One of the many undertakings of the Grid Modernization Laboratory Consortium is to develop a multiyear program plan for grid modernization. The plan will outline an integrated systems approach to transforming the nation's grid by incorporating numerous program activities within DOE as well as activities undertaken by national stakeholders. As a first step, the leaders of the Consortium are focused on coordinating all of DOE's grid-related activities to ensure connectivity, avoid redundancies, and identify gaps in the R&D needs of a modern grid.[25]

The CEDS Program operates with the goal that, by 2020, resilient EDS will be designed, installed, operated, and maintained to survive cyber-incidents while sustaining critical functions. To help achieve this vision, OE fosters and actively engages in collaborations among energy stakeholders, utilities, vendors, national labs, and academic institutions. Through these collaborations, OE seeks to solve the right problems hand-in-hand with industry, and to transition next-generation research from the national labs and academia into commercial products operating in the energy sector.[24]

14.9 Protecting Critical Infrastructure Sectors

In the United States, the DHS has provided a leadership role in promoting threat analysis and security efforts. DHS and The Office of the President have identified 16 critical infrastructure sectors whose assets, systems, and networks are important to sustaining national interest including economic stability and sustainability.[26] The DHS Office of CS&C, within the NPPD, is responsible for enhancing the security, resilience, and reliability of the cyber and communications infrastructure. CS&C works to prevent or minimize disruptions to critical information infrastructure in order to protect the public, the economy, and government services. CS&C leads efforts to protect the federal.gov domain of civilian government networks and to collaborate with the private sector to increase the security of critical networks in the.com domain. In addition, the NCCIC serves as a 24/7 cyber monitoring, incident response, and management center and as a national point of cyber and communications incident integration.[27]

On February 12, 2013 President Barack Obama signed an EO designed to move the federal government rapidly forward on the mission to improving critical infrastructure cybersecurity. The premise behind the order was that repeated cyber intrusions into critical infrastructure demonstrate the need for improved cybersecurity. The national and economic security of the United States depends on the reliable functioning of the critical infrastructure in the face of such threats. NIST was designated to lead the research on and the development of a framework to reduce cyber risks to critical infrastructure (the Cybersecurity Framework). The Cybersecurity Framework was to include a set of standards, methodologies, procedures, and processes that align policy, business, and technological approaches to address cyber risks and incorporate voluntary consensus standards and industry best practices to the fullest extent possible. In addition, the Cybersecurity Framework was to provide a prioritized, flexible, repeatable, performance-based, and cost-effective approach, including information security measures and controls, to help owners and operators of critical infrastructure identify, assess, and manage cyber risk with a focus on identifying cross-sector security standards and guidelines applicable to critical infrastructure.[28]

The U.S. GAO found that SSAs (those agencies charged with leadership in homeland security for a specific critical industry sector) determined the significance of cyber risk to networks and industrial control systems for all 15 of the sectors in the scope of GAO's review. Specifically, they determined that cyber risk was significant for 11 of 15 sectors. Although the SSAs for the remaining four sectors had not determined cyber risks to be significant during their 2010 sector-specific planning process, they subsequently reconsidered the significance of cyber risks to the sector. For example, commercial facilities SSA officials stated that they recognized cyber risk as a high-priority concern for the sector as part of the updated sector planning process. SSAs and their sector partners are to include an overview of current and emerging cyber risks in their updated sector-specific plans.[29]

14.10 Working to Protect Consumers

Even though a considerable amount of U.S. government cybersecurity research is directed at protecting the national infrastructure and the military capability of the United States, there are several research initiatives that are definitely focused on protecting consumers. Agencies like the FDA, the NHTSA, and the FAA have specific responsibilities to protect the general public.

A top USDOT priority is enhancing vehicle cybersecurity to mitigate cyber threats that could present unreasonable safety risks to the public or compromise sensitive information such as consumers' personal data. On behalf of USDOT, the NHTSA is actively engaged in vehicle cybersecurity research and employs a proactive and collaborative approach to protect vehicle owners from safety-related cybersecurity risks.[30]

The FAA has been focusing some of its cybersecurity research efforts on the rapidly changing design of commercial aircraft. Aircraft OEMs are developing eEnabled technologies that they are being increasingly deployed into aircraft. The introduction of eEnabled technologies into new commercial aircraft is leading to unprecedented global connectivity that creates a new environment for the aviation sector. Aircraft navigation and communication functions are transitioning from operating as isolated and independent systems, to being integrated into a networked system that is dependent on exchanging digital information between the eEnabled aircraft and external networks located on the ground and on other eEnabled aircraft. Due to the proliferation of these new connective technologies, it became necessary to reexamine security and safety of the aircraft to protect it against unwanted cyber intrusion. It will be essential to include cybersecurity within the certification criteria and processes. In addition, the FAA recommends that the cybersecurity approach of the new eEnabled aircraft should be coordinated with the move toward the Next Generation Air Traffic Control (NextGen) system, NextGen. In that major initiative, the FAA will be addressing cybersecurity throughout the aviation and air transportation sectors.[31]

The FDA is researching cybersecurity issues in medical devices and recommends that manufacturers and health care facilities take steps to assure that appropriate safeguards are in place to reduce the risk of failure due to cyberattack, which could be initiated by the introduction of malware into the medical equipment or unauthorized access to configuration settings in medical devices and hospital networks.[32]

MDS poses a unique set of challenges to individuals and enterprises. A set of security controls and countermeasures that address mobile threats in a holistic manner must be identified, necessitating a broader view of the entire mobile security ecosystem. This view must go beyond devices to include, as an example, the cellular networks and cloud infrastructure used to support mobile applications and native mobile services.[33]

The IoT has the potential to offer enormous benefits to consumers. Innovative companies are already selling connected devices, apps, sensors, services, etc., unlike anything that has been done before. As with any online activity, it is important to protect consumers' sensitive data from thieves. The IoT, however, adds new security dimensions to consider. For example, an insecure connection could give a hacker access not just to the confidential information transmitted by the device, but to everything else on a user's network. And in the IoT, the risk is not just to data. If that home automation system is not secure, a criminal could override the settings to unlock the doors. And just think of the consequences if a hacker were able to remotely recalibrate a medical device.[34] An UA with associated support equipment, control station, data links, telemetry, communications, and navigation equipment necessary to operate it is just one example of how the IoT keeps expanding and some of vulnerabilities that come with such rapid expansion.[35]

14.11 The Struggle for Cybersecurity Usability

Usability has only recently become an important concern in the cybersecurity field. The cybersecurity field is relatively young and but there is a growing recognition of the fact that users themselves are a key component in organizational security programs. If users find a cybersecurity measure too difficult, they will try to circumvent it which of course harms organizational and personal security. Therefore, it is in every organization's interest to design cybersecurity measures in such a way that they take into account the perceptions, characteristics, needs, abilities, and behaviors of users themselves.[36]

All in all the cybersecurity research activities of the U.S. government are addressing cybersecurity from as many perspectives as possible. This is not only important, it is absolutely necessary. If the IoT will ever live up to its full potential, it will need security. Without security it might not exist beyond a few million little gadgets that do not work or communicate with each other the vast majority of the time.

References

1. The White House. *The Comprehensive National Cybersecurity Initiative.* Retrieved November 8, 2016, https://www.whitehouse.gov/issues/foreign-policy/cybersecurity/national-initiative
2. *S.2521—Federal Information Security Modernization Act of 2014 113th Congress (2013–2014).* December 18, 2014. Retrieved November 8, 2016, https://www.congress.gov/bill/113th-congress/senate-bill/2521
3. The White House. *The Cybersecurity National Action Plan.* February 9, 2016. Retrieved November 8, 2016, https://www.whitehouse.gov/the-press-office/2016/02/09/fact-sheet-cybersecurity-national-action-plan

4. U.S. GAO. *Cybersecurity National Strategy, Roles, and Responsibilities Need to Be Better Defined and More Effectively Implemented*. February 2013. Retrieved November 10, 2016, www.gao.gov/products/GAO-13-187

5. The White House. *Internet of Things: Examining Opportunities and Challenges*. August 30, 2016. Retrieved November 10, 2016, https://www.whitehouse.gov/blog/2016/08/30/internet-things-examining-opportunities-and-challenges

6. U.S. Commission on National Security 21st Century. *Road Map for National Security: Imperative for Change the Phase III Report of the U.S. Commission on National Security 21st Century*. February 15, 2001. Retrieved December 17, 2016, http://govinfo.library.unt.edu/nssg/PhaseIIIFR.pdf

7. DHS. *Department of Homeland Security*.

8. The National Institute of Standards and Technology. *About NIST*. Retrieved November 16, 2016, https://www.nist.gov/about-nist

9. GAO. *Defense Advanced Research Projects Agency: Key Factors Drive Transition of Technologies, but Better Training and Data Dissemination Can Increase Success*. GAO-16-5. November 18, 2015. Retrieved December 21, 2016, http://www.gao.gov/products/GAO-16-5

10. Intelligence Advanced Research Projects Activity (IARPA). *About IARPA*. Retrieved November 10, 2016, https://www.iarpa.gov/index.php/about-iarpa

11. Looking Ahead. *U.S. Central Intelligence Agency*. January 03, 2012. Retrieved November 22, 2016, https://www.cia.gov/library/reports/archived-reports-1/Ann_Rpt_2002/looking.html

12. *Should Congress Establish "ARPA–E," The Advanced Research Projects Agency–Energy? Hearing before the Committee on Science House of Representatives One Hundred Ninth Congress Second Session*. March 9, 2006. Retrieved November 22, 2016, http://commdocs.house.gov/committees/science/hsy26480.000/hsy26480_0.HTM

13. The Networking and Information Technology Research and Development Program. *Report on Implementing Federal Cybersecurity Research and Development Strategy*. Retrieved November 11, 2016, https://www.nitrd.gov/PUBS/ImplFedCybersecurityRDStrategy-June2014.pdf

14. Office of The Secretary of Defense. *Cybersecurity Operational Test and Evaluation Priorities and Improvements*. July 27, 2016. Retrieved November 21, 2016, http://www.dote.osd.mil/pub/policies/2016/20160727_Cybersec_OTE_Priorities_and_Improvements(11093).pdf

15. U.S. National Security Agency. *Science of Security*. June 21, 2016. Retrieved November 28, 2016, https://www.nsa.gov/what-we-do/research/science-of-security/index.shtml

16. U.S. National Security Agency. *Research*. May 3, 2016. Retrieved November 28, 2016, https://www.nsa.gov/what-we-do/research/ia-research/

17. NSA Office of Research and Technology Applications Technology Transfer Program. November 18, 2016. Retrieved November 28, 2016, https://www.nsa.gov/what-we-do/research/technology-transfer/

18. U.S. National Security Agency. *National Centers of Academic Excellence in Cyber Defense*. May 3, 2016. Retrieved November 28, 2016, https://www.nsa.gov/resources/educators/centers-academic-excellence/cyber-defense/

19. NSF. *At a Glance*. Retrieved November 28, 2016, https://www.nsf.gov/about/glance.jsp

20. NSF. *Awards $74.5 Million to Support Interdisciplinary Cybersecurity Research*. October 7, 2015. Retrieved November 29, 2016, https://nsf.gov/news/news_summ.jsp?cntn_id=136481&org=NSF&from=news

21. NSF. *About Funding.*
22. NSF. *Master Government List of Federally Funded R&D Centers.* Retrieved December 4, 2016, https://www.nsf.gov/statistics/ffrdclist/#activity
23. GAO. *Federally Funded R&D Centers: Issues Relating to the Management of DOD-Sponsored Centers.* NSIAD-96-112. August 6, 1996. Retrieved December 5, 2016, http://www.gao.gov/products/GAO/NSIAD-96-112
24. DOE. *Office of Electricity Delivery & Energy Reliability. Mission.* Retrieved December 1, 2016, http://www.energy.gov/oe/mission
25. DOE. *Launch of the Grid Modernization Laboratory Consortium.* November 17, 2014. Retrieved December 1, 2016, http://energy.gov/articles/launch-grid-modernization-laboratory-consortium
26. U.S. Department of Homeland Security Critical Infrastructure Sectors. October 2015. Retrieved December 8, 2016, https://www.dhs.gov/critical-infrastructure-sectors
27. DHS. *Office of Cybersecurity and Communications.* Retrieved December 8, 2016, https://www.dhs.gov/office-cybersecurity-and-communications
28. The White House Office of the Press Secretary. *Executive Order Improving Critical Infrastructure Cybersecurity.* February 12, 2013. Retrieved December 8, 2016, https://www.whitehouse.gov/the-press-office/2013/02/12/executive-order-improving-critical-infrastructure-cybersecurity
29. GAO. *Critical Infrastructure Protection: Sector-Specific Agencies Need to Better Measure Cybersecurity Progress.* GAO-16-79: November 19, 2015. Retrieved December 9, 2016, http://www.gao.gov/products/GAO-16-79
30. USDOT. *National Highway Traffic Safety Administration. Cybersecurity Best Practices for Modern Vehicles.* (Report No. DOT HS 812 333). October, 2016. Retrieved December 7, 2016, http://www.nhtsa.gov/staticfiles/nvs/pdf/812333_CybersecurityForModernVehicles.pdf
31. FAA. *2016 National Aviation Research Plan (NARP).* Retrieved December 7, 2016, https://www.faa.gov/about/office_org/headquarters_offices/ang/offices/tc/about/campus/faa_host/rdm/media/pdf/2016narp.pdf
32. FDA. *Cybersecurity for Medical Devices and Hospital Networks: FDA Safety Communication.* June 17, 2013. Retrieved December 7, 2016, http://www.fda.gov/Safety/MedWatch/SafetyInformation/SafetyAlertsforHumanMedicalProducts/ucm357090.htm
33. NCCoE. *Mobile Device Security.* Retrieved December 4, 2016, http://nccoe.nist.gov/projects/building_blocks/mobile_device_security
34. FTC. *Careful Connections: Building Security in the Internet of Things.* Retrieved December 7, 2016, https://www.ftc.gov/tips-advice/business-center/guidance/careful-connections-building-security-internet-things
35. Florida Department of Transportation. *Unmanned Aircraft Systems (UAS).* Retrieved December 8, 2016, http://www.fdot.gov/aviation/uas.shtm
36. NIST Security. *Usability of Security.* Retrieved December 10, 2016, http://csrc.nist.gov/security-usability/HTML/about.html

Glossary

ablation tests: are used to determine the impact of a data feed being added or subtracted from an information feed used to generate warnings

anonymous networks: enable users to access the World Wide Web while blocking any tracking or tracing of their identity on the Internet

assured and resilient semiconductors: are semiconductors that are free of any malicious code that can compromise cyber operations or cybersecurity

attack surface: is the set of interfaces (the attack vectors) where an unauthorized user can try to enter data to or extract data from a system, or modify a system's behavior

attack vector: refers to the interfaces or paths an attacker uses to exploit a vulnerability

automated driving: operating a vehicle that performs one or more driving functions through the use of vehicle automation systems

backdoor: a backdoor generally circumvents security programs and provides access to a program, an online service, or an entire computer system. It can be authorized or unauthorized, documented or undocumented

best practices: are techniques or methodologies that, through experience and research, have reliably led to a desired or optimum result

biometrics: is the science of using one or more unique physical characteristics or behavioral traits to identify individuals

Border Gateway Protocol (BGP): was developed in the late 1980s to exchange routing information and compute routes between the networks that comprise Internet. Overtime, BGP has evolved into the fundamental "glue" that enables the commercial Internet

Bose–Einstein condensate: Eric A. Cornell of the National Institute of Standards and Technology and Carl E. Wieman of the University of Colorado at Boulder led a team of physicists at JILA, a joint institute of NIST and CU-Boulder, in a research effort that culminated in 1995 with the creation of the world's first Bose–Einstein condensate—a new form of matter. Predicted in 1924 by Albert Einstein, who built on the work of Satyendra Nath Bose, the condensation occurs when individual atoms meld into a "superatom" behaving as a single entity at just a few hundred billionths of a degree above absolute zero

capability package: identifies critical architectural components, while describing the role each component plays in protecting data and also identifies approved Commercial Solutions for Classified (CSfC) products

category: the subdivision of a function into groups of cybersecurity outcomes, closely tied to programmatic needs and particular activities. Examples of categories include asset management, access control, and detection processes

censorship resistance: is the ability of a digital publishing tool to overcome the capabilities of censors and the censorship resistance tools that researchers develop that can serve the needs of citizens who need them to communicate

chat group: is an Internet site that allows users to engage in large group conversation

cognitive fingerprint: is the unique pattern arising from an individual's interaction with existing technology without the need for specific data collection technology and without the need for cooperation from the user

common operating picture: is the mutual understanding and common vision of what actions all players will take to address a situation

composable: technologies that that are able to exist, happen, or work together

computer fraud: is crime involving deliberate misrepresentation, alteration, or disclosure of data in order to obtain something of value (usually for monetary gain)

computer use surveillance: is a process that tracks and records what users do or attempt to do when using corporate computer systems

computing substrate: is a complex of processors and sensors, or collectors, that combined provide arrays of processing abilities interconnected by a communication channel

configurable embedded computer systems: a computer system that is embedded in another device which can be configured prior to embedding as well as after installation

consolidated registry: is a mechanism the U.S. government and military services is using to inventory, approve, and authenticate social media use throughout all levels of the services

consumer-generated content: is digital content that is produced by self-publishers and sometimes picked up or referenced in traditional media

controller area network (CAN): is the dominant serial communication network protocol used for intra-vehicle communication

counterintelligence capabilities: are the knowledge, skills, technology, and organization that provide a comprehensive security program and constant evaluation of the intentions and targets of foreign intelligence services. Counterintelligence capabilities and programs also work to detect and neutralize the impact of espionage against national interests

criminal groups: are comprised of people that are organized for the purpose of committing criminal activity for economic gain or political clout or dominance in a specific geographical area

criminal enterprise: the FBI defines a criminal enterprise as a group of individuals with an identified hierarchy, or comparable structure, engaged in significant criminal activity

criminal intelligence information: is data which meets criminal intelligence collection criteria and which has been evaluated and determined to be relevant to the identification of criminal activity engaged in by individuals or organizations which are reasonably suspected of involvement in criminal activity

critical infrastructure: systems and assets, whether physical or virtual, so vital to the United States that the incapacity or destruction of such systems and assets would have a debilitating impact on cybersecurity, national economic security, national public health or safety, or any combination of these matters

critical infrastructure cybersecurity: is designed to protect the critical infrastructure which includes all technology functions that are required to support the national economy and security

cross-community research: is research than serves several related organizations by employing expertise from government agencies, private companies, and academic institutions that can provide complementary knowledge and skills

cryptocurrencies: are digital assets designed to work as a medium of exchange using cryptography to secure transactions and to control the creation of additional units of the currency

critical industry sectors: are those industries and business sectors that provide essential infrastructure support for economic activity that enables a country to function economically, politically, and socially

critical intelligence: is intelligence that requires immediate attention by a commander or policymaker and which may enhance or refute previously held beliefs about hostilities or actions, leading to a change of policy

culture of security: is an organization culture in which security pervades every aspect of daily life as well as all in all operational situations

cyber analytics: analytical data generated by specialized tools that enable network security managers to address pressing information security problems

cyber health: is the state of the ability of cyber-human systems to be resilient in the face of attacks and the level that the systems will not be compromised by attacks or human error and provide access and availability as needed when needed and where needed

cyberbullying: is bullying that takes place using electronic technology including devices and equipment such as cell phones, computers, and tablets as well as communication tools including social media sites, text messages, chat, and websites

cyber physical systems: are engineered systems that are built from, and depend upon, the seamless integration of computational algorithms and physical components that enable capability, adaptability, scalability, resiliency, safety, security, and usability of physical systems through cyber connections

cybersecurity event: a cybersecurity change that may have an impact on organizational operations (including mission, capabilities, or reputation)

cybersecurity metrics: help organizations verify that cybersecurity controls are in compliance with a policy, process, or procedure and help to identify security strengths and weaknesses

cyber-stalking: is the use of the Internet, email, social media, or other electronic communication devices to stalk another person

dial functionality: provide the ability to change modes or settings that change the trade-offs between recall and false discovery rate (FDR), or between lead time, utility time, or warning quality score

digital government: is a system of electronically accessible utilities and applications that provides access to government services and information

eEnabled: is any device, system, or combination of devices/components and systems that communicate with technologies other than point-to-point including interfaces between aircraft components and interfaces between aircraft and off-aircraft entities

electronic aggression: is the use of any electronic device to commit such acts as cyberbullying, Internet harassment, and Internet bullying

enterprise-level security metrics: measure the security posture of an organization and allow system administrators and nontechnical users alike to use a system while still maintaining security

experimental infrastructure: is the established ability to conduct experimental cutting edge research on extraordinary and previously unexplored areas of science and technology

facial recognition technologies: are technologies that are able to identify human subjects in an idle position or while in motion and the identification and images are used to improve security and security officer safety

framework core: a set of cybersecurity activities and references that are common across critical infrastructure sectors and are organized around particular outcomes. The framework core comprises four types of elements: functions, categories, subcategories, and informative references

framework implementation tiers: a lens through which to view the characteristics of an organization's approach to risk or how an organization views cybersecurity risk and the processes in place to manage that risk

framework profile: a representation of the outcomes that a particular system or organization has selected from the framework categories and subcategories

freedom of information law: is a law defining the public's right to access the records of government

gaps in security: are security measures or mitigation methods that are inadequate to protect an asset or do not thoroughly protect the asset that they were deployed to protect

geolocation: is the location of a user's wireless device or computer location via a GPS chip or triangulation of nearby wireless network towers. The user's device then transmits this information when the website or content provider asks for it. Other geolocation services obtain information from the user's device that does not immediately identify the user's location such as an IP address; then they consult external databases that associate that data with location information such as country and state and pass this information on to the website

Global Information Grid (GIG): is the communications system necessary to accomplish mission and theater superiority anywhere in the world as and when needed

hackathon: is an event in which computer programmers and others have a specific focus, which can include the programming language used, the operating system, an application, an API, the subject, or the demographic group of the programmers. In other cases, there is no restriction on the type of software being created

incident report: is a document that describes an occurrence of a security incident, or a violation or imminent threat of violation of computer security policies, acceptable use of policies, or standard security practices (NIST SP800-61)

indistinguishability obfuscation: a method that transforms a computer program into a "multilinear jigsaw puzzle." Each piece of the program mixes in carefully chosen random elements so that the randomness cancels out and the pieces fit together to compute the correct output. The idea has the potential to transform cybersecurity

industry leader: is a company or organization that performs better than its competitors bringing innovations to its field of endeavor and whose products or services become the industry standard to match or beat in open market competition

infrastructure reinforcement: is the physical and logical technological and human capability required to create and maintain the necessary organizational ability and resources to meet mission needs

infringement of intellectual property: can be the unauthorized reproduction or distribution of copyrighted material, the misappropriation of trade secrets for commercial gain, or the unauthorized use of a trademarked name or logo

innovation ecosystem: multidisciplinary research is key and is often driven by military or industrial needs. Disciplines are brought into the innovation ecosystem from many types of universities, national laboratories, private industry, and military laboratories to perform rapid, efficient innovation that could have a transformative economic impact on an industry or sector

insider misconduct: conduct by an employee that is against organization policies or procedures or that otherwise can harm the employing organization

insider–outsider team: is two or more people that jointly conspire to act maliciously against an organization with which one of them (the insider) is employed or has privileged access

insider–outsider threat: is a threat that emerges as a result of a relationship between one of your employees and a person working for an outside organization or who is otherwise not related to the organization

install-time permissions: require the developer to identify all of the protected resources that an application can access, and to declare these permissions at the time of installation. Based on the permissions displayed, the user can choose whether or not to install the application

lessons learned process: is a structured method of evaluating incidents or events and determining what individuals or organizations could have done better to deal with the situation and transforming that lesson into positive actions through employee training, improving procedures, or improving mitigation methods or technology

logical narrative: an uncomplicated straightforward explanation or directions

malvertising: is the undisclosed and often unauthorized insertion of advertising or misleading content in social media posts, webpage content, and email messages

media convergence: is the melding of different media types into multifaceted streams of information and entertainment including video, text, photos, sound, and graphics which were at one time all delivered from separate platforms and applications

medical device security: medical applications are often not designed with security and privacy in mind and the Trustworthy Health and Wellness project is designed to develop mobile- and cloud-computing systems that respect the privacy of individuals and the trustworthiness of medical information

microgrid: is a localized grouping of electricity sources and loads that normally operates connected to and synchronous with the traditional centralized grid (macrogrid), but can be disconnected and function autonomously as physical and/or economic conditions dictate

moving target defense: is a rotational environment that runs an application on several different operating system platforms to thwart attacker reconnaissance efforts and improve application resilience to the threat of zero-day exploits

multi-factor authentication: uses a combination of two (or more) different methods to authenticate a user identity. The first is what users know, usually a password, but this can also include a user response to a challenge question which is generally known as knowledge-based authentication, and by itself, is insufficient for authentication to sensitive information. The second is what users have such as a physical object (token), for example, a smart card, or hardware token that generates one-time-only passwords. It might also be some encrypted software token installed on an individual's system. The third is who users are, as indicated by some biometric characteristic such as a fingerprint or an iris pattern

nanoscale: technology or physical items that have dimensions measured in nanometers which is one billionth of a meter

natural language generation: plain uncomplicated jargon-free language that does not require specialized training to understand

need-to-know: is the necessity for access to, knowledge of, or possession of specific information required to carry out official duties

netiquette: is a group of principles and concepts that encourage the socially proper use of social media and other Internet applications

next generation Internet architectures: are those which will support future Internet applications and environments such as the Internet or things and the smart grid

online alias: is an online identity encompassing identifiers, such as name and date of birth, differing from the employee's actual identifiers that use a nongovernmental Internet Protocol address. Online alias may be used to monitor activity on social media websites or to engage in authorized online undercover activity

ontology: describes a system of concepts and its associated properties for a specific area often intended to support computer applications and exist on a continuum rather than completely distinct types of artifacts

personally identifiable information (PII): is information that can be used to distinguish or trace an individual's identity, either alone or when combined with other personal or identifying information that is linked or linkable to a specific individual

personal technologies: include individually owned devices such as cell phones, tablets, laptops, and digital media

personal use: means using a service or an item only for personal reasons and goals that do not have any relationship to the organization employing the individual using the item or service

plain language: is the straightforward writing that enables readers of all types and levels of education to better understand written content in any media through which it is delivered

platform of security and privacy: means securing how data are stored, processed, or transmitted

policy-governed secure collaboration: is the process of providing a collaborative platform, normative requirements, and standard policies for handling data with differing usage needs and among users in different authority domains

privacy impact assessment (PIA): is an analysis of how information is handled by ensuring handling conforms to applicable legal, regulatory, and policy requirements regarding privacy, determining the risks and effects of collecting, maintaining, and disseminating information in identifiable form in an electronic information system, and examining and evaluating protections and alternative processes for handling information to mitigate potential privacy risks

public/private partnerships: joint efforts for a mutual cause and benefit between government agencies and private corporations, foundations, or nongovernment organizations

public safety issues: encompass actions or conditions that impede the everyday functioning of a community and the protection of life and property

publicly available social media: is social media applications and content that can be accessed and viewed by the general public without restrictions

replication test: the repeated duplicate answer derived when analyzing a data set

research ecosystems: research capabilities and resources are brought into a research ecosystem from many types of universities, national laboratories, private industry, and military laboratories to perform complex and effective research with each organization contributing their specific expertise and organizational capabilities

run-time permissions: are the permissions that users give to a computing device when a system dialog box prompts the user when an application attempts to access a particular resource. Users can then decide, on a case-by-case basis, whether to give an application access to that resource

science of security (SoS): is science that is needed to mature the broad range of cybersecurity disciplines necessary to establish a foundation to achieve advances in cyber defense

security awareness: is the basic level of understanding of security and recognition of the importance of security

security-metrics: are the necessary standardized measures that are rigorously tested and universally applied to evaluation, design, development, and deployment to security solutions

security threats: are conditions, people, or events that can jeopardize the security of a nation, organization, a facility, or any asset belonging to the threatened entity

security vigilance: is a constant attention given to security during day-to-day operations and contributes to security by encouraging the reporting of security violations and makes suggestions on how to improve security when weaknesses are observed

sensitive information: is that information held by or created by an organization that if revealed to the wrong party would cause harm to the organization owning or creating the information

shared platform approach: is the use of a common computer systems or architecture used by all government agencies to reduce inefficiencies created by fragmented procurement and development practices that waste money and result in inconsistent adoption of new technologies and approaches

siloed: separate systems, each with a separate function or environment that are often duplicated rather than integrated into a whole system

single use code delivered in a text message: is an authentication technique that is used to assure controlled access to online applications or databases by sending the user a text code that can be used only once to access an application and expires within minutes if not used

smart grid: is the secure and resilient electrical grid that enables support for critical infrastructures and the national economy

social media applications: are any existing or future networked computer program that facilitates communication between individuals or individuals and groups

social media policies: specify who in an organization is responsible for social media operations and specify when, why, where, and how social media can be used on behalf of an organization and provides guidance on the inappropriate use of social media by corporate media staff and employees

social media presence: is an organization's use of social media accounts and applications to communicate to individuals or groups as well as the mention, comments, discussions, and display of any material on any social media application that relates to or depicts an organization

spatiotemporal network dynamics: is the interaction and activity that occurs in communities on social networks and can provide direct clues as to the nature of an individual's identity and their role within both online and offline communities, allowing for the creation of cyber-geodemographic profiles

spoofing: is an attempt to gain access to a system by posing as an authorized user. Synonymous with impersonating, masquerading, or mimicking

stochastic: is an event or system that is unpredictable because of a random variable

strategic environment: the environment that military branches must be capable of establishing, maintaining, and adapting in order to achieve the mission at hand

steganographic channels: steganography means covered writing or covered, concealed, or messages in image, or video within another file, message, image, or video. A steganographic channel in a communications network is when hidden in another channel or made difficult to detect in some manner

synchrophasor: is a sophisticated monitoring device that can measure the instantaneous voltage, current, and frequency at specific locations on the electric grid giving operators a near real-time picture of what is happening on the system, and allows them to make decisions to prevent power outages

system usability scale (SUS): is widely used reliable tool for measuring usability of a wide variety of products and services, including hardware, software, mobile devices, websites, and applications

tailored trustworthy spaces: a security architecture and strategic federal cyberse-curity research theme tailored for the smart grid and other cyber environments that assure that all elements in the space are secure

The Code of Federal Regulations (CFR): is the legal code formed by rules published in the Federal Register by executive departments and agencies of the Federal Government. A CFR Citation Number is used to reference each rule

theft of intellectual property: is the illegal obtaining of copyrighted or patented material, trade secrets, or trademarks (including designs, plans, blueprints, codes, computer programs, software, formulas, recipes, graphics) usually by electronic copying

theft of personal or financial data: is the illegal obtaining of information that potentially allows someone to use or create accounts under another name (individual, business, or some other entity). Personal information includes names, dates of birth, social security numbers, or other personal information. Financial information includes credit, debit, or ATM card account or PIN numbers

trade secrets: are any forms or type of business process, scientific formula, technical specification, economic data, or engineering designs that the owner has taken measures to protect and from which economic value can be derived

transfer or transition of technology: is the process of moving technology from one of the national laboratories into use in the private sector or in another organization other than the laboratory

Trojan Horse: is a computer program with an apparently or actually useful function that contains additional (hidden) functions that surreptitiously exploit the legitimate authorizations of the invoking process to the detriment of security or integrity

truck platooning: is an extension of cooperative adaptive cruise control and forward collision avoidance technology that provides automated lateral and longitudinal vehicle control to maintain a tight formation of vehicles with short following distances

trustable foundation in cyberspace: is a basic underlying structure that is reliable, defensible, and available when and where needed to protect national and economic security

unauthorized use: is the reading, recording, transmitting, or storing of data that belongs to a specific party and is meant for a specific and restricted use by the owning or custodial organization or its designees

unstructured data: are data that are more free-form, such as multimedia files, images, sound files, or unstructured text. Unstructured data do not necessarily follow any format or hierarchical sequence, nor follow any relational rules but is usually computerized information which does not have a data structure which is easily readable by a machine

usability testing: is the evaluation of a product or service by testing it with representative users during which participants will try to complete typical tasks while observers watch, listen, and take notes

usenet newsgroups: there are more than 29,000 topic-oriented message bases that can be read and posted to (Also called newsgroups.)

user experience (UX): is what happens during human–computer interaction from the human perspective

virtual currency: are financial systems that usually provide greater anonymity than traditional payment systems and sometimes lack a central intermediary to maintain transaction information and can be accessed globally to make payments and transfer funds across borders

vulnerability assessment: is a structured process by which to evaluate how secure a nation, organization, or individual is, based on the perception of threats and security needs

zombie cyberattacks: spam and denial-of-service attacks that come from compromised computers (zombies) that have been infected with malware and are now controlled remotelyz by the attacker

Index